Demographic Dynamics and Development

SCIENCES

Geography and Demography, Field Director – Denise Pumain

Demography, Subject Head – Brigitte Baccaïni

Demographic Dynamics and Development

Coordinated by

Yves Charbit

iSTE

WILEY

First published 2022 in Great Britain and the United States by ISTE Ltd and John Wiley & Sons, Inc.

ISTE Ltd
27-37 St George's Road
London SW19 4EU
UK

www.iste.co.uk

John Wiley & Sons, Inc.
111 River Street
Hoboken, NJ 07030
USA

www.wiley.com

Library of Congress Control Number: 2021947914

British Library Cataloguing-in-Publication Data
A CIP record for this book is available from the British Library
ISBN 978-1-78945-050-7

ERC code:
LS8 Ecology, Evolution and Environmental Biology
LS8_3 Population biology, population dynamics, population genetics
SH1 Individuals, Markets and Organisations
SH1_3 Development economics, health economics, education economics
SH3 The Social World, Diversity, Population
SH3_8 Population dynamics; households, family and fertility

MIX
Paper from responsible sources
FSC® C013604

Contents

Introduction

Demographic Dynamics

Yves CHARBIT
CEPED, University of Paris, France

I.1. What are demographic dynamics?

Demographic dynamics come down to a fundamental equation. Every year the growth or decline of a given population (P) is reduced to the interaction of four variables:

(2020 Total population) = (2019 Total population) + (2019 births) – (2019 deaths) + (2019 immigration) – (2019 emigration)

From this, three simple definitions follow:

– the difference between births and deaths in a year is the *natural increase* (*natural surplus* or *natural deficit*);

– the difference between immigration and emigration is the *net migration* (which can be either positive or negative). From the point of view of demographic dynamics *stricto sensu*, international migrations are much less important than births and deaths;

– the *total growth rate* is the sum of the two indicators (natural increase and net migration), divided by the population of the previous year. It is expressed as a percentage per year.

Before 1750, when mortality and birth rates were balanced, the world population growth rate never exceeded 0.5%. Between 1750 and the 1930s, it did not exceed 1%. It reached a maximum of 2.1% per year, on average, between 1950 and 1970, when mortality in developing countries fell sharply, without a decline in birth rates. Subsequently, more and more developing countries saw their fertility rate decline, as it did in industrialized countries with the end of the baby boom of the 1950s. The combined effect of these two developments led to a steady decline in the world population growth rate: 1.95% in 1970, 1.26% in 2000 and 1.09% in 2020.

Another aspect of demographic dynamics that is directly related to changes in flows must be mentioned. Their very accumulation determines *population stocks*. Thus, the rural exodus leads to changes in the distribution between urban and rural areas, which is the process of urbanization. As for the evolution of mortality and birth rates, this is translated by the population's age–sex distribution, conventionally represented by a pyramid. After the Second World War, developing countries experienced a large annual number of births but, due to high mortality, very few people reached adulthood. This was reflected by broad-based pyramids. In these populations, although there certainly were adults, very few were elderly people. With the gradual decline in the fertility of couples, annual birth rates decreased and the proportions of children and adults rebalanced. The population became older and demographers spoke of "aging from the bottom". In developed countries, on the other hand, where annual birth rates are lower, the age pyramid has more adults. Over the years, these fall into the category of the third age and we speak of "top-down aging".

These relative proportions of children, adults and the elderly led to several indicators being established, which address the issue of development. It is common to draw a distinction between consumers and producers or, more precisely, to differentiate the inactive from the active. We thus calculate a *dependency ratio*, where the numerator includes 0–19 year olds (young people) and those aged 60 and above (the elderly), and the denominator is the working population (20–69 year olds). Globally, the dependency ratio – equal to 75 inactive people dependent on 100 working people in 1970 – decreased to 56 in 2000 and to 53 in 2020. Another analysis was recently developed. Due to the decline in fertility, the cohorts now under the age of 15 will be replaced by smaller cohorts. But, above all, they will access the economically active ages and the relationship between consumers and producers – hitherto unfavorable due to spending on health and education weighing on national budgets – will become favorable. So far, we have provided data on world population, but is this concept actually useful?

I.2. The world population, now a useless concept?

From a demographic point of view, after the end of the Second World War, the world appeared to be divided into two major groups: developed countries and the so-called "Third World". The former included North America, Japan, Europe, Australia and New Zealand, whereas the latter included Asia (except Japan), Africa, Latin America and the Caribbean. According to this typology, in 2020, developed countries totalled 1,273 billion inhabitants, i.e. 16.3% of the total world population of 7,794 billion inhabitants[1]. But this dichotomy is now outdated, at least in demographic terms, due to the growing disparities between the three continents in which developing countries are located (Table I.1 and Figure I.1).

	Population	%
Worldwide	7,794	1.09
Developed countries	1,273	0.26
Developing countries	6,521	1.26
Per region:		
Africa	1,340	2.51
Latin America	653	0.94
Asia	4,641	0.92

Table I.1. *Population (2020, in millions) and annual growth rate in the major groups (2015–2020 average, in %) (source: UN DESA 2019)*

Annual growth rates reveal that it is necessary not only to contrast the virtual stagnation of developed countries (0.26%) against the demographic dynamism of developing countries (1.26%), but also to differentiate the rapid growth in Africa from the now more moderate growth observed in Asia and Latin America.

An even more detailed analysis reveals differences within these three continents, especially in Asia and Africa. Thus, sub-Saharan Africa is growing at a rate of 2.65% per year, but this average masks deep contrasts: 1.91% in the north and 1.39% in the south, against 3.05% in Middle Africa and 2.67% in the continent's east and west. Western and Central Asia are growing faster (1.64%) than East (0.40%) and Southern (1.20%) Asia. The differences between countries in the same

1 All the data quoted in this introduction are from the United Nations (UN DESA 2019).

region are just as remarkable (Table I.2 and Figure I.2). Size effects play a large part: highly populated countries (South Africa, India, China), often giants relative to their neighbors, weigh heavily on the averages of the sub-regions. South Africa, with its 59.3 million inhabitants (85% of the total) and a rate of 1.37%, largely determines the rate of growth in the sub-region (1.39%), whereas Botswana, which barely totals 2.3 million, is growing much faster (2.07%).

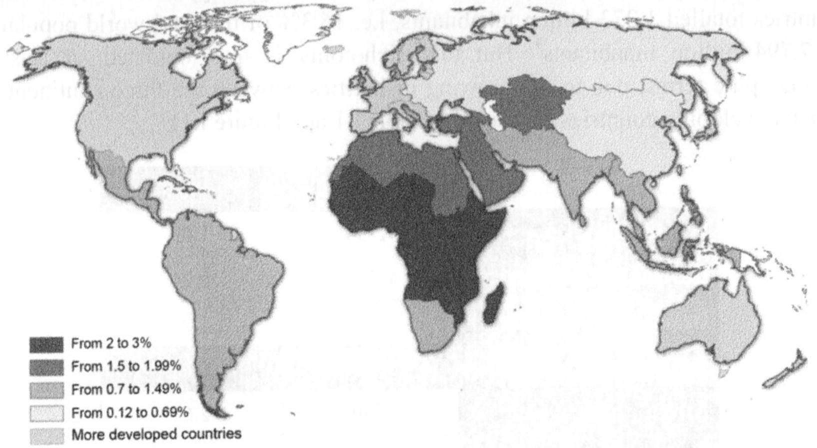

Figure I.1. *Annual growth rate of major groups (2015–2020 average, in %) (sources: Charbit (design); Opurez, IRD-Ceped (realization)). For a color version of this figure, see www.iste.co.uk/charbit/demographic.zip*

Similarly, in Central and Southern Asia, India (1,380 billion with a growth rate of 1.04% per year), Pakistan (220 million and 2.05%) and Bangladesh (164 million and 1.05%) largely determine the sub-regional rate (1.20%), since these three countries on their own account for 90.9% of the sub-region's total population. Finally, Western Asia, which includes countries with high growth rates (Iraq 2.46%, Palestine 2.38%, Yemen 2.37%), contrasts with other Asian sub-regions: 1.64% against 0.40% in East Asia, for example. This low rate is explained by China's slow growth (0.46%), a demographic giant of 1,344 billion inhabitants, which represents 80.3% of the population in this sub-region.

What is more, the major dichotomy between developed and developing countries is questionable because, in some countries considered to be developing, fertility rates are lower than in some industrialized countries. This is the case for China (1.69 children per woman) compared to France (1.85), the United Kingdom

(1.75) and the United States (1.78). From this brief statistical analysis, it is clear that, although convenient, the concept of world population covers an extraordinary diversity of demographic situations. For this reason, two typologies will be used in the following chapters when providing indicators of the relationship between population and development: the continents, on the one hand, and, on the other, the countries classified according to their level of income (high, middle and low).

Region and country	%	Region and country	%
Southern Africa	**1.39**	**West Asia**	**1.64**
Botswana	2.07	Armenia	0.26
Eswatini	0.99	Azerbaijan	1.05
Lesotho	0.79	Bahrain	4.31
Namibia	1.86	Cyprus	0.78
South Africa	1.37	Georgia	–0.18
Southern Asia	**1.20**	Iraq	2.46
Afghanistan	2.47	Israel	1.63
Bangladesh	1.05	Jordan	1.93
Bhutan	1.17	Kuwait	2.15
India	1.04	Lebanon	0.88
Iran	1.36	Oman	3.59
Maldives	3.45	Qatar	2.32
Nepal	1.51	Saudi Arabia	1.86
Pakistan	2.05	Palestine	2.38
Sri Lanka	0.48	Syria	–0.56
		Turkey	1.43
		United Arab Emirates	1.31
		Yemen	2.37

Table I.2. *Annual growth rate per country in certain sub-regions (2015–2020 average)*

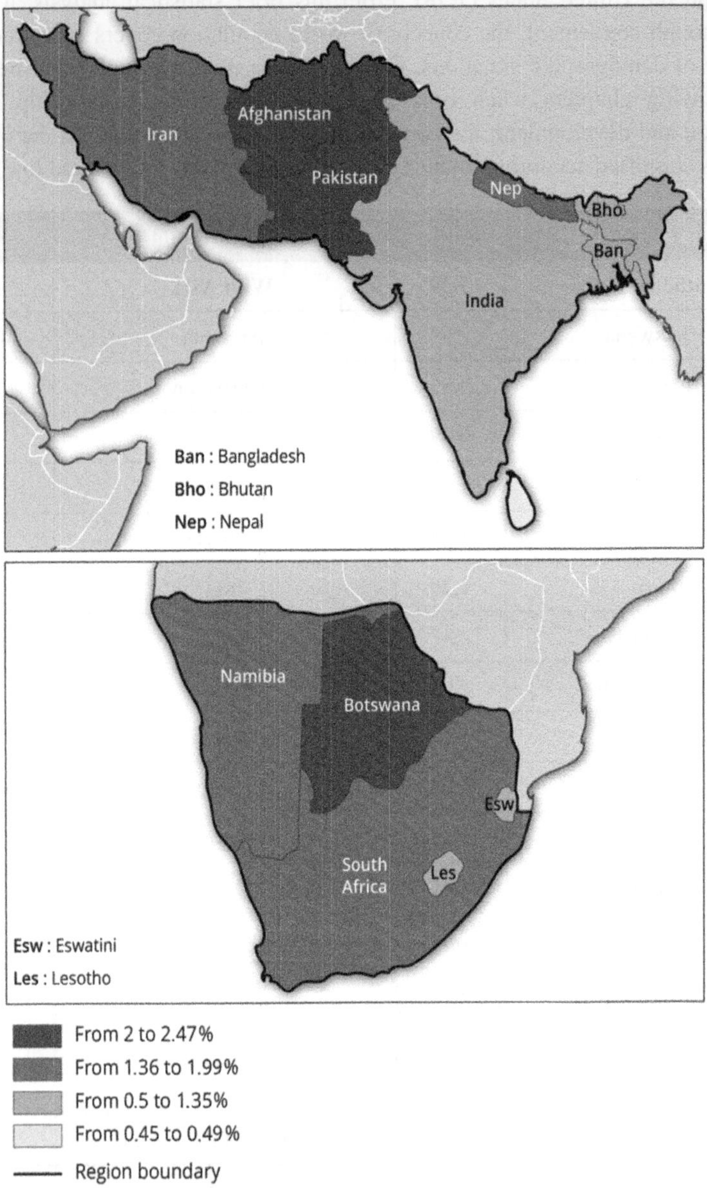

Figure I.2. *Annual growth rate of countries in Southern Africa and Southern Asia (2015–2020 average) (sources: Charbit (design); Opurez, IRD-Ceped (realization)). For a color version of this figure, see www.iste.co.uk/charbit/demographic.zip*

I.3. The double Malthusian progression

Let us move on to economy, the other term of the dialectic between population and development. Alongside China, which has now become the world's second economic power, we have seen the emergence of the Dragons (South Korea, Taiwan, Hong Kong and Singapore) and the Tigers (Malaysia, Thailand, Indonesia, Vietnam and the Philippines) in Southeast Asia. Several countries in the Middle East (the Gulf countries and Iran), Latin America (Venezuela) and Africa (Algeria and Libya) have used oil and gas revenues politically and economically. As for the enormous potential of mining resources in Africa, the soaring prices of raw materials and of basic foodstuffs have resulted in a much higher gross domestic product (GDP) than in Europe, between 2000 and 2015. All of a sudden, the classic parallel drawn between demographic and economic growth has lost much of its meaning and, moreover, the pithy claim that the cause of poverty is the rapid growth of the population, itself driven by a high fertility rate, has been denied by developments in recent decades. This central question is therefore: Is demography the *cause* of underdevelopment?

Why is this claim so widely accepted today? Here, it is appropriate to recall the theory proposed by Thomas Robert Malthus in 1798. In his view, just like animal species, England's poor behaved completely irresponsibly: unable to control their sexual impulses, they had far too many children relative to their meager resources (Malthus 1798). Under these conditions, they had to be held responsible for their misery. In this way, the economic and social inequalities created or reinforced by the policies of 19th-century European conservative governments (Charbit 1983, 2009) were legitimized. However, Malthus fell into oblivion from the mid-19th century with the decline in fertility of industrialized countries, to the point of fearing that low birth rates would eventually lead to the demographic decline of old Europe. The situation then took a new turn from the 1950s onwards with the realization of growing demographic trends in poor countries, especially in Asia. Western scientific and political circles were alarmed at the risk of an explosion in world population. In 1968, the work of biologist Paul Ehrlich, *The Population Bomb*, had a huge impact. But while Ehrlich focused on the global level and addressed the issue of natural resource reserves in particular, it quickly appeared that the problem was not so much world population but rapid population growth in "Third World" countries – to use the term of those times – namely India with its demographic mass of 543 million in 1969 out of a world total of 3,625 billion that year. In short, according to the vision of the 1960s, largely inspired by neo-Malthusian ideas, the population of the Third World was increasing too quickly in relation to resources. Why "the Third World"?

In the Ancien Régime, besides the nobility and the clergy, the rest of the French people were regarded as members of the third state ("*Tiers état*"). The expression

"Third World" is inspired by the declaration of one of the actors of the French Revolution, Abbé Sieyès, who proclaimed: "What is the third state? Everything. What has it been up to now in the political order? Nothing. What does it aspire to? To be something". The concept was proposed in 1957 by demographer Alfred Sauvy, founder of the National Institute of Demographic Studies, and by anthropologist Georges Balandier, professor at Sorbonne University (Balandier 1956). In their mind, the issue was not only demographic, it was also economic and political, since compared to the capitalist world and the Soviet blocks, all the poor countries made up a third group. It is, therefore, hardly surprising that from the 1960s onwards a considerable effort was made, since it was absolutely necessary to keep the population growth of poor countries under control. Private foundations (Population Council, Rockefeller Foundation), non-profit organizations (International Planned Parenthood Federation, Mary Stopes International, etc.), international institutions (the United Nations Population Fund), and later the World Bank all joined forces in order to achieve this. The methods used were generally incentive-based, sometimes coercive with total disregard of human rights, especially in the case of abortion and of male/female sterilization. The pressure exerted by Western countries soon aroused strong opposition. In Bucharest in 1974, during the first World Population Conference, an Action Plan was drawn up with the aim of reducing the growth rate in world population. Since the population of rich countries grew slowly, it was clear that this plan involved considerable effort on the part of developing countries to control their population growth, and consequently their fertility. This was strongly opposed by two countries, Algeria and Argentina, which argued the opposite: the problem was not too many children but was instead underdevelopment. One statement was particularly successful: "The best contraceptive is development".

As for the concept of the Third World, it is clear that it reflected the ideology of the Cold War and the rivalry between capitalism and communism. Furthermore, this was translated into the formation of a group of non-aligned countries during the Bandung conference in 1955. While the concept was in keeping with the times, it had negative effects on research because of its globalizing nature: the term Third World, coined to describe Asia, Latin America and Africa, meant that no distinctions were made between them. And yet, how can we claim that behavior and cultural, social and economic contexts are the same in Peru, Indonesia or Namibia? To understand the reasons for high fertility in these three countries, it is necessary to contextualize research. The theory of modernization was proposed in 1953 by an American demographer, Frank Notestein, a major figure of the Population Council in New York. Typical of the dominant ideology of the time, it described a development model inspired by the rich countries: the reduction in fertility presupposed the existence of urban, educated women and couples, employed in the formal sector who would use modern contraception "rationally" to maintain or even improve their standard of living, having only a few children. Shortly after in 1960, sociologist William Goode published a book which affirmed that the Western model of the monogamous nuclear family would triumph worldwide. However, in 1974, anthropologist David Mandelbaum showed that in India, for example, the economic, social and cultural logics hardly went in the direction predicted by Goode.

The second observation concerns the evolution of the social stakeholders involved since the times of Malthus. The stark contrast between the demographic behavior of the bourgeoisie and the workers, highlighted during the 19th century in European countries, was replaced by that of rich Western and poorer countries in the period following the Second World War. But the evolution of the above-mentioned economic growth rates leads us to propose another analysis grid. Indeed, the gaps in wealth, as well as differences in consumption patterns and access to health or education between developed and developing countries, are dramatic. However, as we saw at the beginning of this introductory chapter, even this dichotomy should be rejected because of the ever-widening gap between the countries where population growth rates are high (mainly certain regions in Africa and Asia) and countries where growth is under control.

I.4. Outine of the book

After this brief general introduction, the dominant theory among demographers, the demographic transition, is presented (Chapter 1). The following two chapters focus on the developmental consequences of changes in age structures caused by the demographic transition. Chapter 2 is devoted to one of its avatars, the demographic dividend. Likewise, the National Transfer Accounts methodology (Chapter 3) makes it possible to study intra-family transfers between generations and, as such, is part of the reflection on structural changes related to age. Fertility and nuptiality (Chapter 4) determine population dynamics. Particular attention is given to one of the variables that regulate fertility: contraception (Chapter 5). The other major driver of the dynamics is mortality. In a book that is centered on the relationship between population and development, morbidity and therefore health could not be neglected (Chapter 6). Although the demography of developing countries is the focus of this book, it was important to include an in-depth analysis of the situation in Europe, from the 16th to 20th century (Chapter 7). This choice is clearly justified by the fact that at the beginning of that period, Europe was truly underdeveloped. A historical approach is therefore useful to help better understand the economic, social, cultural and political dynamics at work – today and in the past – in migration with in developing countries. As for current migration, Chapter 8 provides a broad overview of migration *flows* from countries of origin and migration *stocks* residing in immigration countries where employment prospects are better. While developing countries are associated with the idea that they suffer from the burden of young populations that must be fed, cared for, educated and soon to be employed, it seems paradoxical to raise the question of their aging (Chapter 9). In fact, with an undeniable decline in fertility, developing countries will in turn enter into an aging process. But, while the management of old age is largely socialized, the elderly in Asia, Latin America and even more in Africa will have to be economically supported by their children. Table I.3 summarizes the main contributions of the chapters.

To conclude this introduction, we should mention that in general the chapters present the problem, the hypotheses retained and the sources used. A "general" section provides useful statistical or demographic data. Where appropriate, the following geographical levels are distinguished: global, continental, some of the main sub-regions of the three continents, and countries are classified according to level of development (developed countries, developing countries and least developed countries). Finally, the chapters include one or more in-depth case studies that focus on a country, sub-region or a particularly important scientific sub-topic (Table I.3).

Chapter title	Case study
Introduction: Demographic Dynamics (Charbit)	Malthus and development
1. The Demographic Transition (Cosio Zavala)	Latin America and the Caribbean
2. Demographic Dividend and Dependency Ratios (Turbat)	Sub-Saharan Africa
3. From the Demographic Dividend to Generational Economics (Dramani)	Dividend profiles in Africa
4. Fertility and Nuptiality (Charbit)	Precocious nuptiality
5. Contraception and Reproductive Rights (Dasgupta)	Reproductive rights
6. Mortality and Health, the Factors Involved in Population Dynamics (Gaimard)	Mortality of women and children
7. Dynamics of Migration History in Western Europe (Moch)	Migratory systems
8. Current International Migrations (Feld)	The emigration of the highly qualified workforce
9. Aging (Sandron)	Three models: Cuba, Age-Friendly Cities, Sub-Saharan Africa

Table I.3. *Chapter titles and in-depth case studies*

I.5. References

Balandier, G. (ed.) (1956). *Le Tiers-monde, sous-développement et développement.* PUF-INED, Paris.

Casterline, J.B. and Bongaarts, J. (eds) (2017). *Fertility Transition in Sub-Saharan Africa, Population and Development Review 43.* The Population Council, New York.

Charbit, Y. (1983). The fate of Malthus's work: History and ideology. In *Malthus Past and Present*, Dupaquier, J. (ed.). Academic Press, London.

Charbit, Y. (2009). *Economic, Social and Demographic Thought in the XIXth Century. The Population Debate from Malthus to Marx.* Springer, Dordrecht.

Ehrlich, P. (1968). *The Population Bomb.* Ballantine Books, New York.

Goode, W.J. (1963). *World Revolution and Family Patterns.* Collier-Macmillan, New York.

Malthus, T.R. (1798). *An Essay on the Principle of Population, as it Affects the Future Improvement of Society, with Remarks on the Speculations of Mr. Godwin, M. Condorcet and Other Writers.* Penguin Books, Harmondsworth.

Mandelbaum, D.G. (1974). *Human Fertility in India.* University of California Press, Berkeley.

Notestein, F.W. (1953). Economic problems of population change. In *Proceedings of the Eighth International Conference of Agricultural Economists.* Oxford University Press, London.

Piketty, T. (2013). *Le Capital au XXIe siècle.* Le Seuil, Paris.

UN DESA (2019). *World Population Prospects 2019.* United Nations, New York.

1

The Demographic Transition

Maria Eugenia COSIO ZAVALA
El Colegio de México, Mexico, and Paris Nanterre University, France

1.1. Introduction

The demographic transition refers to the passage from a regime of high mortality and high fertility to a regime with low mortality and reduced fertility. In-depth work[1] has brought to light a large heterogeneity of contexts and variation in stages, such as the demographic situation at the start of the transition, the anteriority of the decline in mortality or fertility, medical progress, urbanization, the pace of the main demographic changes (mortality, nuptiality, fertility and migrations) and the period when the transition has been completed. We cannot, therefore, speak of a single model of demographic transition, but of a great diversity which can be explained by economic, social, cultural and institutional factors, across time and space.

Demographic transitions began in European countries in the 18th century, and afterward spread widely to countries populated by European emigrants, such as Australia, New Zealand, the United States, Canada, Argentina and Uruguay. From the mid-20th century onwards, they reached the majority of Asian and Latin American countries, and later Southeast Asia, the Middle East and sub-Saharan Africa. Demographic transitions were at first related to the "modernization" of economies and societies, but this explanation has proven insufficient. Many authors have highlighted other dimensions, such as spoken language, religion, education,

1 One of the most comprehensive pioneering studies on demographic transition at the regional level in Europe is that of the team led by Ansley Coale within "The European Fertility Project" at Princeton University (Coale and Cotts Watkins 1986).

Demographic Dynamics and Development,
coordinated by Yves CHARBIT.

family models, the value of children, social interactions, intergenerational relationships, and social, racial and gender inequalities.

The concepts developed offer an extremely rich field of study for the history of the world's population, spanning more than three centuries. Indeed, far from a single model of demographic transition – which would be a replica of the evolutions of European countries – temporalities, as well as the variety of demographic changes along the 20th and 21st centuries in developing countries, show a plurality of models.

In this chapter, we will successively analyze the genesis of the demographic transition model and its generalization, the current trends in population growth, as well as the demographic transitions around the world, particularly in Latin America and the Caribbean. The main results of the chapter should provide an in-depth understanding of the relationship between population and development.

1.2. Genesis of the demographic transition

The earliest reference to the consequences of a decline in birth and death rates was first described as a "demographic revolution" by Rabinowicz in 1929 (Adeev 2011, p. 9). Landry chose this reference as the title for his famous work (Landry 1982). Notestein introduced the term "transitional growth" as a reference to the moment when mortality declined, provoking strong population growth, followed by a decline in fertility[2] (Notestein 1945, p. 46). For Notestein, the demographic transition was associated with modernization, urbanization and industrialization; the development of education and public health; increased living standards; fertility control and the adoption of new values (Notestein 1945, p. 57). Davis would in turn publish an article called *The World Demographic Transition* in 1945. According to Chesnais, the original theory of demographic transition, in its European (Landry) or North American (Davis, Notestein) versions, was achieved by 1953 (Chesnais 1986b, p. 1061).

Demographers agree to evoke the "passage from a demographic situation characterized by high mortality and high fertility with a 'high' quasi-equilibrium to a situation of low mortality and low fertility with a 'low' quasi-equilibrium" (Meslé *et al.* 2011, p. 482) and significant population growth between the two phases. The first demographic transition took place as early as the 18th century, in north-western Europe, when the fight against major epidemics and infant mortality spread toward

2 Notestein explicitly mentions fertility, whereas older texts focus more on birth rates as a component of population growth (Notestein 1945).

the whole continent (Meslé and Vallin 1995). In turn, fertility fell from a level of more than five children per woman to about two children per woman. The case of France is an exception, since the reduction in fertility began in the mid-18th century, whereas in other European countries, it started in 1870 (Vallin 2003). It should be noted that, on average[3], the European population multiplied by four in 150 years (Chesnais 1986a; Vallin 2003, pp. 28–30).

By analyzing 67 countries between 1720 and 1984, Chesnais wanted to show that the demographic transition is a general theory, "reduced to a few central empirically testable propositions and [which] can be enriched on certain points that the history of facts deems essential for the understanding of the mechanisms at work" (Chesnais 1986b, p. 1061). He further mentions:

> [T]hree paradigms, which can be drawn from the founding texts: the principle of antecedence in the decrease in mortality; the two-phase reproductive transition module (limitation of marriages, and consequent limitation of births); and the influence of the access to modern economic growth (in the sense of Kuznets) on the triggering of the secular decline in fertility. (Chesnais 1986b, p. 1061)

In addition, he stresses:

> [T]he insufficiencies of the original theory and therefore the necessary amendments [which] concern, for their part, three aspects: the concept of pre- and post-transitional balance, the absence of international openness and the exclusive focus on fertility, considered as a dependent variable. (Chesnais 1986b, p. 1061)

He mentions the role of international migrations in controlling strong population growth (like the massive flows from Europe to the Americas in the 19th century) and the differences in periods and in the speed of national transitions, across time and space (Chesnais 1986b, p. 1061).

Since the publication of Chesnais' book (Chesnais 1986a), empirical observations have called into question these postulates: in Europe fertility may have declined at the same time or before mortality (Coale and Cotts Watkins 1986; Vallin 2003). However, in Africa, Asia and Latin America, the differences are even greater in the timing and speed of demographic changes, as well as in the underlying factors

3 Chesnais proposed the calculation of a transitional multiplier which depends on the value of death and birth rates, as well as on the length of the transition period (Chesnais 1986a).

(Guzmán *et al.* 2006; Attané and Barbieri 2009; Koba *et al.* 2019). In Latin America, the three-phase reproductive transition pattern did not occur in the same form, in that order, or at the same speed (Cosio Zavala 2011).

Below, we will present the various changes in world population, which have been determined by the history of demographic transitions.

1.3. World population changes and trends (2019–2100)

According to the United Nations Population Division, the world population is expected to continue to grow for several decades (United Nations 2019a)[4]. The population might increase from 7.7 billion inhabitants in 2019 to 9.7 billion in 2050 and 10.9 billion by 2100 (medium-variant projection). Between 2019 and 2050, projections predict a near doubling of the population in Africa, whereas the European population might decrease during this period (Table 1.1). Leridon confirms the likelihood of the population exceeding 9 billion by 2050, "unless one considers catastrophes of unprecedented magnitude at a global scale" (Leridon 2020)[5].

On the basis of the theory of demographic transition, the perspectives of the United Nations foresee a reduction and a convergence in mortality and fertility levels[6]: by 2060, fertility might reach 1.75 children per woman in developed countries and 2.15 children per woman in developing countries (United Nations 2019a, Fert/4). Table 1.2 shows the populations of different regions in the world, between 2019 and 2100, classified into six groups, according to the stages of their demographic transitions. We consider the demographic transition to be complete when life expectancy is over 70 years old (average for both sexes) and when fertility is equal to or lower than 2.1 children per woman.

4 The United Nations Population Division regularly produces estimates on population and projections for all countries. It is responsible for studies on various essential demographic themes, the methodological revision of projections and demographic monitoring of international policies, such as the Sustainable Development Goals (SDG) policy. It is the main source of comparable and high-quality demographic data at the global level (United Nations 2019a). Available at: www.un.org/en/development/desa/population/theme/trends/index.asp [accessed 2 July 2020].

5 Moreover, it has been calculated that two-thirds of population growth until 2050 will be a consequence of world population age structures due to "demographic inertia" (Leridon 2020, p. 4).

6 At the world population level, there is zero net migration. We, therefore, only retain mortality and fertility as factors accounting for population growth.

Region	Population		
	2019	2051	2100
Africa	1,308,064	2,489,275	4,280,127
Asia	4,601,371	5 290,263	4,719,907
Europe	747,183	710,486	629,563
North America	366,601	425,200	490,889
Latin America and the Caribbean	648,121	762,432	679,993
Oceania	42,128	57,376	74,916
Total	7 713,468	9,735,034	10,875,394

Table 1.1. *Estimates and projections of the population of the world's geographic regions in 2019, 2050 and 2100 (thousands of inhabitants) (source: Population Prospects 2019; United Nations 2019a)*

The composition of the six demographic transition groups is as follows:

– For 2019, group 1 brought together the countries of Europe, North America and Oceania (1.1 billion inhabitants), which completed their demographic transition before 1970. In 2019, they represented 14% of the world population. The European population is expected to decline (with the exception of Northern Europe) and that of North America and Oceania is expected to increase. This first group could reach a total of 1.2 billion inhabitants by 2100, with low growth between 2019 and 2100, around 10% (according to estimates and medium-variant) (United Nations 2019a).

– Group 2 brings together countries whose demographic transition was completed at the end of 20th century. Japan joined this group in 1970, the Republic of Korea in 1985, China in 1990 and the Democratic Republic of Korea in 1995. These East Asian countries had nearly 1.7 billion inhabitants in 2019 (21% of world population). By adding all the countries whose fertility is lower than or equal to 2.1 children per woman – such as Chile, Brazil, Colombia and Uruguay, many small island countries, a large part of the Middle East's countries, Bangladesh, Iran and Sri Lanka – there are a total of 2.4 billion inhabitants (31% of the world population). However, this population should decrease to approximately 2 billion inhabitants by 2100 (18% of the world population). The population of East Asia, including China, might start to decline in 2050, reaching 1.2 billion people in 2100, half a billion less than in 2019 (according to estimates and medium-variant) (United Nations 2019a).

– Group 3 includes countries that will have completed their fertility transition by 2030. During the second half of the 20th century, they experienced a sharp decline in mortality, a rapid reduction in fertility as well as exceptional population growth. In 2019, these countries narrowly exceeded those of the second group, with 2.5 billion inhabitants (33% of the world population). These are large countries in Southern Asia (India) and countries in Southeast Asia (except Cambodia, Laos and the Philippines). The majority of Latin American and Caribbean countries are in group 3 (except Bolivia, Guatemala, Haiti, Panama and Paraguay). In Africa, this group brings together a few North African countries (Libya and Tunisia) as well as small island countries (Mauritius, Reunion and Cape Verde). By 2100, this set of populations will have grown to 2.1 billion, a fifth instead of a third of the world population (according to estimates and medium-variant) (United Nations 2019a).

– For group 4, the fertility transition will be completed in around 2050. These are Pakistan, Cambodia, Laos and the Philippines in Asia; Algeria and Morocco in North Africa; some Latin American countries (Bolivia, Guatemala, Haiti, Panama and Paraguay) and some sub-Saharan African countries (Botswana, small island countries and South Africa). Group 4 had around 550 million inhabitants in 2019 (7% of the world population), and will count 860 million by 2100, 8% of the world population (according to estimates and medium-variant) (United Nations 2019a).

– Group 5 consists of countries in sub-Saharan Africa (Benin, Burkina Faso, Cameroon, Nigeria, Chad, Togo and Senegal), which will be close to completing their fertility transition by 2100 (between 2.1 and 2.3 children per woman). In 2019, this group brought together approximately 557 million inhabitants (7% of the world population). By the end of the projections, its population will have multiplied more than three times (nearly 1.7 billion inhabitants in 2100), that is to say, 15% of the world population (according to estimates and medium-variant) (United Nations 2019a).

– Finally, group 6 includes countries where fertility will be higher than 2.4 children per woman by 2100. There are not many countries in this group, but its population growth will be extremely high. This group includes Angola, Congo, Côte d'Ivoire, Mauritania, Niger, Somalia, Tanzania and Zambia. It includes 187 million inhabitants in 2019 (2.4% of the world population), and will count 931 million by 2100, that is to say, 8.6% of the world population (according to estimates and medium-variant) (United Nations 2019a).

In summary, in a few decades, based on past and current demographic trends, global demographic change has been radical and a complete geopolitical redistribution is underway, according to the United Nations' medium-variant (United Nations 2019a).

	Complete demographic transition by 2019	Complete demographic transition by 2030	Complete demographic transition between 2030 and 2100
Group 1	1.1 billion Europe, North America, Oceania		1.2 billion
Group 2	2.4 billion Japan, China, Republic of Korea, Democratic People's Republic of Korea, Chile, Brazil, Colombia, Uruguay, Western Asia, Bangladesh, Iran, Sri Lanka		2 billion
Group 3	2.5 billion	India, Southeast Asia[7], Latin America[8], Libya, Tunisia, Mauritius, Réunion Island, Cape Verde	2.1 billion
Group 4	0.550 billion		0.860 billion Pakistan, Cambodia, Laos, Philippines, Algeria, Morocco, Bolivia, Guatemala, Haiti, Panama, Paraguay, Botswana, South Africa
Group 5	0.557 billion		1.7 billion Sub-Saharan Africa[9]
Group 6	0.187 billion		0.931 billion

Note: The definition of a complete demographic transition considers a life expectancy of over 70 years and a total fertility lower than 2.1 children per woman. We only counted the most populated countries in 2019.

Table 1.2. *Groups of countries per demographic transition and population in 2019, 2030 and 2100 (in billions of inhabitants) (source: World Population Prospects 2019 (estimates and medium-variant); United Nations 2019a)*

7 With the exception of: Cambodia, Laos, Pakistan and the Philippines (estimates and medium-variant) (United Nations 2019a), which are in group 4.

8 With the exception of: Bolivia, Haiti, Guatemala, Panama and Paraguay (estimates and medium-variant) (United Nations 2019a), which are in group 4.

9 With the exception of: Angola, the Republic of the Congo, Ivory Coast, Mauritania, Niger, Somalia, Tanzania and Zambia (estimates and medium-variant) (United Nations 2019a) which are in group 6.

If we add to the main countries that completed their demographic transition in 2019 (groups 1 and 2), those of the third group (ending in 2030), this set comprises 78% of 2019's world population (6.1 billion). But this will significantly decrease: by 2100, it will bring together 5.3 billion inhabitants, or 48% of the world population (estimates and medium-variant) (United Nations 2019a). Indeed, the countries which are currently completing their demographic transition will experience a modest population growth, with an older age structure.

However, the population of the main countries where the demographic transition is still "awaiting completion" (groups 4, 5 and 6), which reached 1.3 billion and 16% of the world's population in 2019, will rise to 3.5 billion inhabitants by 2100 and its proportion will double (32%). Its population growth will be high due to the gap between the decline in mortality and the decline in birth rates, and a young age structure.

1.4. The demographic transition in the world

The demographic transition started in the mid-18th century in Europe, prompting two centuries of extraordinary progress reducing the mortality rate, because of the control of epidemics and famine. In France, between 1780 and 1840, life expectancy rose from under 30 to over 40 years of age, and from 1880 to 1940, from 43 to almost 60 years. Infant mortality also fell sharply. Advances in mortality did not take place in all European countries at the same time, or at the same pace. They were interrupted by wars (War of 1870, First World War) and the flu of 1918. Medical discoveries, in particular those of Pasteur on the microbial origin of infectious diseases, health progress and a rise in the standard of living, significantly contributed to reducing epidemics and food shortage (Vallin 2003, pp. 9–14). In addition, the increase in life expectancy continued to soar, reaching over 80 years between 2015–2020 (in Australia, Canada, South Korea, Europe, Japan, Singapore, etc.). In 2019, at a global level, life expectancy for both sexes was 72.3 years: in developed countries, it was 79.2 years, and 72 years in developing countries (United Nations 2019a, Table A.28).

After 1870, the decline in fertility in Europe started later than that of mortality, falling from almost five children to around two or three children per woman on the eve of the Second World War. Only France started limiting births in the mid-18th century, more than a century before other European countries (Festy 1979). The gap between the dates of the beginning of the decline in mortality and that in fertility was responsible for a strong population growth. Thus, the population of England and Wales increased from 6.5 million in 1750 to 42 million in the early 1940s (Vallin 2003, p. 27).

In the mid-20th century, the demographic transition spread to Asia and Latin America, with mortality declining after 1950, followed by fertility circa 1970 (Chesnais 1986a). The decrease in mortality was further accelerated by the effectiveness of health policies resulting from previous experiences in developed countries (Omran 1971). For four decades, between 1940 and 1990, the birth rate greatly exceeded the crude death rate, leading to strong population growth, higher than 2% per year. This figure had never been reached in Europe or in Japan (Chesnais 2002, p. 458). Finally, during the second half of the 20th century, the decline in fertility became widespread. Contrary to what happened in Europe, "the explosion of the Third World" (Vallin 2003, p. 60) resulted in the implementation of birth control policies, thus rapidly reducing fertility. As Vallin wrote, "there are few cases when one can say that the introduction of a birth control program is the main factor underlying a desired reduction in fertility" (Vallin 2011, p. 344). But he rightly emphasized that access is made easier, for couples and for women who wish to limit their births, when such programs exist (Vallin 2011, p. 344).

1.4.1. *The factors which can explain demographic transitions*

To explain the decline in mortality in Europe since the end of the 18th century, Abdel Omran (1971) proposed the theory of epidemiological transition, or the passage from an old mortality regime (the "age of pestilence and famine"), through a transition period of a "decline in pandemics", to finally reach the last age of "degenerative" and "societal" diseases (Omran 1998). Then appeared the more general concept of "health transition" (Meslé and Vallin 2002). During this period, medical advances for reducing infectious and cardiovascular diseases were accompanied by the development of food, agriculture and education, as well as an improvement in the living standards, the establishment of a sanitation infrastructure (drinking water, sewers) and the development of health systems. But, within these dimensions, inequalities have widened, because the entire population does not have equal access to them (Meslé *et al.* 2011, p. 484).

In Europe, the delays in the age for marriage[10] accompanied the secular decline in fertility, in the absence of effective contraception methods for couples. In 1840, Festy made a distinction between countries with late marriages, over the age of

10 Malthus also advocated for this delay in marriage, associated with chastity in celibacy, as a preventive brake on population growth (Malthus 1980).

27 – Scandinavian countries (Denmark, Norway, Sweden), Belgium, the Netherlands, Switzerland – and countries with early marriages, under the age of 26 – Finland, Great Britain, Germany, Austria, Southern Europe (Spain, Italy and Portugal) and North America (Festy 1979, p. 28). He showed the complex relationship between late marriage, low fertility, breastfeeding habits and differences in fecundity between the rich and the poor in 1870 (Festy 1979, p. 42). In addition, "intermediate fertility variables", which are biological, social and economic as well as cultural, work together in the reduction of fertility (Davis and Blake 1956). Bongaarts calculated that they could be reduced to four determining variables, which alone explain the majority of changes in fertility: the age of the first union, the duration of breastfeeding, the use of contraception methods and abortion (Bongaarts 1978). In Asian and Latin American countries, modern contraception and abortion have played a predominant role in birth limitation, because "the contraceptive revolution" reached all the regions in the world (Leridon and Toulemon 2002). In Africa, the duration of prolonged breastfeeding has a reducing effect on the number of children per couple (Tabutin and Schoumaker 2004).

Coale grouped the main macrosocial causes that explain fertility changes in the RWA model (Coale 1973):

– a first factor is the reasoned choice to give birth to a child. The advantages and disadvantages of an additional birth should be accepted by couples. This factor is called *readiness* (R). It determines the beginning of controlled fertility, in particular due to economic reasons;

– a second factor is the perception that low fertility is socially and economically beneficial for mothers and fathers. This factor is called *willingness* (W). It points to the social legitimacy of fertility control within families and a normative/cultural change in values;

– the third factor is the availability of birth control methods and their effective use. This factor is called *ability* (A). It depends on the diffusion of contraception methods, birth control infrastructure, and health and sanitation policies.

According to Coale, the main factors for the fertility transition to come about must simultaneously be economic, cultural and institutional. The three RWA preconditions act mutually, and if only one is lacking, the decline in fertility will not take place (Coale 1973; Lesthaeghe and Vanderhoeft 2001). As not all individuals change their behavior at the same time, and only pioneer groups adopt them, the diffusion toward the rest of the population is conveyed by means of "social interactions" (Bongaarts and Cotts Watkins 1996). But it can be slowed down or accelerated depending on the cultural, religious and linguistic standards of each region[11]. Bourgeois-Pichat (1976) stressed the importance of group effects: "Of course, the couple decides, but they do so according to the social criteria and cultural heritage which, although quickly driven out, paradoxically maintain their rights" (p. 1077).

To explain contemporary demographic transitions, Coale's (1973) diffusion model has been enriched by many authors. McNicoll (1980) analyzed the consequences of political and institutional factors in the behavior of families. Becker (1991) explained the limitation of births within couples due to microeconomic factors. Caldwell (1982) highlighted the role of intergenerational wealth flows: these are transferred from children to parents in high-fertility contexts and their direction changes, from parents to children, when the costs in children's education and health increase, leading to fertility control. From a psychosocial perspective, Fawcett (1983) proposed to take into account the perceptions of the value of children. Simons (1982) was interested in the impact of religious practice on reproductive behavior.

Another theoretical proposition is that of the second demographic transition, which refers to the diversification of family configurations in post-modern societies, marked by the increase in cohabitation outside marriage, the increase in divorces and new cohabitations after union breakdowns, the delay in age for having the first child, the increase in births outside marriage and childless couples. These changes in nuptiality and fertility are probably derived from the primacy of individual choices, more equitable gender relations, greater autonomy for women, macrostructural factors, microeconomic calculations and new cultural models and values, which are expressed individually and collectively (Lesthaeghe 2010). While these movements may have taken place in some European countries, they have not yet spread to all other parts of the world, where family and gender systems are extremely resistant to change.

1.4.2. *Questions*

The observation of contemporary demographic evolution raises questions about the universal validity of the three paradigms by Chesnais to explain the demographic transition: first, on the likelihood of the stabilization hypothesis when the transition is complete; then, on the reproductive transition in two phases (limitation of

11 For example, in 1870, England, the most industrialized country in Europe, maintained a high fertility rate, whereas France, which controlled births since 1750 onwards, was much more rural. Another example is that of Sweden and Germany, where universal primary education was completed in 1870, without reducing family offspring (Coale 1973, p. 65).

marriages, limitation of births); finally, on the influence of entry into modern economic growth (Chesnais 1986a, p. 1061).

The first question concerning the transition's completion is based on the observation of recent upward and downward oscillations in contemporary low fertility. In 1979, Bourgeois-Pichat asked: "Is the current decline in fertility in Europe part of the demographic transition model?" To this question, he gave the following answer:

> What we are currently observing seems to indicate that this last phase is not characterized by constant fertility, but rather by a succession of waves produced by modifications in family structures, which themselves result from variations in fertility. (Bourgeois-Pichat 1979, pp. 293–294)

Vallin also stressed that "the evolutions observed in the most advanced countries are moving further and further away from the model of demographic transition, and, while convergence is still possible, it is unlikely that it will lead to stabilization" (Vallin 2003, p. 75). Moreover, Myrskylä *et al.* (2009) have shown that the relationship between fertility in the most developed countries and the high level in the Human Development Index (HDI)[12] has become positive, which explains the recovery in fertility levels in countries having reached the higher level of development.

The second question concerns the paradigm of the two-phase reproduction transition module (limitation of marriages, and consequent limitation of births), which is not always confirmed. For example, in Mexico, nuptiality is still early: in the 30 generations between 1951 and 1980, the median age for the first union[13] of Mexican women was stable at age 21, despite a significant increase in their education. This did not prevent fertility from decreasing rapidly, and other factors explain this, such as the diffusion of modern contraception methods, including female sterilization (Zavala and Paéz 2016). A comparison between Algeria and Mexico showed that the reduction in fertility was similar between 1970 and 2005: decreasing from 7 to 2.4 children per woman. However, the average age for the first

12 The Human Development Index (HDI) is a multidimensional index, calculated since 1990 by the United Nations Development Program (UNDP), based on three components: life expectancy at birth, education index and GDP (income level) per capita (PNUD 1990). Over time, it has been supplemented by other dimensions (indicator adjustments, gender perspective).

13 These are all consensual unions and marriages. As a matter of fact, co-habiting couples have the same reproductive behavior as married couples (Zavala and Paéz 2016).

union evolved differently throughout the period: while it remained roughly stable in Mexico (from 21 to 23 years old), it sharply increased in Algeria (from 18 to 30 years old) (Cosio Zavala 2012).

Finally, the other paradigm that does not hold true everywhere is that of economic growth to explain changes in fertility. As a matter of fact, in developing countries, there are two fertility transition models: the first model is that of the urban and educated population, which controls their births, following an improvement in their standard of living. The second model, *Malthusian poverty*, has its origin in weak economic growth and poor living conditions. This has been the case in Mexico for three decades, in a situation of interminable economic crisis, where families limit the number of children because they lack the means to raise them (Cosio Zavala 1996). These two fertility transition models are also present in sub-Saharan Africa: in Kenya and Côte d'Ivoire (Vimard and Fassassi 2001), Benin (Capo-Chichi 1999), Nigeria (Caldwell *et al.* 1992) and in a number of countries in the region (Lesthaeghe and Jolly 1995). Therefore, the postulate of a negative relationship between fertility levels and economic growth does not apply to developing countries or to highly developed populations, as mentioned above (Myrskylä *et al.* 2009). It is, therefore, not a global relationship, neither in all places nor at all times, capable of explaining the generalization of the demographic transition worldwide.

In the next section, we will analyze the demographic transition in Latin America and the Caribbean in order to illustrate the diversity and particularity of developments. Having begun around 1900 in the south of the subcontinent, it has barely started in some countries today. The temporal and spatial disparities are very important, depending on social, economic and cultural contexts.

1.5. The demographic transition in Latin America and the Caribbean

The first phase of the Latin American demographic transition began at the end of the 19th century, when mortality declined in countries with high European immigration (Argentina, Cuba, Uruguay) and large cities, with the best urban and hygiene services of the time, inspired by Paris or New York[14]. At the beginning of the 20th century, the lowest crude death rates were found in Uruguay (14 per thousand), Argentina (20 per thousand), Cuba (24 per thousand) and Panama (21 per thousand), whereas the rest of the countries recorded crude death rates above 30 per thousand (Delaunay and Cosio Zavala 1992, p. 17).

14 Buenos Aires was considered one of the most modern cities in the world. The first metro in Latin America was built there in 1914 (Rivière d'Arc and Schneier 1993, p. 220).

For the whole of Latin America[15], Arriaga estimated life expectancy at 25 years around 1825, and at 27 years around 1900 (Arriaga 1968), a considerable delay compared to European levels, which reached around 41 years for life expectancy by 1840 in Sweden, England, Wales and France (Vallin 2003, p. 5). Large differences were also observed within the subcontinent, depending on regions, infrastructure and economic and social development levels. In Cuba, for example, life expectancy in 1910 reached 34 years for men and 37 years for women (Albizu-Campos 2000). The decline in Cuban mortality was particularly rapid and Cuba has the lowest infant mortality rate in Latin America, with a rate of four deaths of children under the age of 1 per thousand births between 2015–2020 (United Nations 2019a, Mort/1-1).

Table 1.3 shows the changes in life expectancies and the infant mortality rate between 1950 and 2020.

1.5.1. *The modes of accelerated mortality reduction*

In the mid-20th century, the rapid decline in mortality spread throughout Latin America and the Caribbean (Table 1.3). In two decades, between 1950–1955 and 1970–1975, life expectancies at birth increased by almost 10 years, and between 1980–1985 and 2000–2005, the increase was 7 years. Over the last period, between 2000–2005 and 2015–2020, the increase was 3 years. Then, during the 1980s, the "lost decade"[16], the progress in mortality slowed down (Table 1.3) due to the Latin American economic crisis. The end of the 2000s also saw a stagnation in mortality, as the health transition now tackles chronic, degenerative diseases and violent causes, in a context of increasing social inequalities, demographic aging and great disparities between cities and rural areas, depending on gender and educational level.

However, over the whole 1950–2020 period, life expectancy at birth increased by 23.8 years (3.4 years per year on average). The infant mortality rate decreased from 126 deaths in 1950–1955 to 59 in 1980–1985, then to 15 deaths of children under the age of 1 per 1,000 births in 2015–2020. Therefore, according to these two

---

15 Latin America comprises the member countries of the United Nations Economic Commission for Latin America and the Caribbean (ECLAC). In a first definition, comprising 20 countries in total, the former English and Dutch possessions as well as the French departments were excluded. Since 1984, the ECLAC region has included all the countries or territories, whether independent or not (38 countries in 2020).

16 In Latin America, the "lost decade" refers to the years 1980–1990, a period of crisis in the Latin American development model, marked by the weight of foreign debt and structural adjustment programs (CEPALC 2019).

indicators, the decline in mortality was particularly swift, reaching 75 years of life expectancy at birth in 2020 for both sexes (Table 1.3).

	1950–1955	1970–1975	1980–1985	2000–2005	2015–2020
Life expectancy (years)	51.4	61.2	65.3	72.3	75.2
Infant mortality rate (per thousand)	126	80	59	25	15

Table 1.3. *Life expectancy at birth and infant mortality in Latin America and the Caribbean: 1950–2020 (sexes combined) (source: United Nations 2019a, File/Mort 1-1 and Mort 7-1)*

Between 1950–1955 and 2015–2020, life expectancies at birth converged among nations. Between 1950–1955, the lowest values were 38 years in Haiti and 40 years in Bolivia; the highest, 63 years in Argentina and 66 years in Uruguay: the difference was 28 years between the two extreme values. Between 2015–2020, Costa Rica reached 80 years of life expectancy at birth; Haiti had the lowest value (64 years), which is a 16 years difference between extreme values (Figure 1.1). Spanning seven decades, mortality declined more rapidly in countries with high initial levels (Honduras, Peru and Nicaragua). Bolivia gained 31.5 years of life expectancy at birth, which is considerable from its initial level of 39.6 years. In Mexico, rapid progress has stalled since 2000, following an increase in homicides (Cosio Zavala 2017, pp. 25–27). In Argentina, the increase is steady, whereas Costa Rica has drawn level with and then overtaken Cuba (Figure 1.1).

For Latin America and the Caribbean as a whole, between 2015–2020, female life expectancy at birth (78.5 years) was 6.5 years higher than that of men (72 years). For women, the two extreme values in 1950–1955 were those of Uruguay and Haiti (69 and 39 years, respectively), a difference of 30 years, whereas in 2015–2020, the difference between Costa Rica (83 years) and Haiti (66 years) was 17 years. Among men, in 1950–1955, the difference between extreme values was 27 years (63 years in Uruguay versus 36 years in Haiti), and 16 years in 2015–2020 (77 years in Chile and Costa Rica, and 61 years in Haiti) (United Nations 2019a, Mort/7-2 and 7-3). There is, therefore, a certain convergence in mortality between countries over time, although that of men continues to be higher than that of women.

Between 2015 and 2020, we can classify the mortality of Latin American countries into three groups, based on life expectancy at birth for women, which have the most favorable values:

– In a first group, it exceeds 80 years in Cuba, Argentina and Uruguay, which had low mortality levels since the beginning of the demographic transition[17]. This also includes countries that experienced rapid progress in the medical field and in health (Chile, Costa Rica, Panama) and many Caribbean islands in relation to their metropolises (Barbados, Curaçao, Guadeloupe, Martinique, Puerto Rico, Virgin Islands). Infant mortality rates are low within this group: between 4 (Cuba) and 18 (Panama) deaths of children under the age of 1 per thousand births (United Nations 2019a, Mort/7-3).

– The second group is between 75 and 80 years: Brazil, Colombia, Ecuador, Peru, Paraguay, Venezuela in South America; Belize, El Salvador, Guatemala, Honduras, Mexico, Nicaragua in Central America; Antigua, Aruba, Bahamas, Dominican Republic, Jamaica, Saint Vincent and Trinidad and Tobago in the Caribbean. These countries reached 70 years in the late 1980s, except El Salvador, Guatemala, Honduras and Nicaragua, with around 60 years around 1980. But these Central American countries quickly drew level, reaching the values of the second group in the 1990s. Infant mortality rates reached between 15 and 20 deaths of children under the age of 1 per 1,000 births in Venezuela (15), Mexico (17), Peru (18) and Brazil (20); they ranged from 23 to 31 deaths of children under the age of 1 per 1,000 births in Honduras (23) and Nicaragua and Guatemala (31), reflecting poor living conditions and high economic and social vulnerability (United Nations 2019a, Mort/7-3).

– The third group includes four countries, Haiti, Bolivia, Guyana and Suriname, whose female life expectancy at birth is lower than 75 years. These are the poorest countries in Latin America, with many economic and political difficulties, and high social inequality (CEPAL 2019). Infant mortality in Haiti is 64 and in Bolivia it equals 42 deaths of children under the age of 1 per thousand births, which are very high levels (United Nations 2019a, Mort/7-3).

It should be noted that the remarkable progress made in the fight against mortality has been achieved in a coordinated manner. The Pan American Health Organization (PAHO)[18], founded in 1902, has organized medical and sanitation programs in all Latin American countries (installation of drinking water, sewage systems, massive vaccination campaigns, fight against yellow fever, malaria, tuberculosis, measles and other infectious and parasitic diseases). From 1950, they effectively reduced infectious and parasitic mortality, as well as infant mortality,

---

17 They were populated mainly by immigrants of European origin at the end of the 19th century and early 20th century (Cosio Zavala 1998), with relatively low mortality rates upon arrival.

18 All Latin American countries are members of PAHO, and France, the United Kingdom and the Netherlands also take part in it. Puerto Rico is an associated member.

regardless of the population's living standards, by taking advantage of the discoveries of developed countries. However, during the economic crisis of the 1980s (the lost decade), programs to combat mortality experienced funding restrictions, causing the return of malaria and measles (Cosio Zavala 1998, pp. 39–40). With time, new infectious diseases came into existence, such as AIDS, dengue, Zika, chikungunya and Covid-19.

In 2017, the PAHO declared that in Latin America and the Caribbean, the Millennium Development Goals (MDGs) had all been achieved in 2015, except for MDG5 on maternal mortality. The PAHO is also responsible for monitoring the sustainable development goals (SDGs) in progress, including SDG3 on good health and well-being (PAHO 2017).

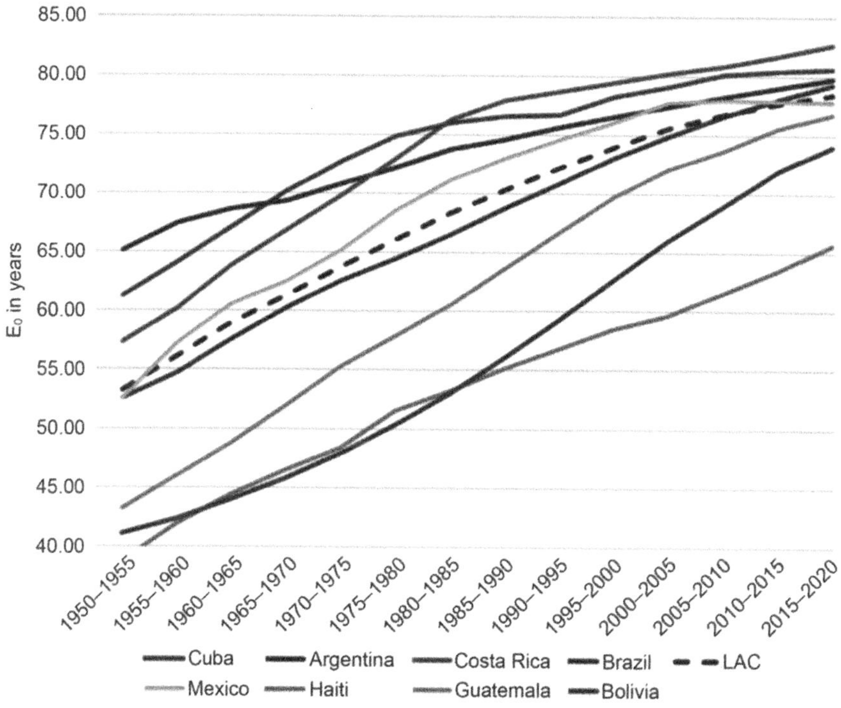

Figure 1.1. *Female life expectancy at birth per 5-year periods, 1950–2020. LAC (Latin America and the Caribbean) group and selected countries (source: United Nations 2019a, Mort/7-3). For a color version of this figure, see www.iste.co.uk/charbit/demographic.zip*

1.5.2. *The period of strong population growth*

A period of strong growth in the Latin American population began in the mid-20th century, following the decline in mortality. Between 1950 and 1970, natural increase rates rose to over 2.5%, reaching 2.75% per year between 1960 and 1965 (Cosio Zavala 1998). This was a consequence of the decrease in mortality, increase in nuptiality and high fertility. Indeed, a Latin American *union boom* was observed between 1950 and 1960[19]. The percentages of women in union increased, with particularly early unions and universal nuptiality (as was the case of Nicaragua between 1950 and 1960, where 60% of women between 20 and 24 years old were in union, as well as 97% of women aged 50). It was only in the southern countries of South America (Argentina, Chile, Uruguay) that unions came later, although these increased during the period of the union boom (Camisa 1978).

Fertility in Latin America remained very high before 1965, and all countries showed indicators of between 6 and 7.4 children per woman, with the exception of a few countries with moderate fertility (between three and five children per woman), such as Argentina, Chile, Cuba and Uruguay (United Nations 2019a, Fert/4). High fertility was the result of the association of a lasting marital life, *natural* fertility in couples (who did not control their births), early and intense nuptiality, the decline in mortality which reduced intrauterine mortality and widowhood (divorce being very rare in those times) and the reduction in the infertility of couples, thanks to medical, nutritional and health progress.

1.5.3. *New reproductive behavior*

After 1965, fertility was quickly transformed in Latin America and the Caribbean. We can identify four fertility transition models, as follows:

– An early transition that occurred, since 1900, in Argentina and Uruguay, with a total fertility rate in 1960–1965 of 3.1 and 2.9 children per woman, respectively (United Nations 2019a, Fert/4). These countries had a particular history: strong immigration of European origin, fast urbanization and good living conditions since the end of the 19th century. Immigrants from Italy, Spain and Eastern Europe arrived as carriers of the family standards from their home countries, where the fertility transition had already started. Fertility decreased throughout the 20th century, and did so until 2015–2020, slowly but steadily, then accelerated at the end of this period (Figure 1.2).

---

19 Non-legal (*consensual*) unions have always been extremely common in Latin America and the Caribbean, and therefore must be considered in the nuptiality study together with legal marriages. We therefore refer to unions, and not only to marriages, for studying nuptiality (Camisa 1978).

– A transition that started around 1965 in Cuba[20] (4.7 children per woman in 1960–1965) and in Chile (4.6 children per woman in 1960–1965) (United Nations 2019a, Fert/4). High education and urbanization made it possible to reduce fertility, reaching 1.9 and 2.6 children per woman in 1980–1985, with a drop of 60% and 40%, respectively. In the second period (1980–2015), the decline continued in these two countries, but at a slower pace (Figure 1.2).

– An accelerated transition that occurred between 1965 and 2015 in Brazil, Colombia, El Salvador, Ecuador, Mexico, Peru, Panama, Dominican Republic and Venezuela. In this group of countries, fertility in 1960–1965 oscillated between 6 and 7.4 children per woman, then between 3.5 and 5 children per woman in 1980–1985, and finally, in 2015–2020, between 1.7 and 2.5 children per woman. In Colombia and Costa Rica, the reduction in the total fertility rate was 46% between 1960 and 1985, and greater than 30% in Brazil, Mexico, Panama and Venezuela (United Nations 2019a, Fert/4).

– A late and extremely rapid transition that occurred in Bolivia, Guatemala, Haiti, Honduras, Nicaragua and Paraguay. These countries maintained a high fertility level in 1980–1985, with values between five and six children per woman. The decline in fertility after this date reached a reduction equal to or greater than 50%, and fertility in 2015–2020 oscillated between 2.5 and 3 children per woman (United Nations 2019a, Fert/4).

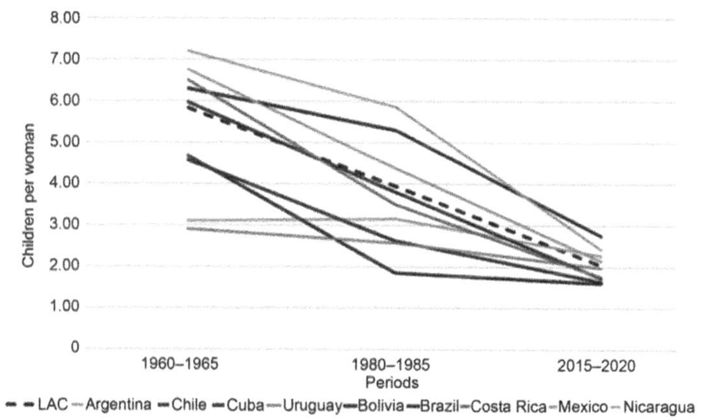

Figure 1.2. *Total fertility rate in Latin America and the Caribbean (LAC): 1960–1965, 1980–1985, 2015–2020 (source: United Nations 2019a, Fert/4; LAC group and selected countries). For a color version of this figure, see www.iste.co.uk/charbit/demographic.zip*

---

20 Cuba experienced a post-revolutionary baby boom between 1959 and 1970 (Cosio Zavala 1998).

Consequently, fertility converged in the region after 1965. All countries, regardless of their reproductive history, showed fertility levels between 1.6 and 3 children per woman in 2015–2020, whereas the starting levels in 1960–1965 ranged from 2.9 in Uruguay to 7.4 children per woman in the Dominican Republic. This transformation of Latin America's fertility rate can be explained by the contraceptive revolution that occurred between 1965 and 1990, and by Malthusian poverty.

In 2019, contraceptive prevalence in Latin America and the Caribbean rose to 58% of women aged between 15 and 49 years using contraception methods. Female sterilization predominated, with 16% users for the whole region, 30% in the Dominican Republic and more than 20% in El Salvador, Colombia, Ecuador and Mexico. The pill follows with 15% for the Latin American average, but 30% in Brazil. Sterilization is the first female method in Cuba (25% of users), and 24% of Cubans use the IUD, in a country where many legal abortions occur[21] (United Nations 2019b).

The diffusion of modern contraception methods explained the decrease in fertility in Latin America after 1965, as family planning programs were established in the majority of countries, making it possible to meet the demand for birth control on the part of educated, economically active women living in large cities, with high standards of living (Cosio Zavala 1992). The use of modern contraception methods spread rapidly in these well-situated social categories, which followed the path of the societies that started the modern contraceptive revolution (Leridon and Toulemon 2002).

However, for disadvantaged social categories, a different fertility transition model took place, in the form of a late and rapid decrease. Until 1985, the poorest and least educated populations maintained high fertility, between five and six children per woman, as in Bolivia, Guatemala, Haiti, Honduras, Nicaragua and Paraguay (United Nations 2019a, Fert/4). Then, their fertility dropped extremely quickly. *Malthusian poverty* came about when disadvantaged families had to limit their births in order to be able to survive given that modern contraception methods were widely available to them:

> Far from conveying a harmonious social development, this stresses the bankruptcy of the economic model, the deterioration of the living standards and the effects of the crisis which dramatically hit the most disadvantaged social strata, while an abundant parallel offer of family planning services were developing. (Cosio Zavala 1998, p. 67)

21 It is difficult to know how many legal abortions are practiced in Cuba, because the most common method is aspiration at an early stage of pregnancy, called menstrual regulation, for which there are no statistics.

In Table 1.4, we present a summary of the Latin American transitions in mortality and fertility, in 2015–2020, resulting in 10 differentiated groups depending on the different combinations.

Mortality transitions	Fertility transitions: Highly advanced TFR < 2.0	Advanced TFR = 2.0	Major 2.4 ≥ TFR > 2.1	Moderate TFR = 2.5	In progress TFR > 2.5
Advanced $E_0 \geq 78$ years	Chile 80/1.7 Costa Rica 80/1.8 Cuba 79/1.6	Uruguay 78/2.0		Panama 78/2.5	
Average 78 years $< E_0 \geq 75$ years	Brazil 76/1.7 Colombia 77/1.8		Argentina 76/2.3 Ecuador 77/2.4 Mexico 75/2.1 Peru 76/2.3	Honduras 75/2.5	
In progress 72 years $\geq E_0 \leq 74$ years			Dominican Republic 74/2.4 El Salvador 73/2.1 Nicaragua 74/2.4 Venezuela 72/2.3	Paraguay 74/2.5	Guatemala 74/2.9
Starting $E_0 < 72$ years					Bolivia 71/2.8 Haiti 64/3.0

Table 1.4. *Latin American and Caribbean countries according to mortality and fertility transitions (2015–2020) (source: United Nations 2019a; Tables Mort/7-1 and Fert/4)*[22]

1.6. Conclusion

The story of the demographic transition in Europe and its subsequent generalization in the world is part of a common demographic framework, despite

22 In Table 1.4, the 20 countries are those belonging to the CEPAL in 1984. E_0 is the life expectancy at birth (in years, both sexes combined) and TFR is the total fertility rate (number of children per woman). The numbers after the country name represent the E_0/TFR between 2015–2020.

great economic, social and cultural differences among different regions and periods. Challenging the concept of a universal theory is based on the diversity of stages and factors which provoke it, as well as on the lack of evidence for the hypothesis of population convergence and stabilization (Vallin 2003).

Furthermore, beyond the analyses at a global scale, if one takes into account social and territorial inequalities, migrations, as well as cultural and religious dimensions, different models of demographic transition arise, depending on historical, economic, social and institutional contexts.

We can indeed conclude:

> That there is no single model of demographic transition, since the conditions under which it occurs are under the influence of temporal and spatial variables, the values and standards of each society, of its economic and social organization. (Unesco 1996, p. 8)

And therefore, it is necessary to study the social, regional and cultural dimensions of demographic trends in more depth. This is what has led to a considerable number of works on the subject, for decades and still nowadays.

It is in fact paradoxical and stimulating that the concept of demographic transition has been criticized from all sides, but that it is at the origin of fundamental investigations to understand the common history and the possible future of demographic changes worldwide.

1.7. References

Albizu-Campos Espiñeira, J.C. (2000). *Mortalidad y supervivencia en Cuba en los 90*. Centro de Estudios Demográficos, Barcelona and Universidad de La Habana, Cuba.

Arriaga, E.E. (1968). Components of city growth in selected Latin American countries. *The Milbank Memorial Fund Quarterly*, 46(2), 237–252.

Avdeev, A., Eremenko, T., Festy, P., Gaymu, J., Le Bouteillec, N., Springer, S. (2011). Populations and demographic trends of European countries, 1980–2010. *Population*, 66(1), 9–129.

Becker, G. (1991). *Fertility and the Economy*. Population Research Center/University of Chicago, Chicago.

Bongaarts, J. (1978). A framework for analyzing the proximate determinants of fertility. *Population and Development Review*, 4, 105–132.

Bongaarts, J. and Cotts Watkins, S. (1996). Social interactions and contemporary fertility transitions. *Population and Development Review*, 22(4), 639–682.

Boserup, E. (1985). Economic and demographic interrelationships in sub-Saharan Africa. *Population and Development Review*, 11(3), 393–398.

Bourgeois-Pichat, J. (1976). Baisse de la fécondité et descendance finale. *Population*, 31(6), 1045–1097.

Bourgeois-Pichat, J. (1979). La baisse actuelle de la fécondité en Europe s'inscrit-elle dans le modèle de la transition démographique ? *Population*, 2, 267–305.

Caldwell, J.C. (1982). The wealth flows theory of fertility decline. In *Determinants of Fertility Trends: Theories Re-examined*, Hohn, C., Mackensen, T. (eds). Ordina, Liège.

Caldwell, J.C., Orubuloye, I.O., Caldwell, P. (1992). Fertility decline in Africa: A new type of transition? *Population and Development Review*, 18(2), 211–242.

Camisa, Z.C. (1978). La nupcialidad de las mujeres solteras en América latina. *Notas de Población*, 18, Naciones Unidas Comisión Económica para América Latina (CEPAL), Santiago.

Capo-Chichi, P.V.A. (1999). Fertility transition in Benin: New reproductive patterns or traditional behaviours? PhD Thesis, London School of Hygiene & Tropical Medicine, London [Online]. Available at: http://researchonline.lshtm.ac.uk/682287 [Accessed 22 February 2020].

CEPAL (2019). *Panorama Social de América Latina 2019*. United Nations, Comisión Económica para América Latina y el Caribe, Santiago.

Chesnais, J.-C. (1986a). *La transition démographique : étapes, formes, implications économiques. Étude de séries temporelles (1720–1984) relatives à 67 pays*. INED, Paris.

Chesnais, J.-C. (1986b). La transition démographique : étapes, formes, implications économiques. Etude de séries temporelles (1720–1984) relatives à 67 pays. Présentation d'un Cahier de l'INED. *Population*, 41(6), 1059–1070.

Chesnais, J.-C. (2002). La transition démographique : 35 ans de bouleversements (1965–2000). In *La Population du monde. Géants démographiques et défis internationaux*, 2nd edition, Chasteland, J.-C., Chesnais, J.-C. (eds). INED, Paris.

Coale, A.J. (ed.) (1973). The demographic transition reconsidered. In *International Population Conference*. UIESP, Liège.

Coale, A.J. and Cotts Watkins, S. (eds) (1986). *The Decline of Fertility in Europe*. Princeton University Press, Princeton.

Cosio Zavala, M.E. (1992). La transición demográfica en América Latina y en Europa. *Notas de Población*, Centro Latinoamericano de Demografía (CELADE), 20(56), 11–32.

Cosio Zavala, M.E. (1996). Malthusianisme de la pauvreté au Mexique. In *Populations. L'État des connaissances*, Leridon, H. (ed.). INED/La Découverte, Paris.

Cosio Zavala, M.E. (1998). *Changements démographiques en Amérique latine*. Estem, Paris.

Cosio Zavala, M.E. (2011). Démographie, pauvreté et inégalités. In *Les enjeux du développement en Amérique latine. Dynamiques socioéconomiques et politiques publiques*, Quenan, C., Velut, S. (eds). Institut des Amériques et Agence française de développement, Paris.

Cosio Zavala, M.E. (2012). Les transitions démographiques du XXe siècle dans les pays en développement, des contre-exemples théoriques ? *Les Cahiers D'EMAM*, 21, 13–31.

Cosio Zavala, M.E. (2017). Les jeunes en Amérique latine, un point de vue démographique. *Problèmes d'Amérique latine*, 105(2), 13–28.

Cosio Zavala, M.E. and Paéz, O. (2016). Tendencias y determinantes de la fecundidad en México: las desigualdades sociales. In *Generaciones, cursos de vida y desigualdad social*, Coubès, M.L., Solís, P., Cosio Zavala, M.E. (eds). El Colegio de México/El Colegio de la Frontera Norte, Mexico/Tijuana.

Davis, K. (1945). The world demographic transition. *The Annals of the American Academy of Political and Social Science*, 237(1), 1–11.

Davis, K. and Blake, J. (1956). Social structure and fertility: An analytic framework. *Economic Development and Cultural Change*, 4, 211–235.

Delaunay, D. and Cosio Zavala, M.E. (1993). Populations et sociétés. In *L'Amérique du Sud aux XIXe et XXe siècles. Héritages et territoires*, Rivière d'Arc, H. (ed.). Armand Colin, Paris.

Fawcett, J.T. (1983). Perceptions of the value of children: Satisfactions and costs. In *Determinants of Fertility in Developing Countries: A Summary of Knowledge, volume 1. Supply and Demand for Children*, Bulatao, R., Lee, R. (eds). Academic Press, New York.

Festy, P. (1979). *La fécondité des pays occidentaux de 1870 à 1970*. INED/PUF, Paris.

Guzmán, J.M., Rodríguez, J., Martínez, J., Contreras, J.M., González, D. (2006). La démographie de l'Amérique latine et de la Caraïbe depuis 1950. *Population*, 61(5), 623–733.

Landry, A. (1982). *La Révolution démographique : études et essais sur les problèmes de la population*. INED, Paris.

Leridon, H. and Toulemon, L. (2002). La régulation des naissances se généralise. In *La Population du monde. Géants démographiques et défis internationaux*, 2nd edition, Chasteland, J.-C., Chesnais, J.-C. (eds). INED, Paris.

Lesthaeghe, R. (2010). The unfolding story of the second demographic transition. *Population and Development Review*, 36(2), 211–251.

Lesthaeghe, R. and Jolly, C. (1995). The start of the sub-Saharan fertility transition: Some answers and many questions. *Journal of International Development*, 7(1), 25–45.

Lesthaeghe, R. and Vanderhoeft, C. (2001). Ready, willing and able. A conceptualization of transitions to new behavioral forms. In *Diffusion Processes and Fertility Transition*, Casterline, J.B. (ed.). US National Research/Committee on Population, Washington.

Malthus, T.R. (1980). *Essai sur le principe de population*. INED, Paris.

McNicoll, G. (1980). Institutional determinants of fertility change. *Population and Development Review*, 6(3), 441–462.

Meslé, F. and Vallin, J. (1995). *La mortalité dans le monde : tendances et perspectives*. Centre français sur la population et le développement, Paris.

Meslé, F. and Vallin, J. (2002). La transition sanitaire : tendances et perspectives. In *Démographie, analyse et synthèse, volume III. Les déterminants de la mortalité*, Caselli, G., Wunsch, G., Vallin, J. (eds). INED, Paris.

Meslé, F., Toulemon, L., Véron, J. (2011). *Dictionnaire de démographie et des sciences de la population*. Armand Colin, Paris.

Myrskylä, M., Kohler, H., Billari, F. (2009). Advances in development reverse fertility declines. *Nature*, 460, 741–743 [Online]. Available at: www.semanticscholar.org/paper/Advances-in-development-reverse-fertility-declines-Myrskyl%C3%A4-Kohler/2a24121c15b0715a086b0635e6a530d49250aaba#paper-header [Accessed 22 February 2020].

Notestein, F.W. (1945). Population. The long view. In *Food for the World*, Schultz, E. (ed.). University of Chicago Press, Chicago.

Omran, A. (1971). The epidemiological transition: A theory of the epidemiology of population change. *The Milbank Memorial Fund Quarterly*, 49(4), 509–538.

Omran, A. (1998). The epidemiological transition theory revisited thirty years later. *World Health Statistics Quarterly*, 51(2–4), 99–109.

OPS (2017). Informe quinquenal 2013–2017 del Director de la Oficina Sanitaria Panamericana. Abogar por la salud a favor del desarrollo sostenible y la equidad: En el camino hacia la salud universal. Report, Organización Panamericana de la Salud, Washington [Online]. Available at: http://iris.paho.org [Accessed 2 February 2020].

PNUD (1990). *Rapport mondial sur le développement humain 1990*. Economica, Paris.

Rabinowicz, L. (1929). *Le problème de la population en France précédé d'une Histoire générale de la population : étude de sociologie de la population*. Marcel Rivière, Paris.

Rivière d'Arc, H. and Schneier, G. (1993). De Caracas à Rio et Buenos Aires : un siècle d'aspiration à la modernité urbaine. In *L'Amérique du Sud aux XIXe et XXe siècles. Héritages et territoires*, Rivière d'Arc, H. (ed.). Armand Colin, Paris.

Simons, J. (1982). Reproductive behaviour as religious practice. In *Determinants of Fertility Trends: Theories Re-examined*, Hohn, C., Mackensen, T. (eds). Ordina, Liège.

Tabutin, D. and Schoumaker, B. (2004). La démographie au sud du Sahara des années 1950 aux années 2000. Synthèse des changements et bilanstatistique. *Population*, 59(3–4), 521–622.

Unesco (1996). Population and quality of life: Synopsis of the theme papers solicited by the independent commission on population and quality of life. Paper, EPD-96/WS/3, Unesco, Paris.

United Nations (2019a). World Population Prospects 2019, volume I: Comprehensive tables (ST/ESA/SER.A/426). Department of Economic and Social Affairs, Population Division [Online]. Available at: https://population.un.org/wpp/Download/Standard/Population/ [Accessed 2 July 2020].

United Nations (2019b). Contraceptive use by method 2019 (ST/ESA/SER.A/435). Department of Economic and Social Affairs, Division de la Population, New York [Online]. Available at: www.un.org/en/development/desa/population/publications/pdf/family/ContraceptiveUseByMethodDataBooklet2019.pdf [Accessed 2 February 2020].

Vallin, J. (2011). Faut-il une politique de population ? In *Dictionnaire de démographie et des sciences de la population*, Meslé, F., Toulemon, L., Véron, J. (eds). Armand Colin, Paris.

Vimard, P. and Fassassi, R. (2001). Vers deux modèles de transition de la fécondité en Afrique subsaharienne ? In *Les transitions démographiques des pays du Sud*, Gendreau, F., Poupard M. (eds). AUPELF-UREF/ESTEM, Montreal/Paris.

2

Demographic Dividend and Dependency Ratios

Vincent TURBAT
Georgetown University, Washington, DC, USA

2.1. Introduction

In recent years, discussions on how to capture a demographic dividend have come to dominate the debate on international development in sub-Saharan Africa. The demographic dividend concept, which was developed in the seminal paper by Bloom *et al.* (2003), is encapsulated in the rapid economic growth (about 7% per year) that resulted from a rapid demographic transition experienced by the four East Asian countries (the Four Asian Tigers) between the early 1960s and 1990s. This chapter's common point of discussion is whether sub-Saharan Africa can replicate the policies implemented by the Four Asian Tiger countries and thus benefit from a first demographic dividend. To answer this question we focus on the dependency burden as assessed through the dependency ratio. In section 2.2, we revisit the first demographic dividend concept and focus on the pivotal role of the dependency ratio concept. We then analyze three different dependency ratios: a demographic dependency ratio (DDR), an employment dependency ratio (EDR) and a socioeconomic dependency ratio (SDR), and provide estimated data for each. In section 2.3, we study several sub-Saharan Africa's dependency ratios, which we compare with East Asia's dependency ratios, assess the prospects of sub-Saharan African countries to benefit from a first demographic dividend and execute the main actions to be undertaken to increase their potential to benefit from a demographic dividend. In conclusion, we evaluate the prospects for sub-Saharan Africa countries to capture a first demographic dividend by 2035.

Demographic Dynamics and Development,
coordinated by Yves CHARBIT.

2.2. The dependency ratios, main indicators of the potential of a first demographic dividend

Today's development projects, such as the World Bank's Sahel Women Empowerment and Demographic Dividend project (World Bank 2014), put the demographic dividend at the top of the priorities that less developed countries should pursue. They aim to help these countries to develop the policies that would (1) open up a demographic dividend window of opportunity; (2) employ the working age population bulge that results from the demographic transition; and (3) ensure that an increasing number of people are self-sufficient.

2.2.1. *The demographic dividend*

The concept of demographic dividend is an addition to the long list of works that aim to assess the impact of population growth on economic growth. It is now well documented that the concept of demographic dividend has been developed on the basis of an ex post analysis of the rapid growth in the four East Asian countries (that are called "tigers" or "dragons") between the early 1960s and 1990s. The Four Asian Tiger countries are as follows: Hong-Kong, Singapore, South Korea and Taiwan.

Just before they experienced what Rostow (1960) calls a "take off" (characterized by an exponential economic growth rate), the Tiger countries experienced a *demographic transition*. The latter begins with a marked decrease in mortality rates, especially infant (under 1 year or U1) and child (U5) mortality rates. This translates into a rapid growth of the general population, and especially the youth.

After a period of variable duration, the total fertility rate also starts to decrease. If the decline is sharp, this translates into a marked reduction of the crude birth rate and therefore of the population growth rate. In the case of the Tiger countries, it is worth noting that (i) the time lag between the start in the reduction of mortality and the start in the reduction of fertility rates was quite short (about 10–15 years), and (ii) the decrease rate in both mortality and fertility rates was rather sharp (see below). These two elements, along with favorable macroeconomic conditions, and the choice of the right macroeconomic policies, explain the high impact of the demographic transition on the economy of these countries.

The "baby boom" or "population swell" (Bloom *et al.* 2003) that results from the period between the decrease in mortality rates and the decrease in population growth, due to a decrease in fertility rates, will progressively be accompanied by a change in the age structure of the population. And when the "baby boomers" reach the working age (which, so far, is generally defined as being 15–64), the dependency ratio starts also to change, and with it, an opportunity to benefit from a demographic dividend.

The demographic dividend can be defined as an economic surplus resulting from a relative increase in the employed working-age population compared to the dependents, in particular, the young dependents (Turbat 2017). This economic surplus is generated by two elements: (i) the release of resources due to a decrease in the dependency ratio and (ii) an increase in gross domestic product (GDP) due to the arrival of the "boom generation" on the labor market. This economic surplus translates into a greater amount of resources, expressed in terms of GDP. These additional resources are in excess of what is needed to cover the current needs of the dependents, and are available either for investment in both fixed and human capital or for additional consumption (May and Turbat 2017). It should be noted that a second demographic dividend could be triggered, but in a longer term. This second demographic dividend would result from an increase in adult longevity, which causes individuals to save more in preparation for old age. This increase in savings can thus contribute to capital accumulation and economic growth (see Lee and Mason (2006)). In this chapter, we only address the prospects of, and the policies for, a first demographic dividend in sub-Saharan Africa.

Besides the time lag and the pace of the demographic transition, a second element will be key in the occurrence and magnitude of a first demographic dividend: the timing of the opening of the demographic window of opportunity (Parant and Hommel 2019) to generate a demographic dividend. There are three main formulations (May and Guengant forthcoming) of this opening. The first is to consider that the window of opportunity opens when (i) the percentages of those aged less than 15 years reach 30% and below of the total population, and (ii) those aged 65 years remain below 15% of the total population. Using the UN 2019 population projections, May and Guengant (forthcoming) obtained different results for the projection of low and high variants. As of 2020, only five sub-Saharan African countries meet the two age conditions above.

A second formulation is that the window of opportunity opens when the demographic dependency ratio (the number of persons aged less than 15 years and 65 years and above, divided by those aged 15–64 years) becomes equal to or less than 0.6. May and Guengant (forthcoming) found that six sub-Saharan African countries already have such a dependency ratio.

The third formulation, which we are adopting in this chapter, is that the window of demographic opportunity opens when the working age population (15–64 or

19–64) is growing faster than the total population, and especially the young population (U15 or U19) as a result of a decrease in the fertility rate. As all sub-Saharan African countries have started their fertility decline, this implies that all sub-Saharan Africa countries have already entered the demographic window of opportunity. However, some Central and West African countries have just entered this window, and very timidly, as they still have high dependency ratios. Others, mostly in East and Southern Africa, are in the middle, and a few, mostly in Southern Africa, are entering the last stage of this process.

2.2.2. *The dependency ratios*

The concept of dependency burden is in many respects similar to the global burden of disease, as dependency is considered as a global cost that should be borne by the whole economy of a country, and especially by those who are contributing to the GDP of this economy. This global cost includes all direct (at household level) and indirect (at meso- and macro-levels) expenditures that are needed to bring an educated and healthy youth to working age and ensure that the elderly receive a decent retirement. To measure a dependency burden, the common indicator is the ratio of young and old dependents to the working age population, a ratio that varies as a country moves through its demographic transition (Bongaarts 2009). In this chapter, we call the dependency ratio based on age groups a demographic dependency ratio (DDR). Following a modest initial rise, the DDR typically undergoes a prolonged period of decline that is closely linked to the decline in fertility. The timing, duration and magnitude of the decrease in the dependency ratio in mid-transitional societies are largely determined by the timing, duration and magnitude of fertility declines.

The DDR's formula has the dependents (U15 or U19, and 65+) as the numerator, and the working age population as the denominator. The working age population will be labeled as providers (also called supporters in the National Transfer Accounts), as they are providing for (or supporting) the dependents. The higher the ratio, the heavier the dependency burden (with each provider supporting a higher number of dependents).

$$\text{DDR} = \frac{(\text{Number of people aged } 0-14 \text{ and } 65 \text{ and over})}{(\text{Number of people aged } 15-64)} \times 100$$

However, this first estimate of the burden of dependency needs to be re-examined for two main reasons. First, on the dependents' side, today's children remain dependents well beyond the age of 15 in less developed countries (as in more developed countries), and older people often fall into the dependents' category again before they reach the age of 65. As expected, our calculation of DDRs with U19 and 65 and over as the numerator and 19–64 as the denominator shows that the DDR U15 underestimate the actual demographic dependency burden. Second, and more importantly, on the providers' side, a sizeable portion of the working age population might be unemployed and, therefore, should be added to the dependents in the numerator and subtracted from the number of working age people in the denominator. It could be argued that people who are under-employed should be treated similarly, although accurate data on under-employment are usually difficult to obtain. Therefore, we calculate an "employment dependency ratio" (EDR), which we define as the number of people that are unemployed (or inactive), whatever their age, *divided* by the number of people that are working (or active), whatever their age. The formula is as follows:

$$\text{EDR} = \frac{(\text{Under 15} + \text{Over 65}) + (\text{Unemployed 15 to 64}) - (\text{Employed U15 and 65} +)}{(\text{15 to 64}) - (\text{Unemployed 15 to 64}) + (\text{Employed U15 and 65} +)} \times 100$$

or, in short,

$$\text{EDR} = \text{Unemployed/Employed} \times 100$$

The comparison between the DDR and the EDR shows that the DDR systematically underestimates the dependency burden (see Table 2.1). However, the EDR is still not an accurate assessment of the dependency burden (i.e., the financial burden on the active people who need to support the dependents), as it does not consider the situation of those who are employed at a wage that is under the minimum needed to support themselves and family, as well as those who are unemployed but self-sufficient. We therefore need to calculate a dependency ratio that assesses the ratio between people who are financially self-sufficient and those who are not. This ratio is usually called a support ratio (see Cutler *et al.* 1990; United Nations 2013), and it focuses on the evolution of the ratio between workers and consumers. However, this ratio is defined in different ways. Some count each person in the 15–64 age range as one worker and each member of the population as one consumer (the demographic approach). The National Transfer Accounts (NTAs) use a more economic approach: the effective number of workers, the numerator, is a composite number that incorporates age variation in labor force participation, hours worked, unemployment and productivity or wages, while the effective number of consumers, the denominator, incorporates age-specific variation in consumption.

To assess the ratio between the people who benefit from a financial assistance and those who do not, we use the "socioeconomic dependency ratio" (SDR), which we define as the number of people who have a total consumption higher than their total income – and therefore need to be financially supported – divided by the number of people who have a total income – generated by an economic activity higher than their total consumption. In other words, the dependents under the SDR are all of the people who are not self-sufficient and need some financial assistance to cover their basic needs.

The SDR formula reads as follows:

$$\text{SDR} = \frac{(\text{Number of People whose Income is} < \text{Consumption})}{(\text{Number of People whose Income is} > \text{Consumption})} \times 100$$

or in short,

$$\text{SDR} = \frac{(\text{Unemployed} + \text{Employed but not self-sufficient})}{\text{Employed and self-sufficient}}$$

This dependency ratio is similar to the "Support Ratio", as spelled out by the CREFAT for the SWEDD countries (see World Bank (2014)), but different from the NTAs (ratio between the number of effective workers and the number of effective consumers, i.e. the whole population). The main difference resides in the fact that the CREFAT has the supporters as the numerator and the dependents as the denominator. As for the EDR, the SDR calculation is made difficult by the paucity of relevant primary data.

2.2.3. *Data*

As can be seen in Table 2.1, the DDR of the four regions of sub-Saharan Africa and East Asia grossly underestimates the real dependents' burden on the economy of a region, when compared to the EDR. The latter is no doubt a much better, albeit insufficient, indicator of the "dependency burden".

In Table 2.2, we compare the three DRs for a selected number of sub-Saharan African and East Asian countries as we could not come up with regional averages for the SDR, due to a lack of data. Several elements are worth noting: (1) there are large discrepancies among regions and countries for each of the DRs; (2) in all countries, (i) the EDR is systematically higher than the DDR and

(ii) the SDR is systematically higher than the DDR; and (3) in most countries, the SDR is lower than the EDR.

Sub-Saharan Africa and Asia Regions	(DDR)	(EDR)
Western		
Total	85.31	146.81
Central		
Total	84.26	130.01
Eastern		
Total	78.95	120.21
Southern		
Total	52.78	151.37
East Asia		
Total	59.43	76.39

Table 2.1. *Comparison DDR with EDR, 2016 (source: author's calculations based on ILO, UNDP and WBG data collected for 2016)*

Countries	DDR	EDR	DDR vs. EDR	SDR	SDR vs. DDR	SDR vs. EDR
Ghana (GHA)	70.0	157.7	87.6	141.5	71.4	–16.1
Mali (MLI)	101.9	193.0	91.1	151.8	49.9	–41.1
Benin (BEN)	86.1	153.4	67.3	144.5	58.4	–8.9
Burkina Faso (BFA)	92.2	195.1	102.9	123.2	30.9	–71.9
South Africa (ZAF)	52.2	245.8	193.5	80.5	28.2	–165.3
Ethiopia (ETH)	83.9	119.3	35.4	104.9	21.0	–14.4
Mozambique (MOZ)	93.5	140.5	47.0	107.4	13.9	–33.0
Republic of Korea (KOR)	36.3	92.6	56.3	93.0	56.7	0.4
China (CHN)	37.7	83.0	45.3	87.9	50.2	4.9
Japan (JPN)	63.9	98.3	34.3	121.7	57.7	23.4

Table 2.2. *DDR, EDR and SDR in selected countries, 2016 (source: Linyu Li[1] and author)*

1 Linyu Li is an experienced programmer with a Master's degree in Health Information and Data Science. As the author's research assistant, she did most of the calculations, including the previsions, of this chapter. The author wants to thank her for her dedication and quality of work.

The large discrepancies reflect several elements. First, the selected regions and countries are not at the same phase of the demographic transition. For example, Japan has already started its second demographic transition (Lesthaege 2010), in which the Total Fertility Rate (TFR) is under the replacing rate of 2.1 and the 65+ population is the fastest growing part of the population. South Korea is also entering its second demographic transition, China is at its lowest DDR because of the One Child policy, Ethiopia is currently experiencing a stalled TFR, and Burkina Faso and Mali have yet to experience a significant decline of their TFR. Second, the economic development level varies from highly developed to low income, and it directly impacts the employment and income levels. Third, the population and economic policies that have been implemented, and greatly vary in magnitude and efficacy, have had diverse impacts on the dependency ratios.

As expected, as it includes the unemployed working age population in the dependents' category, the EDR is reflecting this additional burden (which is far from being compensated by the employed non-working age population). Most less developed countries, especially in sub-Saharan Africa, have a very weak labor market absorptive capacity and, as a result, a large share of the population bulge generated by the demographic transition goes directly from the status of dependent (because of the absence of a legal working age) to dependent (because of unemployment).

The SDR is also systematically higher than the DDR, but the difference is generally less than that between the EDR and the DDR. Contrary to what we may expect, the EDR is mostly higher than the SDR. We could find several explanations for this rather unexpected result. First, employment, income and consumption data are not collected uniformly. In this instance, we have used ILO data and filled the gaps using World Bank data for employment, and the National Transfer Accounts for the income/consumption data. Second, many people that are informally employed are not recorded as employed, but can be more or less self-sufficient. Third, the category "employed" as in ILO and "self-sufficient" do not fit in the logical progression that goes from working age to self-sufficient, as a self-sufficient person might not be recorded as employed. What is needed at this point is an evaluation of the population, which is both employed and self-sufficient (as in the support ratio of the NTAs).

The first finding is that one cannot base a study on the prospects of a first demographic dividend in sub-Saharan Africa on the sole DDR, as it underestimates the burden of dependency. As we will see in section 2.3, the DDR can improve while the EDR deteriorates. For more accurate previsions, the EDR and/or the SDR will be needed.

2.2.4. *Policies*

In order to capture a demographic dividend, a developing country will need to not only improve the DDR, but also the EDR and the SDR. In a brief paragraph on policies that a country needs to implement to benefit from a demographic dividend, this chapter will focus on the necessary conditions, as well as the sufficient conditions needed to achieve this goal (Groth *et al.* 2019). The fulfillment of the arrays of these various necessary and sufficient conditions follows a logical and chronological sequence. Figure 2.1 offers a summary of the conditions that policymakers will need to meet in order to capture a first demographic dividend.

First, health and population policies aiming to decrease both mortality and fertility rates need to be put in place. Today, as all sub-Saharan Africa countries have, at minima, entered the first phase of the first demographic transition. The health policies will aim to accelerate the decline in mortality rates, focusing on infant and child mortality rates and maternal mortality ratios. However, a swift and sharp decrease in fertility is the most important policy lever to open a demographic window of opportunity, improve the DDR and benefit from a first demographic dividend (May and Turbat 2017). Such a fertility decline is necessary as it will reduce the growth rate of the young dependents (U15) under that of the working age population, which will result in a decline of the DDR, which in turn will result in an opening of the demographic window of opportunity. The faster the fertility declines, the less dependents and the more resources for investments. However, the demographic window of opportunity will not last forever because the population will inexorably start to age. The older dependents will eventually grow faster than the working age population, and therefore, the dependency burden will increase again.

Figure 2.1. *Policies impacting, respectively, the demographic dependency ratio (DDR), the employment dependency ratio (EDR) and the socioeconomic dependency ratio (SDR) (source: Groth* et al. *2019)*

The first step will be to improve and expand the supply of family planning services, namely programs that offer reliable information and quality services

(May 2012). The current level of contraceptive use for modern methods in sub-Saharan Africa is currently estimated at 28% (Population Reference Bureau 2019), whereas it will be necessary to reach a contraceptive prevalence rate (CPR) of about 75% to achieve the contraceptive revolution and replacement level fertility. Despite some exceptions (e.g. Ethiopia and Rwanda), most sub-Saharan African countries currently experience a very low growth rate of their CPR, to the tune of 0.6 percentage points per year. Therefore, it is necessary to increase the uptake of modern contraception. A rate of increase of contraceptive coverage of at least 1.5 percentage points per year appears to be an ambitious but feasible target. The programmatic challenge is not only to attract new family planning acceptors, but also to retain current users. Also, health programs, especially those targeting children and mothers, should be reinforced to accelerate the decline in mortality rates and especially infant and child mortality rates, and maternal mortality ratios.

If properly implemented, the population and health policies should result in a decrease in the DDR, a necessary condition for the opening of the demographic window of opportunity. However, other policies are needed to significantly increase the prospects of capturing a demographic dividend: (i) labor market policies that aim to increase employment and therefore improve the EDR; (ii) socioeconomic policies that aim to increase the employed population purchasing power and should result in an increase in the number of people who are both employed and self-sufficient, and therefore improve the SDR; and (iii) macroeconomic policies that aim to boost investments, including investments in health and education.

To improve the EDR, a government's priority should be to increase the labor market's absorptive capacity to the level of the youth bulge, which will reach the working age as a result of the decline in child mortality and the modification of the age structure that ensues (Lee *et al.* 2016; Eberstadt 2017). In case of failure to do so, the youth will end up reacting to chronic unemployment either through out-migration or social unrest. And, in both cases, this would negatively impact the prospects of capturing a first demographic dividend.

The International Labor Organization (ILO 2016) estimated that the global youth unemployment rate in developing countries was expected to reach 9.4%, or 7.9 million youths in 2017. In addition, it was noted that wide disparities exist between young women and men, underpinning and giving rise to wider gaps during the transition to adulthood. In 2016, for instance, the labor force participation rate for young men stood at 53.9% compared to 37.3% for young women – representing a gap of 16.6 percentage points. Also, millions of young people in low-income countries continue to leave school to take up jobs when they are still very young.

According to ILO, 31% of youth in low-income countries have no educational qualifications at all, compared to 6% in lower middle-income countries and 2% in upper middle-income countries. And, if we factor in the current Covid-19 pandemic that will have a significant direct impact on girls' education – as many of them will not return to school when the lockdown is lifted – we can foresee a rising unemployment rate among the new comers on the labor market.

In addition to being the most unemployed age group, the youth are more likely to be employed in the informal sector, at a low wage and without social protection. They are constituting a large share of what is called the "working poor", meaning that their income is below the living wage, and therefore cannot cover their basic needs. Finally, there are large discrepancies among the youth. Kipesha and Msigwa (2013) list five criteria, namely gender, geographical location, education, skills and marital status as significant factors explaining the difference in youth employment status.

A relevant employment policy should, therefore, focus on the youth, and not only when they arrive on the labor market. It should start much earlier on in their education, with a special focus on girls education, skills, and health. Rural labor markets need to be boosted to slow down the current out-migration flows that start from the most remote areas to end up in European camps, if not on a slave market or at the bottom of the sea, via the slums of the capital cities. Also, the plague of informality needs to be effectively addressed, especially at the level of urban labor markets. Data clearly show that most people, and especially the youth, who are "employed" in the informal sector live under the poverty line.

Even if a government succeeds in increasing youth employment, the impact on the SDR might be minimal in case of a large number of "working poor". The latter are recorded as employed, and are therefore in the denominator of the EDR. However, because they receive less than a living wage, they are among the dependents in the numerator of the SDR. The working poor condition continues to disproportionately affect youth, albeit with considerable regional differences. For example, sub-Saharan Africa continues to suffer the highest youth working poverty rates globally, at almost 70%. As observed in many economies, there is growing evidence of a shift in the age distribution of poverty, with the youth taking the place of the elderly as the group at the highest risk of poverty (defined for developed economies as earning less than 60% of the median income). The challenge is particularly acute in some countries where the at-risk-of-poverty for young workers exceeds 20%.

Cunningham (2007) suggests that the minimum wage is an attractive policy tool for governments aiming to reduce poverty and promote social justice, as the resulting increase is mostly borne by the employers. However, because the minimum wage is often tied to social programs, an increase in minimum wage might exacerbate deficit issues. Cunningham (2007) also notes that the salaries of workers in both the formal and informal sectors increase as a result of a raise in the minimum wage, and that the minimum wage is more binding in the informal sector than in the formal sector. Terrell and Almeida (2008) confirm Cunningham's conclusion that an increase in the minimum wage tends to have a positive wage effect. They also find a small increase in unemployment among workers covered by minimum wage legislation.

With regard to social policies, a clear distinction should be made between those that aim to increase the benefits of the employed population, and will mostly be paid by the employers, and those that are paid by the active population, mostly via taxes, to support the dependents. The first ones should result in a decrease in the dependency burden for the employed population, while the second would result in an increase in the dependency burden for the employed population. The economic burden of dependency cannot only be measured by the number of dependents. It has to be measured by the amount (amount per dependent multiplied by the number of dependents) that is transferred to the dependents. Only policies that increase the income of the active population would improve the SDR through an increase in the number of employed and self-sufficient. A raise in the social benefits of the unemployed and employed but not self-sufficient would result in an increase in the SDR, and namely a deterioration.

2.3. Sub-Saharan Africa in search of a demographic dividend

Looking at the probable evolution of the DDR (United Nations 2019), we observe that most sub-Saharan African countries will experience a decrease in their DDR while, by comparison, East Asian countries will experience an increase in their DDR due to the rapid growth of their older population. Also, most sub-Saharan African countries have yet to capture a demographic dividend. Some are already experiencing a steady DDR decrease, while others have yet to experience it. The sub-Saharan Africa countries that are most likely to experience a sharp improvement in their DDR are those that are already on a swift path of fertility decline. But prospects of an improved DDR remain unclear for the countries that have a stalled TFR or have yet to experience a steady and swift TFR decline.

A first analysis shows significant discrepancies among the sub-Saharan African regions. Central Africa is behind with a current DDR of 91.6, followed by West Africa (85.0), East Africa (80.9) and Southern Africa (53.6). Between 2020 and 2035, the four regions should experience a decrease in their DDR. However, Central and West Africa would just be in the first stage of the opening of the window of opportunity; East Africa would be in the second stage; and Southern Africa would be in the final stage (the lowest DDR would be reached soon after, in 2040, at 46.8). In 2050, the DDRs of Central (65.6), West (64.3) and East Africa (58.1) would continue to decrease, while the DDR of Southern Africa would start to grow (48.3). Between 2050 and 2075, in Central, West and East Africa the DDR would continue its descent, while in Southern Africa it would continue to ascent. Finally, in 2100, Central and West Africa would reach their lowest DDR, respectively, at 53.3 and 52.3, and the DDRs in East and Southern Africa would pursue their ascent.

A second analysis shows large discrepancies among countries (see Table 2.3), both within and outside the regions (the country selection has been done on the basis of data availability).

In order to get a realistic answer on how wide the window of opportunity is actually opened and how much time remains for sub-Saharan Africa to benefit from a demographic dividend, the assessment needs to be done at the country level. There certainly is a trend at the level of sub-Saharan Africa regions, but some countries are either way ahead (such as South Africa) or far behind (such as Niger) the region's average.

Country	DDR 2015 Observed	DDR 2035 Estimated	DDR 2055 Estimated
Benin	82.6	72.1	61.7
Burkina Faso	87.9	74.0	60.9
Ethiopia	76.8	62.2	51.0
Ghana	67.4	60.3	55.1
Mali	98.0	80.5	62.3
South Africa	52.2	46.6	49.3
China	42.2	54.9	75.8
Japan	69.0	76.9	99.4
South Korea	39.5	64.6	96.6

Table 2.3. *DDR in selected countries 2015–2055 (source: Linyu Li and author)*

Finally, a comparison of the DDR evolution between the Asian Tigers and most sub-Saharan Africa countries reveals that a swift demographic transition is key to not only increasing the probability of benefiting from a demographic dividend but also determining its magnitude. The mortality rates in Asia decreased at a fast and steady rate starting in the late 1960s. This was followed by a decrease in fertility rates that kicked in within 10–15 years. The fertility decreased very fast and impacted the age structure in less than a generation, as can be seen in the evolution of the U19 population in South Korea for the following years.

1960	1970	1980	1990	2000	2005	2010
12,634	16,333	16,943	15,474	13,329	12,083	11,298

Table 2.4. *U19 population in South Korea 1960–2010 (source: United Nations 2019)*

In comparison, Central Africa DDR (U15–65+) continued to increase from 1960 to 1990 (from 90.35 to 97.66), then started to slowly decrease to reach 94.5 in 2010 and 92 in 2020. It is expected to reach 66 in 2050 and 53 in 2100.

The West Africa region DDR (U15–65+) also continued to increase from 1960 to 1990 (from an average of 80.65–95.95) and then started to slowly decrease to reach 90.43 in 2010. However, in countries such as Niger, the dependency ratio was still increasing and reached a peak of 110.1 in 2010. The West Africa DDR is expected to decrease, but rather slowly, to reach 64 in 2050 and 52 in 2100. In East Africa, the U15–65+ DDR increased until 1990 (from 90.3 in 1960 to 97.7) and then went back to its 1960 level in 2010 (90.0). It is expected to decrease until 2075 (at 54) and start to slowly increase to reach 57 in 2100. In Southern Africa, the U15–65+ DDR increased from 1960 to 1980 (from 88.6 to 96.2) and then decreased to reach 81.6 in 2010, 81 in 2020, 57 in 2035, when it will start to increase to reach 57 in 2100.

From these data, we can formulate several main conclusions: (1) As noted by many researchers (Drummond *et al.* 2013), the demographic transition pattern in sub-Saharan Africa is different from the other world regions, mostly due to the fertility pattern (longer time lag between the decline in mortality and fertility and slower decline – even stall – in fertility); (2) the four sub-Saharan African regions are not at the same stage of the demographic transition: Southern Africa has completed it; East Africa is in the midst of it; and Central and West Africa are still in the early stages due to a delayed and slow decrease in fertility; (3) the window of opportunity has recently been opened for most Central and West African countries and they need to put policies in place the that would both accelerate the demographic transition and ensure employment of their 15–64 population to benefit from a first demographic dividend in the upcoming decades; (4) most East African countries should swiftly complete their demographic transition and start benefiting from a first demographic dividend; (5) most Southern African countries will soon experience a closing of their window of opportunity as the rapid aging of the population will slow down the decrease in the dependency ratio. They should put policies in place that would ensure the benefit of a second demographic dividend; and (6) with the demographic window of opportunity being dependent on the pace of decrease in both mortality and fertility rate, as well as the span of time between the decrease in mortality and the decrease in fertility, it appears that, as it is, the "yearly working population bulge" in sub-Saharan Africa, and especially in Central and West Africa, all other things equal, is going to be much smaller than it has been in Asia.

The evolution of the EDR under the assumption of the current level of labor market absorptive capacity remaining constant during the period 2015–2055 shows that several regions in sub-Saharan Africa could be in deep trouble very soon. Unless they implement effective employment policies, their EDR will likely either continue to ascend or stall, which means that the working population will either support more dependents per worker or, at best, the same number as today in the upcoming years, and therefore no resources would be freed up as a result of the demographic transition.

Country	EDR 2015 Observed	EDR 2035 Estimated	EDR 2055 Estimated
Benin	153.0	152.0	152.0
Burkina Faso	195.0	239.0	289.0
Ethiopia	119.3	84.0	48.0
Ghana	157.7	156.0	156.0
Mali	193.0	196.0	196.0
Mozambique	140.0	145.0	151.0
South Africa	245.7	250.0	250.0
China	83.0	91.0	99.0
Japan	98.0	96.0	96.0
South Korea	92.6	64.0	35.0

Table 2.5. *EDR in selected countries 2015–2055 (source: Linyu Li and author)*

Table 2.5 shows that, under their current level of labor market absorptive capacity, (i) even if a country has drastically improved its DDR, as is the case in South Africa, the EDR can be an obstacle to benefiting from a demographic dividend as a result of a lack of effective policies targeting unemployment, and especially the unemployment of the young adults that just transitioned from the U15 age category to the 15–64 age group, and (ii) except for Ethiopia, the sub-Saharan Africa countries selected would not be able to reach EDR levels (less than 100) that would enable them to benefit from a demographic dividend. It is worth noting that China could experience an increase in its EDR, while Japan would remain more or less at its current level and South Korea continues to improve to reach a low level in 2055.

Countries	SDR 2015	SDR 2035	SDR 2055
Benin (BEN)	141.6	119.3	97.6
Burkina Faso (BFA)	151.9	102.0	84.8
Ethiopia (ETH)	144.5	84.8	69.8
Ghana (GHA)	123.2	117.4	93.0
Mali (MLI)	80.5	133.1	104.5
Mozambique (MOZ)	104.9	92.3	76.4
South Africa (ZAF)	107.5	67.5	66.4
China (CHN)	93.0	126.8	158.4
Japan (JPN)	88.0	153.2	181.7
Republic of Korea (KOR)	121.7	129.4	166.7

Table 2.6. *SDR in selected countries 2015–2055 (source: Linyu Li and author)*

Table 2.6 provides a different picture of a demographic dividend prospect for the sub-Saharan Africa countries. Except for Mali (until 2035), each selected sub-Saharan Africa country should experience an improved SDR, which means a decreasing financial dependency burden in the upcoming years. We notice that for the three selected Asian countries, it is the opposite: their respective SDR is deteriorating due to population ageing. Older people keep a relatively high level of consumption (compared to the young population) which, depending on the pension scheme and the social security system, will require an increasing amount of transfers from the self-sufficient population.

2.4. Conclusion

The dependency ratio evolution is a good indicator of a country's chances to benefit from a first demographic dividend. However, the demographic dividend being a surplus generated by a decrease in resources allocated to the dependent population, which is ultimately the fraction of the population which is economically supported by the other fraction of the population (the providers or supporters), there is a need to find a dependency ratio that closely estimates this financial burden. The DDR is not this indicator, even if there is a good correlation between the DDR and the GDP, and especially the GDP per capita.

The EDR is a better indicator as it transfers the working population, which is unemployed on the side of the dependents. However, this indicator has several weaknesses linked to (i) the extreme difficulty to identify "employed" and "unemployed", especially in low-income countries, where the informal sector is dominant, and where there is a large category of "self-employed" that are not recorded as employed; (ii) the large number of "employed" (especially from the informal sector) who receive a lower salary than the living wage, which means that they are not self-sufficient and should therefore be counted as dependents; and (iii) the number of "unemployed" who are self-sufficient and should therefore be on the providers' side. We should note that there is an even better correlation between the EDR and the GDP than between the DDR and the GDP.

Finally, the SDR should be the better dependency ratio to use. However, at this point in time, its calculation needs to be improved in order to get more robust results (e.g. SDR correlation with the GDP should be at least as good as that of the EDR).

Because of our assessment of the capacity to evaluate the dependency burden of each of the dependency ratios, we have been using the EDR to estimate the dependency burden now and in the upcoming years in this chapter.

Based on our current EDR previsions, that will need to be significantly refined by introducing different scenarios based on various hypotheses of labor market absorptive capacity changes, most sub-Saharan African countries have a very low probability of starting to benefit from a demographic dividend by 2035. It seems clear that for the sub-Saharan Africa countries that have already opened their window of opportunity wide, the main bottleneck for benefiting from a first demographic dividend will be their labor market. Employment rate projection data in selected countries tend to show that most Central and West African countries that will experience a working age population bulge will not be able to absorb this bulge and unemployment rates would rise as a result. This would not only translate into an increased dependency burden (as estimated through the EDR), and therefore a lower probability of benefiting from a first demographic dividend, but also increased migration flows toward the more developed countries, especially European countries.

2.5. References

Barrientos, A. and Hulme, D. (2008). Social protection for the poor and poorest in developing countries: Reflections on a quiet revolution. Working document 30, Brooks World Poverty Institute, University of Manchester, Manchester.

Bloom, D.E., Canning, D., Sevilla, J. (2003). *The Demographic Dividend: A New Perspective on the Economic Consequences of Population Change*, 1st edition. Rand, Santa Monica.

Bongaarts, J. (2009). *Human Population Growth and the Demographic Transition*. The Population Council, New York.

Cook, S. (2013). Rescuing social protection from the poverty trap: New programmes and historical lessons. In *Social Protection in Developing Countries. Reforming System*, Bender, K., Kaltenborn, M., Pfleiderer, C. (eds). Routledge, London.

Cunningham, W. (2007). Minimum wages and social policies. Lessons from developing countries. Report, The World Bank Group, Washington.

Cutler, D.M., Poterba, J.M., Sheiner, L.M., Summers, L.H. (1990). *An Aging Society: Opportunity or Challenge?* The MIT Press/Harvard University, Boston.

Drummond, P., Thakoor, V., Yu, S. (2013). *Africa Rising: Harnessing the Demographic Dividend*. The International Monetary Fund, Washington.

Eberstadt, N. (2017). Manpower, education, skills and jobs in sub-Saharan Africa: Past trends and future outlook. In *Africa's Population: In Search of a Demographic Dividend*, Groth, H., May, J.F. (eds). Springer, Cham.

Gribble, J.N. and Bremner, J. (2012). Achieving a demographic dividend. *Population Bulletin*, 67(2), 1–14.

Groth, H. and May, J.F. (eds). (2017). *Africa's Population: In Search of a Demographic Dividend*. Springer, Cham.

Groth, H., May, J.F., Turbat, V. (2019). Policies needed to capture a demographic dividend in sub-Saharan Africa. *Canadian Studies in Population*, 46(1), 61–72.

Guengant, J.-P. (2017). Africa's population: History, current status, and projections. In *Africa's Population: In Search of a Demographic Dividend*, Groth, H., May, J.F. (eds). Springer, Cham.

Guengant, J.-P. and Isaka Maga, H. (2017). Bilan des activités de planification familiale au Niger depuis les années 1990. Institut d'étude du développement économique et social/ Université Paris I Panthéon-Sorbonne, Paris.

ILO (2013). Employment and social protection in the new demographic context. Report IV. *International Labour Conference*, 102nd Session. International Labour Organisation, Geneva.

ILO (2016). Global Youth Unemployment is on the rise again. World Employment and Social Outlook 2016: Trends for Youth. International Labour Organisation, Geneva.

Kipesha, E. and Msigwa, R.E. (2013). Determinants of youth unemployment in developing countries: Evidences from Tanzania. *Journal of Economic and Sustainable Development*, 4(14), 67–76.

Lee, R. and Mason, A. (2006). What is the demographic dividend? *Finance & Development*, 43(3), 16–17.

Lee, M., Christianson, H., Bietsch, K. (2016). Global employment and the sustainable development goals. *Population Bulletin*, 71(2), 1–22.

Lesthaeghe, R. (2010). The unfolding story of the second demographic transition. *Population and Development Review*, 36(2), 211–251.

May, J.F. (2017). The politics of family planning policies and programs in sub-Saharan Africa. *Population and Development Review*, 43, 308–329.

May, J.F. and Guengant, J.-P. (forthcoming). *Demography and Economic Emergence of Sub-Saharan Africa*. Académie royale de Belgique, Brussels.

May, J.F. and Turbat, V. (2017). The demographic dividend in sub-Saharan Africa: Two issues that need more attention. *Journal of Demographic Economics*, 83(1), 77–84.

Population Reference Bureau (2019). 2019 World population data sheet. Report, Population Reference Bureau, Washington.

Terrell, K. and Almeida, R.K. (2008). Minimum wages in developing countries: Helping or hurting workers? Policy note, The World Bank Group, Washington.

Thakoor, V. and Wakeman-Linn, J. (2016). Surf the demographic wave. *Finance & Development*, 53(1), 22–25.

Turbat, V. (2017). The demographic dividend: A potential surplus generated by a demographic transition. In *Africa's Population: In Search of a Demographic Dividend*, Groth, H., May, J.F. (eds). Springer, Cham.

United Nations (2013). National Transfer Accounts Manual: Measuring and analyzing the generational economy. Department of Economic and Social Affairs, Population Division, New York.

United Nations (2019). World Population Prospects 2019. Department of Economic and Social Affairs, Population Division, New York.

World Bank (2007). Capturing the demographic bonus in Ethiopia: Gender, development, and demographic actions. Report, The World Bank Group, Washington.

World Bank (2014). Sahel women empowerment and demographic dividend project phase 1. Report, The World Bank Group, Washington.

World Bank (2015). *Africa's Demographic Transition: Dividend or Disaster*? Africa Development Forum. The World Bank Group, Washington.

World Bank and International Monetary Fund. (2016). Global monitoring report 2015/2016: Development goals in an era of demographic change. Report, The World Bank Group, Washington.

Zuber, A., Blickenstorfer, C., Groth, H. (2017). Governance, transparency and the rule of law. In *Africa's Population: In Search of a Demographic Dividend*, Groth, H., May, J.F. (eds). Springer, Cham.

3

From the Demographic Dividend to Generational Economics

Latif DRAMANI
CREG-CREFAT, University of Thiès, Senegal

3.1. Introduction: transition and demographic dividend, generational economics

The Dragons (South Korea, Taiwan, Hong Kong and Singapore) and the Tigers (Malaysia, Thailand, Indonesia, Vietnam and the Philippines) have taken advantage of the demographic transition to accelerate their socioeconomic development and reduce poverty (Mason 1997; Bloom and Williamson 1998). This phenomenon, known as the demographic dividend, is not automatic and requires the implementation of a set of economic policies consistent with all of the sectors of the economy during the demographic transition (Mason and Lee 2006, 2012; Gribble and Bremner 2012; CEA 2013).

From a theoretical perspective, the changes that occur during the demographic transition can mainly affect the economy through the labor supply, the savings rate and the investment on physical and human capital (Bloom *et al.* 2003a). The increase in the labor supply related to the demographic transition occurs by means of two effects: a mechanical effect and a behavioral effect. The mechanical effect takes place when cohorts with large population sizes enter the active age and actually find productive jobs. The behavioral effects associated with the demographic transition occur when the reduction in mortality and the increase in life expectancy affect retirement and savings-related decisions. Also, the reduction in fertility observed during the demographic transition frees up the time devoted to childcare and

Demographic Dynamics and Development,
coordinated by Yves CHARBIT.

increases female labor supply. Finally, declining fertility can free up resources and promote investment in the health and education of children. To summarize, Mason and Lee (2006) consider that the effect of the labor supply associated with the modification in the population's age structure and the entry of women into the labor market refers to the first dividend. At the same time, the effect related to the increase in savings and investment in physical and human capital makes it possible to induce the second demographic dividend.

Several works have demonstrated these mechanisms related to the demographic dividend. For example, Bloom *et al.* (1998) developed an econometric model to explain the differences observed in cross-country growth rates. In this model, the dividend is measured by the growth of the working age population. They show that the growth of the working age population has had a positive and significant effect on the per capita GDP growth rate in East Asian countries. But this assimilation of the growth of the working age population to the demographic dividend comes up against some methodological difficulties, in particular, setting boundaries in the definition of "working age population". Bloom *et al.* (2003b) have found that the increase in life expectancy is an important explanatory factor for the high savings rates observed in East Asian countries. In relation to behavioral effects, Bloom *et al.* (2009) showed that the decline in fertility improves female participation in the labor market.

Other works, based on growth accounting using microeconomic data to estimate consumption and labor income profiles per age, have been used to estimate the demographic dividend. For example, Lee and Mason (2006) found that the first and second dividends that East Asian countries benefited from throughout the 1970–2000 period accounted for 44% of GDP growth per actual consumer. Mason and Lee (2012) and Dramani and Oga (2017) also showed that there is a trade-off between fertility and investment in human capital. In particular, expenses in education and children's health increase when fertility declines.

The demographic transition – responsible for changes that can improve capital intensity, affect the population's age structure and induce behavioral changes in African countries – is already underway (Canning *et al.* 2016). However, there is a debate around the opening of the window of opportunity for the demographic dividend. For some, the demographic windows of opportunity are not yet opened and measures should be put in place to accelerate the opening (CEA 2013; Guengant 2015). However, recent research in sub-Saharan Africa using the National Transfer Accounts (NTA) approach has shown that the windows of opportunity for dividends are already open in several countries (Dramani and Ndiaye 2012; Biao *et al.* 2014; Dramani and Oga 2016; Dramani and Mbacké 2017; Mason *et al.* 2017). Therefore,

African countries are currently going through a critical moment in their phase of socioeconomic development, as the opening of the window is unique for a country.

Under these conditions, understanding the policies implemented in East Asia is essential for the countries in sub-Saharan Africa, if they wish to accelerate economic reforms and also take advantage of the demographic dividend's window of opportunity. Understanding the way in which reforms are to be conducted and the role of states in this process is also important. It is in this context that this chapter pursues specific objectives. These objectives are to highlight the characteristics of the economic life cycle of African countries compared to that of the Asian Dragons and Tigers; to provide estimates on the opening of demographic windows of opportunity in African countries through a case study of East Asian countries; and to illustrate the policy measures taken in different economic sectors to take advantage of demographic dividend potential, with a particular focus on the relative importance of the state in relation with the market.

Some works have addressed the opening of the window of opportunity for the demographic dividend in Africa. Mason *et al.* (2017) estimated the durations of the phase of the first demographic dividend in the world based on 60 countries with national consumption and labor income profiles. Their sample included 16 African countries, and the estimates on the duration of the dividend phase in the sub-regions of Africa were solely based on the assumption of average fertility provided by the United Nations. Our sample consisted of 22 African countries in order to estimate the phase duration of the first demographic dividend according to three fertility scenarios, whereas Dramani and Oga (2017) have proposed estimates using the United Nations average fertility scenario based on a sample of 16 African countries.

While the concept of demographic dividend describes the interaction between changes in the population's age structure and economic growth (Bloom and Williamson 1998; Bloom *et al.* 2000), generational economics has helped to model it through the economic lifecycle and mechanisms used by economic agents at each age to produce, consume, share and save resources (Mason and Lee 2011). This chapter uses the NTA methodology, an original methodology currently functioning as an international benchmark. The United Nations adopted this methodology in 2013 and developed the NTA manual. In this manual, the calculation of the demographic dividend is based on the economic support ratio.

Another new aspect in this chapter is the comparison of average consumption and labor income profiles with those of East Asian countries having benefited from the demographic dividend, in order to highlight their differences. Mason *et al.* (2002)

have shown that promoting savings and investment, the quality of human resources, as well as the massive jobs creation played a crucial role in capturing the demographic dividend in East Asia. Little is known about the actual combination of state interventions with the role of the private sector in capturing this dividend. A case study of the state's role in these countries sheds new light on the relative importance of the state in relation to the market during the development process. After a presentation of the data and the method for calculating the first demographic dividend (section 3.2), we will present and discuss the results obtained (section 3.3). The conclusion will show the implications of economic policies (section 3.4).

3.2. Data and method for calculating the demographic dividend

In this section, we will present the data used for estimating consumption and labor income profiles per age, as well as the opening and closing dates of the demographic window of opportunity in African countries. Data are drawn from two main sources. First, the population data are extracted from the World Population prospects, 2017 edition. Projections are made according to several fertility scenarios, three of which are used in this study. These are the low, medium and high fertility scenarios. Second, the NTA data were used to calculate the consumption and labor income profiles. These were drawn from the NTA network's website[1], or the Regional Consortium for Research in Generational Economy (*Consortium regional en économie générationnelle* [CREG]) in synergy with the Thiès Applied Economics and Finance Research Center[2] (*Centre de recherche en économie et finance appliquées de Thiès* [CREFAT]), or the NTA Benin team.

The economic support ratio is defined as the ratio between the actual number of producers (L) and consumers (N). Following Mason and Lee (2006), the economic support ratio at a given moment (the reverse of the economic dependency ratio) is obtained using the following formula:

$$SR(t) = \frac{L(t)}{N(t)} = \frac{\sum_x \varphi(x)XP(x,t)}{\sum_x \gamma(x)xP(x,t)} \qquad [3.1]$$

1 The sample countries whose profiles are on the NTA site are as follows: Mozambique, Ghana, Nigeria, Ethiopia, Kenya and South Africa.

2 The other countries in the sample do not have an NTA research team, but they do have technical teams trained by CREG-CREFAT.

where:

– $\varphi(x)$: represents the specific weight related to age that takes into account the variations per age of the participation in the labor market, the number of hours worked, unemployment and worker productivity;

– $y(x)$: represents the specific weight related to age that captures consumption variations per age, depending on the physiological needs of individuals, culture, their preferences, etc.;

– $P(x,t)$: represents the age population x throughout t year.

The previously calculated support ratio is then used to determine the way in which the changes in the population's age structure affect the economy. On the one hand, income per actual consumer $y(t) = Y(t) / (N(t)$ can be written as a two-factor multiplicative function:

$$y(t) = SR(t)xy_l(t) \qquad [3.2]$$

where:

– $SR(t) = L(t) / N(t)$: represents the ratio of the actual number of producers to the actual number of consumers; it counts how the changes in the age structure affect the concentration of the population in relation to the most productive individuals in society, that is to say, those in the 30–49 age group;

– $y_l(t) = Y(t) / L(t)$: represents the average income per worker. It can be influenced by several factors, including technology levels, physical and human capital, the extent of political and economic institutions, as well as the availability of natural resources, among others.

Income growth per actual consumer, $gr[y(t)]$, is the sum of the support $gr[SR(t)]$ ratio growth rate and the growth rate of income per worker $gr[y_l(t)]$:

$$gr[y(t)] = gr[SR(t)] + gr[y_l(t)] \qquad [3.3]$$

The growth rate of the support ratio is called the first demographic dividend. It is equal to the growth rate of the number of effective workers minus the growth rate of the number of effective consumers:

$$gr[SR(t)] = gr[L(t)] - gr[N(t)] \qquad [3.4]$$

The first dividend is positive when the effective number of producers grows faster than that of effective consumers. On the other hand, the standard of living is measured by the total national consumption per actual consumer, $C(t) / N(t)$ (Mason and Lee 2012). This standard of living can be expressed as a function of the consumption produced by each worker ($(1 - s)\ Y/L$) and the support ratio (L/N):

$$\frac{C(t)}{N(t)} = \frac{(1-s)Y(t)}{L(t)} \times \frac{L(t)}{N(t)} \quad [3.5]$$

where:

– s: savings rate;

– $Y(t)$: total income.

This standard of living is the amount of what is produced in the economy, apart from the production which is saved and invested. A number of important factors influence the output per worker, $Y(t)/L(t)$. Among these factors, we have the physical capital per worker, human capital, the availability of natural resources, institutions. However, our variable of interest at this precise moment is the support ratio. Given the consumption per worker, a higher support ratio translates directly into a higher living standard. The effect of an increase in the actual support ratio $C(t) / N(t)$, expressed in absolute terms, depends on the net productivity of workers, which is not the case for the effect expressed as a percentage. An increase in the support ratio by one percentage point also increases consumption per effective consumer by one percentage point, as follows:

$$gr[C(t) / N(t)] = gr[(1 - s)Y(t) / L(t)] + gr[L(t) / N(t)] \quad [3.6]$$

where $gr[(x)]$: growth rate of argument X.

Thus, the dividend related to the demographic transition provides an opportunity to accelerate economic growth and reduce poverty in Africa by improving the population's standards of living.

Calculating the dividend using microeconomic data for the estimation of consumption and labor income profiles per age ensures that arbitrary age limits for dependency are not set. The age groups where people are consumers or net producers are determined by the ages at which consumption and labor income patterns intersect.

Specific weight–age consumption and labor income profiles are those obtained from consumption and labor income profiles. The labor income profile for Africa is the simple arithmetic mean of the normalized labor income profiles of the 22 African countries having intergenerational NTA profiles. The list of these countries is provided in the appendix in section 3.5. The same procedure was used to calculate the normalized consumption profile for the continent. For calculation and projection purposes of the support ratio and the demographic dividend, specific weight–age data were calculated per 5-year age groups. The weights obtained show that the population under 30 is less productive than individuals in the 30–49 age bracket (Table 3.1).

Age	Labor income	Consumption
0–4	0.00	0.45
5–9	0.01	0.59
10–14	0.05	0.74
15–19	0.13	0.91
20–24	0.33	1.05
25–29	0.60	1.06
30–34	0.85	1.04
35–39	1.00	1.01
40–44	1.08	0.99
45–49	1.07	0.97
50–54	1.01	0.96
55–59	0.86	0.93
60–64	0.60	0.91
65–69	0.36	0.89
70–74	0.21	0.86
75–79	0.13	0.84
80–84	0.08	0.81
85–89	0.05	0.78
90+	0.04	0.73

Table 3.1. *Specific weight–age in relation with labor income and consumption in African countries (source: CREG-CREFAT)*

3.3. Results and discussion

According to Lee and Mason (2006), the proportion of the first dividend achieved during the demographic transition depends on the characteristics of economic lifecycle. This is why it is important to analyze the characteristics of consumption and labor income. In Africa, the average consumption of the population aged 20 and under is lower than that in East Asia (Figure 3.1). The importance of consumption of this age group in Asia could be related to higher investment in health and children's education. In addition, the consumption profiles of the sample countries show a decrease in the level of consumption per age in Africa, whereas Asia shows relative stability. This observation highlights the vulnerability of adults and seniors in Africa compared to their counterparts in Asia, who tend to age better.

The observation of labor income shows that in Africa, child labor (5–14 years old) is more present than in East Asia, which could represent an obstacle for the human capital development in Africa. Also, the individual's productivity under 35 is higher in Asia than in Africa. For example, the population aged 20–30 produces on average 63% of the average labor income in Asia, compared to 49% in Africa.

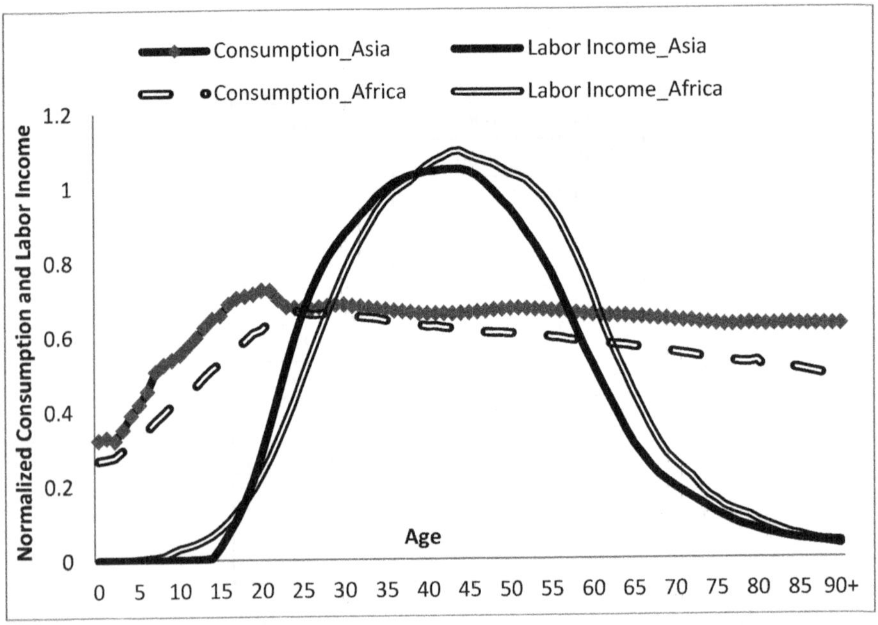

Figure 3.1. *Africa's economic lifecycle compared to that of Asian countries (source: CREG-CREFAT). For a color version of this figure, see www.iste.co.uk/charbit/demographic.zip*

The lifecycle analysis reveals that, in East Asia, it is only between 26 and 57 years that the population produces more than it consumes, whereas this age bracket is between 29 and 62 years in Africa (Figure 3.2). Therefore, the economic dependency of youngsters is higher in Africa than in East Asia.

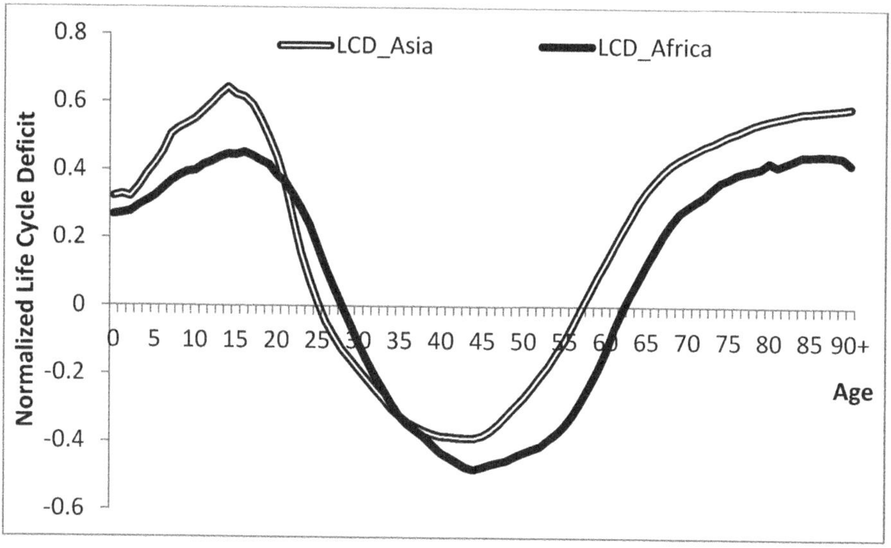

Figure 3.2. *Lifecycle deficit (LCD) in Africa and in East Asia (source: CREG-CREFAT)*

3.3.1. *Demographic dividend profiles in Africa per region*

The dividend phase begins with an increase in the support ratio. The latter has started to grow in all African regions. This increase began in the 1980s in Southern and Northern Africa (Figure 3.3). However, the support ratio is higher in Southern Africa where we will observe up to 60 effective producers per 100 effective consumers in 2065. In terms of support ratio magnitude, Southern Africa is followed by North African countries. In West and East African countries, support ratios started their growth in the mid-1990s and the early 2000, respectively. In contrast, the increase in the support ratio has been more recent in Middle Africa, starting in 2005. As of 2015, the Middle African region had the lowest support ratios in the continent, with 42 effective producers per 100 effective consumers.

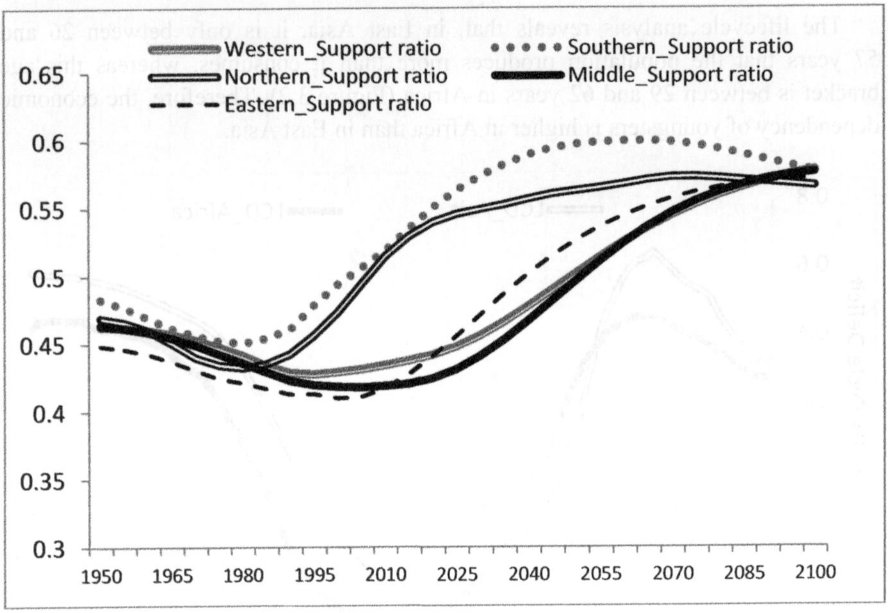

Figure 3.3. *Evolution of the economic support ratio in African countries, 1950–2100 (source: CREG-CREFAT)*

The first dividend phase began in the 1980s in Northern and Southern Africa. In these two regions, the peak of the first dividend was obtained earlier in Southern Africa, with 0.76% in 1990 against 0.87% in Northern Africa in 2000. In the countries of Southern Africa, the growth estimate for the support ratio according to the average United Nations fertility scenario will be positive until 2060 (Figure 3.4). This means that the demographic window of opportunity, which has been open since 1980, is estimated to close on that date. In Northern Africa, the window of opportunity is expected to close in 2065. But from 2020 onwards, the amplitude of the first dividend will be considerably reduced in this region.

Compared to the beginning of the dividend phase, Eastern and Western Africa are in an intermediate position. On average, the first dividend phase started in 1995 in Western Africa and in 2000 in Eastern Africa. On the other hand, the peak of the first dividend, 0.68% on average for the countries of Eastern Africa in 2025, is greater than the one for the countries in Western Africa (0.45% in 2045). In addition, in the countries of Eastern Africa, the support ratio growth remains positive until 2095 (Figure 3.4). The first dividend phase has recently started in Middle Africa, where the peak dividend is 0.62% on average. In Middle and Western Africa, the growth of the support ratio will slightly change beyond 2,100.

As a result, sub-Saharan Africa is likely to reap the first demographic dividend if adequate action is taken now.

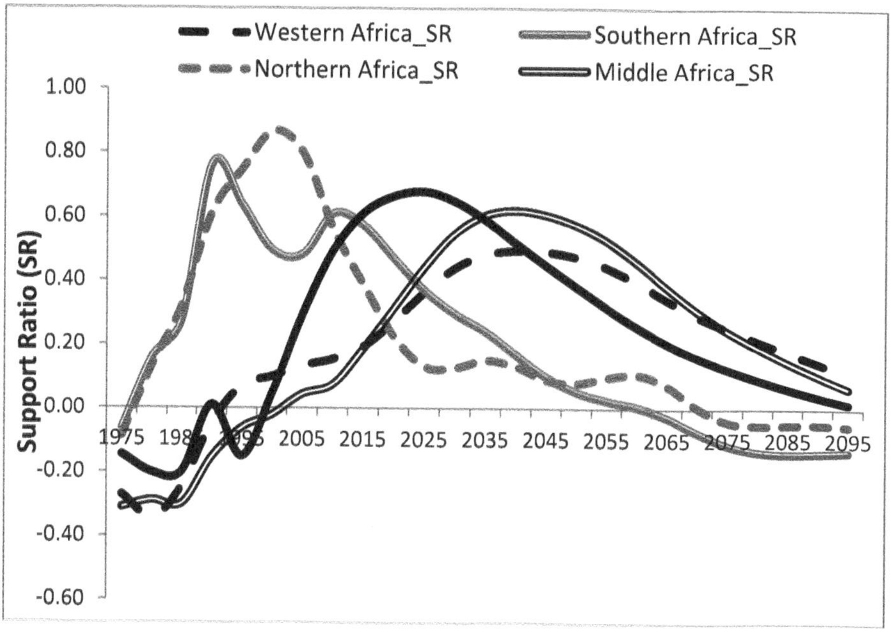

Figure 3.4. *Evolution of the support ratio growth per African sub-region, 1975–2095 (source: CREG-CREFAT)*

However, the estimates of the average duration of the first dividend phase are influenced by the hypotheses relating to the decline in fertility (Table 3.2). So the window of opportunity will close earlier if the speed for fertility decline is significant. For example, if the fertility decline is rapid, the window of opportunity will close, in all regions, no later than 2095. On the other hand, regardless of the fertility hypothesis used for calculating population estimates, the window of opportunity will not close in Western Africa before the end of the century. At the same time, if fertility remains high, only Southern and Northern Africa will see their demographic windows close in 2070 and 2080, respectively.

The mean extent of the first dividend phase observed in each sub-region hides disparities at the country's level. For example, 10 of the 22 African countries with national consumption and labor income profiles will see their demographic windows of opportunity shut down before the end of the century, regardless of the fertility scenario chosen for the projections (Table 3.3).

Sub-region	Opening year	Closing year		
		Low fertility	Average fertility	High fertility
Western Africa	1995	–	–	–
Southern Africa	1980	2050	2060	2070
Northern Africa	1980	2055	2070	2080
Middle Africa	2005	2095	–	–
Eastern Africa	2000	2085	2095	–

Table 3.2. *Estimated duration for the demographic window of opportunity in African regions in relation to fertility scenario (source: CREG-CREFAT)*

Country	Demographic window of opportunity			
	Beginning	Ending		
		Low fertility	Average fertility	High fertility
Ethiopia	2003	2055	2065	2075
Gabon	1999	2060	2065	2090
Guinea	2007	2060	2065	2065
Kenya	1980	2045	2055	2075
Mali	1998	2085	2090	2095
Mozambique	2010	2080	2090	2095
Central African Rep.	2002	2080	2085	2090
Senegal	1998	2070	2095	2100
South Africa	1977	2040	2040	2070
Congo	1990	2090	–	–

Table 3.3. *Extent of the demographic window of opportunity in some African countries according to three population projection scenarios (source: CREG-CREFAT)*

3.3.2. *Discussion*

According to Lee and Mason (2006), most of the economic dynamism of the countries in East and Southeast Asia can be explained by demographic changes. In fact, between 1970 and 2000, demographic change dividends represented 44% of the real output growth per actual consumer. Several works have sought to understand the policies implemented by these countries to capitalize the demographic dividend. For example, Mason (2002) studied how the countries of East Asia capitalized the demographic dividend. Three key factors emerge from the analysis made by this scholar: (i) the availability of qualified human resources, (ii) rapid job creation and rapid increase in productivity and (iii) promotion of savings and increased investment. Other factors such as political stability, the fight against corruption and a prudent fiscal policy have helped to build investor confidence and set up an attractive environment for international financial resources.

Acknowledging the multidimensional nature of the interventions required capitalizing the demographic dividend. The Population Reference Bureau (PRB) developed a conceptual framework called the dividend wheel (PRB 2012). This conceptual framework has helped to explain the demographic dividend in terms of demographic changes, human capital, economic policies and governance. But, in this work, the role played by the state during the process of accelerated development in East Asia countries has been poorly analyzed. From a theoretical point of view, there is a debate on the role of the state in stimulating economic development. On the one hand, there is the neoclassical development theory that emphasizes the importance of a neutral political regime. On the other hand, there are those who advocate for targeted industrial policies (Cheng *et al.* 1998).

Governments in East Asian countries have long adopted a comprehensive approach toward development and been able to shift the focus of their efforts over time (Stiglitz 2008). Their vision for development was to ensure political and social stability. Social stability requires an abundance of jobs and few inequalities. In order to be consistent with this vision of development, the states of these countries mainly focus on the achievement of missions that allow them to be stable at the political and social level, namely the development of education (primary, secondary, higher) and the construction of infrastructure. Actually, success requires both universal literacy and the mentoring of highly qualified individuals. Likewise, infrastructure such as roads and ports facilitate goods transportation and make it less expensive to operate businesses and export merchandise.

Apart from these ordinary missions, these states have played an active role in planning and stimulating development, since markets often fail to coordinate new activities (Stiglitz 2008). For example, we can mention the choice to invest in advanced technologies in South Korea and Taiwan. According to the same source, governments have played an important role in mobilizing local savings in order to finance investments. In that sense, the savings rate was 25% or more in all East Asian countries. In Singapore, there was compulsory placement of 42% of wages in a "contingency fund". In Japan, for example, the state established savings banks in even the remotest rural areas, offering the population suitable and secure means of saving money.

Apart from the mobilization of domestic savings, states have also been very active in other economic areas. Wade (n.d.) discussed the role of the state in relation with three major instruments: the financial system, trade policy and Foreign Direct Investment. Regarding financial instruments, most of these countries had a financial system based on credit and not on the stock market. The choice of this option enabled them to have control over interest rates and collateral conditions required to obtain loans, and to correct stock market failures. In reality, these markets follow short-term thought, which does not make it possible to finance long-term investments.

In relation to trade, East Asian countries used an active trade policy. As a matter of fact, they influenced the volume and composition of imports through a combination of selective controls on trade (tariff and non-tariff measures). These selective controls enabled these countries to build technological capacity and develop an industrial base at the national level (Rodrick 1994). To promote exports, East Asian countries used Foreign Direct Investment. This interconnection between the national economy and the international market has its advantages, especially in relation to the development of national production capabilities and income distribution.

3.4. Conclusion

The goals of this chapter were to highlight the characteristics of the lifecycles of African countries compared to the Asian Dragons and Tigers, and to provide estimates in round figures on the opening of demographic windows of opportunity in African countries. The method used to calculate support ratios and analyze the opening of the windows of opportunity is the NTA approach, based on generational economics. It uses microeconomic data to estimate consumption and labor income profiles per age and does not set arbitrary age limits for dependency. Age groups where people are consumers or net producers are determined by the ages at which consumption and labor income patterns intersect.

The results of data processing show that the window of opportunity related to the first demographic dividend is open in all African regions, regardless of the fertility scenario retained for estimating support ratios. This opening of the window of opportunity corresponding to the phase of the first dividend began in the 1980s in Northern and Southern Africa. In these two regions, the peak of the first dividend took place earlier in Southern Africa (with a value of 0.76% in 1990) than in Northern Africa (with a value of 0.87% in 2000). In addition, the growth estimate for the support ratio according to the United Nations average fertility scenario remains positive until 2060 for the countries in Southern Africa. Thus, the demographic window of opportunity, which has been opened since 1980, is estimated to close on that date. In Northern Africa, the closure of the window of opportunity for the first dividend is scheduled for 2065. But from 2020 onwards, the amplitude of the first dividend will be considerably reduced in this region. There is hope that sub-Saharan African countries will capitalize on the demographic dividend, provided that suitable policies are implemented.

The literature review on capitalization and the demographic dividend in East Asian countries reveals that the state has played a key role in development planning and correcting market failures. Therefore, the state has an active role to play in Africa in terms of human resources training, mobilizing savings and increasing investment for jobs creation. This role must go beyond the classic missions assigned to it. It is necessary for each country to find the right combination between the state and the market for implementing the necessary actions at all times, in order to capitalize on the demographic dividend. Given the need to achieve a global vision of actions to be implemented in all of the economic sectors for capturing the demographic dividend in Africa, the establishment of national dividend observatories is essential. These observatories will provide states with the necessary information to monitor the indicators specifically related to each sector, in order to guide the actions to be implemented.

The second dividend must be prepared during the first dividend phase; it is also important for states to take measures that can anticipate population aging. These measures must go in the direction of the preparation for retirement and supporting the elderly. Offering a complementary option enabling individuals to directly contribute to their own retirement is an integral part of the innovations that policymakers in African countries should anticipate.

3.5. Appendix: country and survey year for consumption and income profiles

Country	Survey year
Africa	
Benin	2015
Burkina Faso	2014
Chad	2011
Ethiopia	2005
Ghana	2005
Guinea	2012
Ivory Coast	2014
Kenya	2005
Mali	2015
Mauritania	2014
Mozambique	2008
Niger	2014
Nigeria	2009
São Tomé and Príncipe	2012
Senegal	2011
South Africa	2005
Togo	2011
Cameroon	2015
Gabon	2005
Central African Republic	2008
Guinea-Bissau	2010
Congo	2011
East Asia	
Indonesia	2005
Philippines	1999
South Korea	2000
Thailand	1998
Taiwan	2004

Table 3.4. *Country and survey year for consumption and income profiles (source: CREG-CREFA)*

3.6. References

Biao, B., Oga, I.J-B., Guidimé, C.D. (2014). Demographic transition and economic growth in Benin. *10th Meeting of the Working Group on Macroeconomic Aspects of Intergenerational Transfers*, 10–14 November, Beijing.

Bloom, D.E. and Williamson, J.G. (1998). Demographic transitions and economic miracles in emerging Asia. *World Bank Economic Review*, 12, 419–455.

Canning, D., Raja, S., Yazbeck, A.S. (eds) (2016). *La transition démographique de l'Afrique, dividende ou catastrophe*. AFD, Paris.

CEA, AUC, AFDB (2013). Creating and capitalizing on the demographic dividend for Africa. Report, CoM 2013, Industrialization for an Emerging Africa, Abidjan.

Cheng, T-J., Haggard, S., Kang, D. (1998). Institutions and growth in Korea and Taiwan: The bureaucracy. *The Journal of Development Studies*, 6(34), 87–111.

Dramani, L. and Ndiaye, F. (2012). Estimating the first demographic dividend in Senegal: The national transfers account. *British Journal of Economics, Management & Trade*, 2(2), 39–59.

Dramani, L. and Oga, I.J.-B. (2017). Understanding the demographic dividends in Africa: The NTA approach. *Journal of Demographic Economics* [Online]. Available at: 10.1017/dem. 2016.30.

ESCWA (2016). Demographic profile of the Arab region: Realizing the demographic dividend. Technical Paper 3, ESCWA.

Gribble, J.N. and Bremner, J. (2012). Achieving a demographic dividend. *Population Reference Bureau Bulletin*, 67(2–5).

Guengant, J.-P. (2015). La révolution contraceptive : une prospective démographique pour les pays du Partenariat de Ouagadougou. Paper, Le Partenariat de Ouagadougou, Cotonou, December.

Lee, R. and Mason, A. (2006). Les dividendes de l'évolution démographique. *Finances et développement*, September.

Lee, R. and Mason, A. (2011). *Population Aging and the Generational Economy: A Global Perspective*. Edward Elgar Publishing Limited, Cheltenham.

Mason, A. (1997). Population and the Asian economic miracle. *Asian-Pacific and Population Policy*, 43(4).

Mason, A. (2002). Capitalizing on the demographic dividend. Working document [Online]. Available at: http://www2.hawaii.edu/~amason/Research/UNFPA.PDF.

Mason, A. and Lee, R. (2012). Demographic dividends and ageing in low-income countries. Working Paper, National Transfer Accounts, December.

Mason, A., Lee, R., Abrigo, M., Lee, S-H. (2017). Support ratios and demographic dividends: Estimates for the word. Technical Paper 1, Population Division, United Nations.

National Transfer Accounts Manual (2013). *Measuring the Generational Economy*. National Transfer Accounts Manual, New York.

Rodrick, D. (1994). Getting interventions right: How South Korea and Taiwan grew rich. NBER Working Paper, 4964.

Stiglitz, J.E. (2008). *Un autre monde contre le fanatisme du marché*. Fayard, Paris.

UN (2013). Manuel des comptes de transferts nationaux Manual, United Nations..

UN (2017). World Population Prospects 2017. Department of Economic and Social Affairs, Population Division, New York.

Wade, R. (n.d.). The role of the government in overcoming market failure, Taiwan, South Korea and Japan. Working document.

4

Fertility and Nuptiality

Yves CHARBIT
CEPED, University of Paris, France

4.1. Introduction: the decline of fertility in the world

With the advances in medicine and increased global agricultural production, which have reduced mortality considerably in developing countries, it is now fertility that governs population growth, because – contrary to popular belief – in any given country, international migratory movements only play a marginal role. If the demographic bomb is currently in the process of being defused, it is due to the current decline in fertility.

We are certainly witnessing the end of the explosion of world population, since the decline in fertility, a decisive variable, has become widespread since 1950 (Table 4.1). The percentages of decline vary noticeably (Figure 4.1). The decrease is especially strong in Asia and Latin America, unlike Africa, and, considering that middle-income countries are mainly located in the first two continents, it is among these that the decline is the most spectacular. The current issue is clear: will the last high fertility regions in the world in turn be characterized by low fertility, so that the world population stabilizes at a maximum of 11 billion around 2100? This is indeed the hypothesis of the United Nations.

Let us look at some examples across different countries and regions (Table 4.2 and Figure 4.2). The number of children per woman is now below five almost everywhere, and below two in a significant number of developing countries (Brazil, China, Iran, Korea, Thailand, Turkey and most countries in Latin America and the Caribbean).

This chapter updates two previous publications (Charbit 2015, 2018).

Demographic Dynamics and Development,
coordinated by Yves CHARBIT.

	Number of children per woman	
	1950	2020
World	4.97	2.47
Africa	6.57	4.44
Latin America and the Caribbean	5.83	2.04
Asia	5.83	2.15
North America	3.34	1.75
Europe	2.66	1.61
Oceania	3.89	2.36
Low-income countries	6.42	4.52
Middle-income countries	5.68	2.35
High-income countries	2.99	1.67

Note: According to the World Bank classification (July 2019), the income brackets in US $ as of July 2019 are the following: Low: >1,026. Middle: 1,026–<12,375. High: >12,375.

Table 4.1. *Number of children of women by continent and income level (1950–2020) (source: UN DESA)*

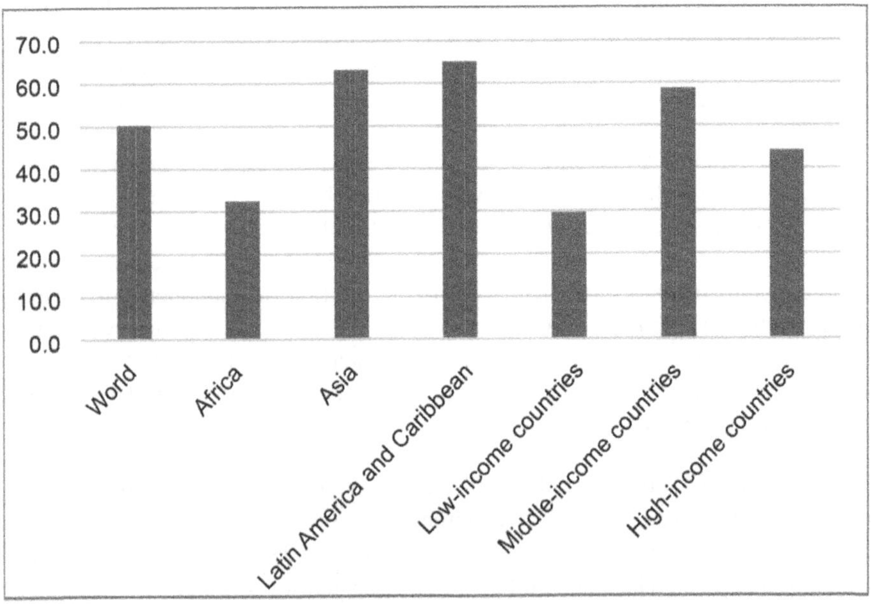

Figure 4.1. *Percentage of fertility decline by continent and income level (1950–2020) (source: UN DESA)*

	Number of children	
	1950	2020
	Africa	
Mali	6.95	5.92
Niger	7.30	6.95
Angola	6.00	5.55
DR Congo	5.98	5.96
	Latin America	
Colombia	6.51	1.82
Mexico	6.75	2.14
Brazil	6.10	1.74
	Asia	
China	6.11	1.69
Thailand	6.14	1.53
Turkey	6.69	2.08

Table 4.2. *Number of children per woman in some countries (1950–2020)*

In 2020, apart from a few rare Asian countries – Afghanistan (4.56), Yemen (3.84), Timor (4.10), Pakistan (3.55) – for the most part, fertility remained high in three African regions: Western (5.18), Eastern (4.43) and Middle Africa (5.53). But in the other two, in Northern (2.93) and Southern Africa (2.50), fertility was close to the levels in Asia (2.15) and Latin America (2.04).

Despite the millions of dollars invested over several years in family planning programs, the results obtained in some African countries are derisory. Between 1970 and 2020, fertility declined slightly in Mali (–14.8%), Niger (–4.8%), Angola (–7.5%) and Somalia (–2.1%), but did not decrease at all (0.3%) in the Democratic Republic of Congo. The contrast is striking with the decrease observed in Asia (China: –72%; Thailand: –75%; Turkey: –68.9%) and Latin America (Colombia: –72%; Brazil: –71.5%; Mexico: –68.3%).

This chapter presents and discusses the main theoretical explanations that can account for the decrease in fertility over the past decades. Then, the topic of nuptiality is addressed and contraception discussed in the following chapter. In the case of developing countries, fertility remains high (mainly in Africa) because marriages occur at earlier ages and the use of contraception is low. These early unions have resulted in a public health problem, described as “teenage pregnancy”, which is also analyzed from a sociodemographic perspective.

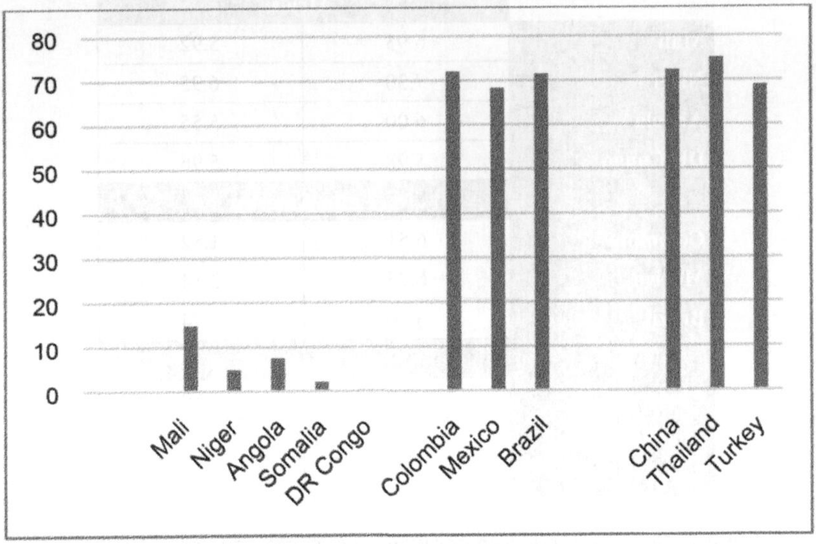

Figure 4.2. *Percentage of fertility decline in some countries (1950–2020) (source: UN DESA)*

4.2. The sociodemography of fertility

But then, how can we explain the fact that populations are now in control of their own reproduction? Research has been oriented in two directions: either focusing on particular factors or, on the contrary, offering more comprehensive explanations. However, we will see that neither the specific factors nor the more global theories can by themselves account for the observed decline in fertility. As is often the case in the human sciences, it is undoubtedly necessary to give up the idea of a universal model and, more modestly, to accept the coexistence of highly diverse processes, which have all contributed in one way or another to the decline in fertility within the same population, or across the same continent.

Entire fields of research, falling under the scope of the population and development paradigm, have been built in a way which is totally independent of the theory of demographic transition, albeit directly related to the two variables underlying the transition pattern: birth and death rates. Thus, nuptiality and family life, intergenerational relationships, the AIDS epidemic, reproductive health and poverty constitute *population issues per se* which can, for example – and have been – fully addressed outside the framework of the theory of demographic transition, defined as an *articulation* of long statistical series. The only way forward then is to start from the facts observed in developing countries, and from there, to try to advance possible explanations for the decline in fertility.

4.2.1. *Insularity*

As fertility had started to decline from the 1960s in small territories which were generally islands (Mauritius, Reunion, Sri Lanka, Fiji, Jamaica), the idea arose that insularity favored the dissemination of new attitudes toward fertility, the only indicator available at the time being birth rates. In itself, as a simple geographical characteristic, insularity explains nothing, but it undoubtedly has a psychosociological and social dimension. In many of these small countries, high density is often associated with insularity and they function as relatively closed social spaces. These places are characterized by a greater mutual acquaintance among individuals than in larger territories. And even when exposed to international emigration, returning migrants disseminate new behavior models in their home society. In addition, health and social action is easier and more efficient, because distances are shorter. Under these conditions, the population's adoption of contraception methods is faster, as proven by a survey we carried out in Guadeloupe and Martinique in 1975 (Charbit and Léridon 1980; Charbit 1987).

This attractive explanation quickly ran up against several major objections: if mutual acquaintance phenomena are relevant, then what is the role of the culture which permeates these societies? This is the case of Confucianism in Hong Kong, Singapore and Malaysia, for example, about which there is general consensus that it promotes an economic pragmatism favorable to the adoption of contraception. In addition, for Guadeloupe, Martinique and Reunion, their status as overseas French departments weighed heavily. Concerned about rapid population growth, France implemented the 1967 law on contraception (Neuwirth law) much faster in those departments than in metropolitan France, relaying the action of very effective private associations in the field for several years. As for Tunisia, neither densely populated nor insular, the key factor was undoubtedly Bourguiba's proactive policy which promulgated the Personal Status Code in 1956, endowing women with a status far ahead of all other Arab countries, and implemented an effective population policy. Finally, how can we explain the decline in fertility which took place later in large States (Mexico, China) or even entire continents (Latin America)?

4.2.2. *The decline in infant mortality*

A remarkable correspondence was observed, even a parallelism, between the drop in infant mortality and birth rates between 1960 and 1980 (Figure 4.3), stimulating an interpretation centered on the change in the behavior of couples in the face of the drop in infant mortality, regardless of the geographical context.

In Singapore, for example, a 35.4% drop in the birth rate was concomitant with a drop of 41% in the infant mortality rate and, in Hong Kong, between 1960 and 1970, the fall in the birth rate was 42% for a fall of 52% in the infant mortality rate. Was this a simple coexistence or a true causal relationship? A chain of causalities seemed to prevail. In societies without a social protection system, children are a true insurance for old age. When infant mortality is high, couples must give birth to many children, so that at least two or three reach adult age and take care of their elderly parents when they are no longer able to provide for their own needs. Thus, infant mortality must fall before fertility and, as soon as populations are fully aware of this, the mechanism for "replacing births" no longer operates.

The weak point of the argument is that infant mortality and the decline in fertility could actually be two consequences of underlying variables, not taken into account in the reasoning: economic development and improvement in living standards. In fact, the reality is much more complex and cannot be reduced to a simple *mechanical relationship* between infant mortality and fertility. On the one hand, development influences infant mortality at the level of the State and the family. On the other hand, it also has an impact on fertility at these two levels. In terms of infant mortality, a country's economic growth favors investments that can improve the health care supply, as well as transportation, thus facilitating the access to care and reducing infant mortality. Likewise, families benefit from higher incomes and once essential needs have been assured – namely the access to food and water – they can spend more on children's health and education, or even improve housing, all of which contribute to reducing the risk of illness, and therefore infant mortality. In addition, the education of mothers is decisive. Fatalism prevails where infant mortality is very high ("God gave it to me, God took it from me", a Senegalese woman told us). Practices which can be harmful to health are more easily defeated if the mother has notions of hygiene (a baby's bottle must be sterilized). In addition, development influences fertility by means of mechanisms which are largely independent of those reducing infant mortality. At the State level, the income generated by development helps to create or improve infrastructure and to extend the health and education supply, most often for the benefit of rural areas, neglected up until then.

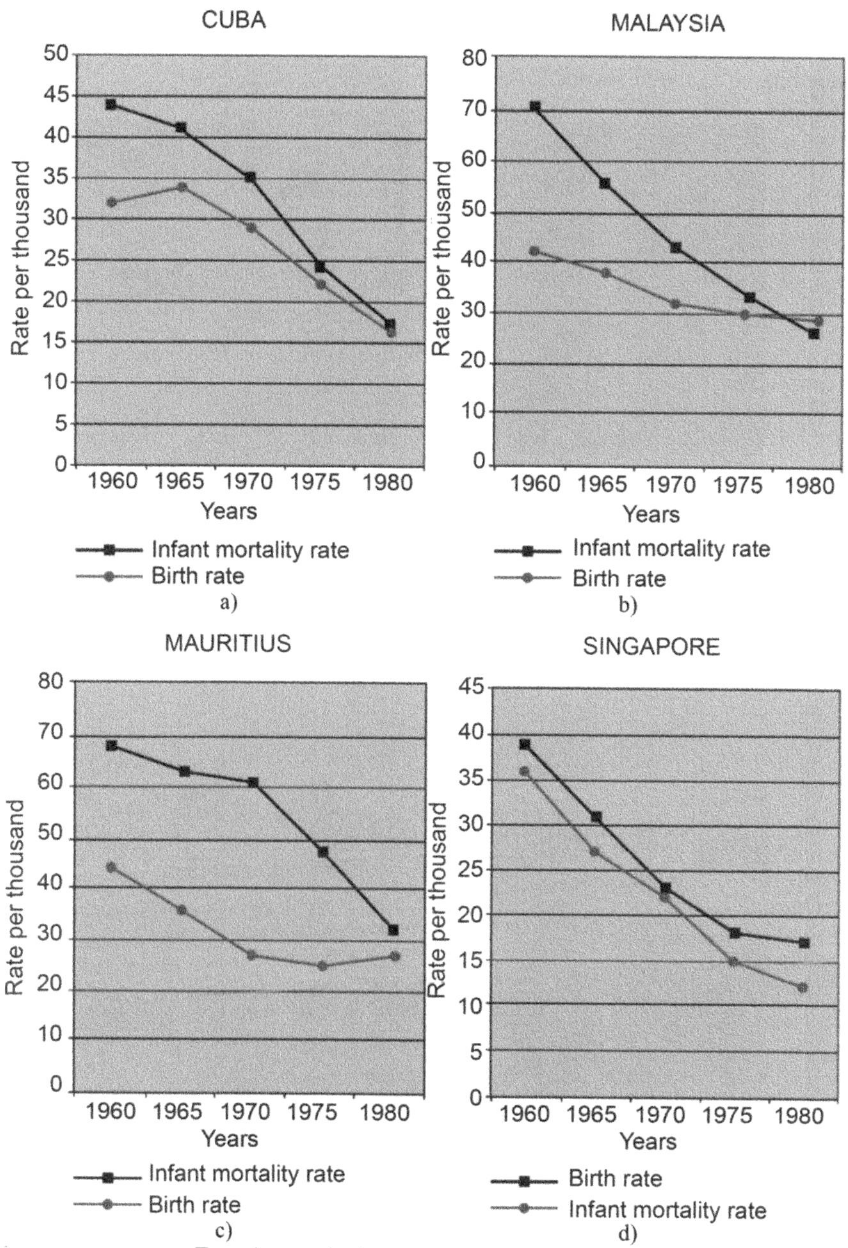

Figure 4.3. *Declines in infant mortality and fertility (1960–1980) (source: Charbit 2015; UN DESA data)*

Figure 4.4 illustrates the reality of sanitary conditions in cities and the resulting epidemiological risks. Figure 4.5 contrasts the practical schooling conditions depending on available means.

a)

b)

Figure 4.4. *Sanitary conditions in Africa (sources: (a) ©IRD P. Gazin; (b) ©IRD C. Costantini). For a color version of this figure, see www.iste.co.uk/charbit/demographic.zip*

a)

b)

Figure 4.5. *Educational conditions in Africa (sources: (a) ©AM-DHDD; (b) ©Merwan Kaoula). For a color version of this figure, see www.iste.co.uk/charbit/demographic.zip*

Family behavior also changes with development. In general, a woman's status improves when her educational level rises because the generalization of education (primary, secondary and higher education) translates into a rebalancing of school attendance rates for the benefit of girls. Until then, they had been sacrificed when parents had to choose between educating their sons or their daughters. Finally, with further education, and often at odds with the parents' position, the idea spread among young couples that it was possible and legitimate to decide on the number of children. At the same time, contraception is better accepted and, above all, used more effectively. In Burkina Faso, for example, 44% of women in secondary school were using modern contraception at the end of 2010, compared to 11% of illiterate women.

Obviously, the positive effect of development is all the more evident when the distribution of wealth is not too unequal. This means that development has a political dimension that should not be underestimated. In some African countries where oil or mining resources had been discovered, this new income was only gained by certain social groups or even by certain regions, sometimes degenerating into conflicts. This is the case with Sudan for example. There is, therefore, no direct explanatory causal relationship between infant mortality and fertility.

4.2.3. *Religion is not in itself a factor for high fertility*

It is common to think that religion promotes high fertility and is a factor of resistance to demographic change. Due to the process of secularization of attitudes and behavior, could declining religion represent a condition for the decline in fertility? In the 1960s, the pronatalism of the Catholic religion ("be fruitful and multiply") was evoked to predict the unlikelihood of couples adhering to contraception and the improbability of the decline in fertility.

But actually, since the 1960s, fertility has halved in 10 or 15 years in several Latin American and Caribbean countries. Whatever the influence of Catholicism may have been, the error in the prognosis is due to several factors. First of all, the positions adopted in the field by the local Catholic clergy may have seriously diverged from the recommendations issued by the Vatican. But this analysis, which *essentializes* religion and ignores the elementary difference between beliefs, attitudes and practices, is coupled with an ignorance of the political dimension of the question of population control in Latin America in the 1960s, a topic properly addressed by Joseph-Mayone Stycos (1971). Opposition first came from extreme left groups, under the influence of the Communist doctrine based on the Marxist theory that the growth of the proletariat would eventually accelerate inherent contradictions in capitalism and precipitate its collapse. But opposition also came from right-wing milieux which were generally in power. Hostile to family planning programs in the name of a nationalist ideology, they set apart from their Yankee big brother, accused of desiring to weaken the demographic base of the States by imposing on their territory what they referred to as a Malthusian behavior model.

Directly opposed, the reformist left ended up winning, together with international contraception programs that were less openly neo-Malthusian than those of the American international aid insofar as they presented contraception as the means for families to get out of the high fertility/poverty vicious circle. Thus, it was generally women (mainly middle-class), clearly assuming their desire to have only one or two children, who served as a model for others.

	Number of children 1970–1975	Number of children 2018	% of Muslims
Afghanistan	7.7	6.2	100
Algeria	7.38	3.0	100
Saudi Arabia	7.3	2.3	97
Bangladesh	6.1	2.1	90
Egypt	5.7	3.3	95
Indonesia	5.2	2.3	88
Iran	6.4	2.1	99
Jordan	7.8	2.8	98
Kuwait	6.9	2.1	95
Libya	7.6	2.2	97
Morocco	6.9	2.4	99
Uzbekistan	6.3	2.4	96
Pakistan	6.6	3.5	96
Syria	7.5	2.8	92
Tajikistan	6.8	3.6	84
Tunisia	6.2	2.2	99
Turkmenistan	6.2	2.8	93
Turkey	5.3	2.1	98
Yemen	8.5	3.8	99

Table 4.3. *Evolution of fertility and % of Muslims in various countries (sources: fertility (UN DESA 2005, 2019); percentage of Muslims: Pew Forum on Religion & Public Life, October 8, 2009)*

The supposed weight of the religious factor has been reaffirmed in recent years in the case of Islam, but what does this really mean? The evolution of fertility in most countries of widespread Muslim religion is characterized by a spectacular drop in fertility numbers over the past 40 years (Table 4.3). The simple list of these countries suggests that as Islam is embedded in so widely different political, social, economic and cultural contexts, it cannot be invoked as a *common* factor of resistance to the decline in fertility. While it is true that Turkey benefited from a forced secularization following Kemal Atatürk, why and how – despite Saudi Arabia's Wahhabi Islam – has fertility declined in other countries?

Iran provides the best demonstration of the error made when considering that Islam, as such, could be a factor blocking the decline in fertility. In 1967, the Shah's government implemented the first family planning program, but, on the eve of the Khomeinist Revolution of 1979, it had not achieved any significant results. The Islamic Republic suspended family planning programs, declared the legal minimum marriage age to be 9 for girls and 15 for boys, gave back to men the unilateral right to divorce and polygamy, by abolishing the law legalizing abortion and, finally, by cultivating the traditional division between the male social sphere and the female family sphere (Ladier-Fouladi 2009) – according to the rules of the *sharia* – the Khomeinist regime asserted itself as strongly pronatalist. Moreover, with the war against Iraq, families were called to fill the ranks of "an Army of twenty million". Yet, despite this unfavorable legal and political context and against all expectations, fertility began to decline (from 6.9 to 5.3 children) in 1989, when the Islamic Republic returned to its initial position and adopted a neo-Malthusian policy. In 1989, the reversal of the population policy (Law No. 13985) was justified by a religious leader from Chom University in these terms: "The Supreme Leader can change Islamic law depending on the circumstances". Insofar as 50% of married women aged 15–49 were already using modern or traditional contraceptive practices, and despite the absence of propaganda on birth control between 1979 and 1989 – which was a sign of strong motivation in women – the second family planning program was well received and accelerated the decline in fertility from 4.8 children per woman in 1990 to 1.9 in 2012, making Iran's demographic transition one of the fastest in the world: in the space of 17 years (1986–2003) fertility fell by nearly 70%. Two factors were decisive: the regular increase in the average age for the first marriage in women (from 19.7 years old in 1976 to 24 years old in 2006) and above all, contraception: as of 2000, three quarters of married women aged 15–49 used modern or traditional contraceptives.

However, this observation only puts off the question. Why this decline in marriage age and this increased use of contraception? The sociocultural and political context is decisive. Urbanization is constantly progressing (from 47% to 68% between 1976 and 2006), literacy has also significantly increased: it evolved from 59% to 89% among men, and from 35% to 80% among women. Thus, the vast majority of urban women and a little over two-thirds of rural women have fairly largely egalitarian couple relationships (Ladier-Fouladi 2009). The second factor is related to the war against Iraq (1980–1988). By dispatching the soldiers and conscripts of the regular army to the front, the *Pasdaran* troops and the volunteers who subsequently became the *Bassij* (the mobilized), the Islamic Republic did not feel the need to decree general mobilization. As a result, the war did not have a direct demographic impact and the number of casualties was much more moderate than expected (during the 8 years the war lasted, the number of military and civilian casualties amounted to 200,000 people).

On top of the cost of war ($500 billion), an extra sum of $300 billion was needed to afford post-conflict reconstruction. And above all, in this type of highly oil-dependent economy, the 1984–1990 oil countershock and the economic crisis worsened unemployment and forced the Islamic State to cut subsidies on all services and consumer products. If the government made such a radical shift in its population policy, as illustrated by the above-mentioned Law No. 13985, despite the constant reaffirmation of the preeminence of the regime's theocratic character, it is because it was forced to compromise. With the crisis, couples badly needed a second salary, while the regime continued to be contested by young people and women, resulting in a weakening of the regime's social base, something which inevitably forced it to soften its position. In summary, Iran is a textbook case on the instrumentalization of religion by politics (see *supra* for the turnaround of 1989) and shows that religion, in itself, explains nothing.

4.2.4. *Land tenure: land saturation*

Since for several decades populations have been essentially rural, the hypothesis of a relationship between population growth and the availability of cultivable land is worth exploring. What happens when there is no pressure on the land, as is the case with populations who live in settlement fronts and perform forest clearing, for instance? Conversely, how is the saturation of the land (related to overpopulation), likely to reduce fertility?

For example, in the Amazon rainforest in 1990, Ecuadorian settlers used to have eight children per woman, comparable to the numbers observed in frontier areas in Brazil (8.3) and Peru (8.4), much higher than anywhere else, either in urban areas or in the rest of the rural areas. Likewise, in the Philippines, in 1952, a survey showed that, among women at the end of their fertile life (45–49 years old), the number of children varied from 4.8 to 7 when the size of the farm increased from 1 to more than 4 hectares. More recent surveys have confirmed this relationship in Bangladesh, India, Mexico, Brazil, Egypt and Thailand. Again, historical comparisons are enlightening: fertility was very high in the United States in the frontier areas, during the conquest of the West. The underlying logic is economic: the survival of colonists depended on their family labor force, therefore on their fertility, whereas the cost of children was almost zero: no school or supply care on these pioneering fronts where everything was yet to be built (data drawn from Carr and Pan 2002).

On the other hand, since population growth saturates space and stabilizes populations, the gradual reduction of available surfaces per family can lead to such parcelization of land that families can no longer live off the land. In the mid-19th century in France, contemporaries pondered about fertility decline in the countryside. They evoked the egalitarian sharing instituted by the Napoleonic Civil Code as the cause for fragmentation; however, customary practices probably circumvented the law in several French regions. But while the real role of this institutional factor has not yet been elucidated, the economic motivation underlying farm size need not be called into question. Confronted with the dismemberment of farms, small peasant owners had developed an effective strategy: they married their only son to the neighbor's only daughter, something which enabled each successive generation to regroup the land.

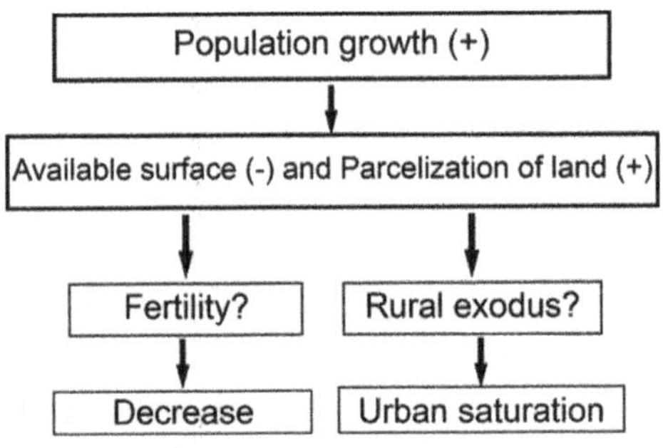

Figure 4.6. *The process of land saturation*

In our time, the land saturation hypothesis is important for developing countries (Figure 4.6). One of the arguments advanced by some ideologues opposed to fertility-decreasing population programs is the underpopulation of the African continent. This amounts to forgetting that the total area of a country is an unsatisfactory indicator, since only the arable land can produce enough to feed the population. In fact, there are considerable differences between the densities along the major rivers (Niger, Senegal, Nile) and those areas barely a few kilometers away from the bed of these rivers. In this sense, it is inaccurate to say that Africa is underpopulated. Finally, faced with land saturation, two solutions are available to rural populations: either fertility reduction or rural exodus. But the second option poses the problem of urbanization in developing countries: cities can only absorb rural surpluses at the cost of increasing difficulties (environmental degradation, saturated infrastructure) and newcomers are faced with major challenges as in rural areas. Moreover, growth forecasts for some cities have had to be revised downwards.

4.2.5. *The modernization of behavior*

An objection arises as to the approach taken so far. Right along with the factor taken in isolation and privileged in the analysis, other factors may have come into play. For example, regarding the role of insularity, the case of Cuba's remarkable public health policy's implementation in these decades cannot be ignored.

We should therefore turn to multifactorial explanations such as the widespread theory of the "modernization of behavior".

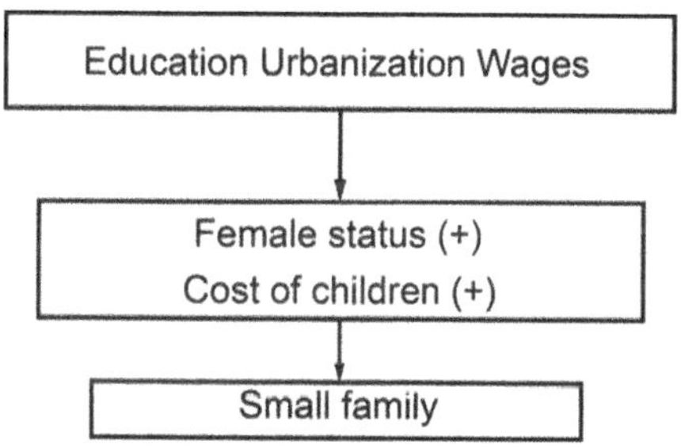

Figure 4.7. *Modernization theory*

According to modernization theory, with economic development, urbanization and the rise in the level of education, the family is losing its importance as a production unit, women increasingly having paid jobs in the modern sector and various activities other than the household or the family. All of these changes increase the costs of raising children and contribute to reducing their participation in family income. The number of children that couples believe they can afford to raise also tends to decrease as the demands of the family's standard of living and of children's education increase (Figure 4.7).

Data drawn from international surveys show that this behavior model applies quite suitably to educated women living in urban areas. They marry later and have fewer children because of a well-controlled use of contraception. They are often referred to as "pioneers", likely to lead other women into the logic of limited fertility, by way of imitation. Specialists have taken up this idea: what explains the decline in fertility is the diffusion of Western ideals, favored by the globalization of culture (Cleland and Wilson 1987).

Modernization theory has the defect of making general assumptions, based on the three aforementioned contextual factors (wages, education, urbanization), which characterized the socioeconomic evolution of industrialized countries, namely the shift of extra-European societies from the rural environment to the modern industrial world. However, the comparison between the cities of the industrial revolution, such as Manchester or Lille, with Bombay or Cairo, must be seriously nuanced. While the former created employment and wealth, the large growth of megalopolises in developing countries, and probably several thousand medium-sized cities, can be explained by the accumulation of poor populations of rural origin striving to survive. They tend to worsen an (already partly anarchic) urbanization, dwelling in the suburbs, without access to water, electricity or the road network. Similarly, the share of paid work in these cities is undoubtedly much lower than it was in Europe in the 19th century, since the economy which developed there is mostly informal. However, this sector, which largely escapes taxation, makes it difficult to organize social protection and retirement systems. Unlike industrialized countries, which organized public prevention and care against disease by means of the State's budget resources throughout the 19th century, in developing countries, this social protection function remains the prerogative of families.

Still, economic growth does not necessarily convey social development. In the oil states of the Persian Gulf, the huge increase in the GDP (Gross Domestic Product) contrasts with the still high female illiteracy rates: 32% in Saudi Arabia, plus 12% of women who have not even completed the primary school cycle, and another 12% who have completed it without pursuing any further studies. In other words, more than half of women (32% in Qatar) do not have a suitable educational level to enable them to assert their autonomy, in particular, in terms of contraceptive choice and, more generally, for playing social roles which are usually associated with modernization, such as economic autonomy and real independence from spouses and relatives.

4.2.6. *The rationality of the large family*

Beyond these criticisms, is modernization the only possible path? The theory's flaw is, ultimately, to presuppose that a whole set of favorable economic and cultural conditions have been met, which is by no means true in the rural world. This still represents more than half of the population of Africa: illiteracy is important, unpaid work predominates and the status as a woman is significantly lower than that of men.

In rural areas, economic factors also shape social reality, but according to a completely different logic. It makes sense to have a large family, because the family is a hardly mechanized production unit mainly relying on the labor of the domestic group (women, children and other parents living there) (Figure 4.8), while child-rearing costs in terms of education, health and housing are non-existent or very low. In the absence of a social security and public retirement system, these constitute genuine comprehensive insurance, at least in terms of health and old age. And, first and foremost, having a lot of children makes it possible to satisfy labor needs for agricultural production, especially in the case of self-sustaining families.

Once this survival condition has been satisfied, "surplus" children can be oriented toward crafts and, better still, the head of the family can invest in their education by sending them to a neighboring city. This certainly amounts to reducing the climate hazard that weighs on agricultural income, and therefore vulnerability. But, in the background, the probabilistic calculation is difficult to dismiss: while each additional child costs almost nothing, and can pay off big (success in the city), then why deprive oneself of this possibility? Everything is based on the head of the family's *Weltanschauung*: does his strategy extend beyond the village's boundaries?

From a sociocultural point of view, the large family is associated with great prestige, while society values the authority of parents and elders, something which does not promote the emancipation of women and maintains traditional values focused on the group's reproduction. This is why women are confined to their breeding role, in addition to their contribution to the family economy. There is no question that in Africa they are expected to fulfill a personal destiny and must marry early in order to meet family expectations, or those of the social or ethnic group. But then, why has fertility also decreased in poor urban areas, in Asia and in Latin America, as well as in rural areas, although admittedly slower than in the cities?

a)

b)

Figure 4.8. *Child labor (sources: (a) ©IRD, O. Barrière; (b) ©IRD, E. Bernus). For a color version of this figure, see www.iste.co.uk/charbit/demographic.zip*

4.3. The sociodemography of precocious nuptiality

While childhood has been a priority at the international level since the end of the Second World War, marked in particular by the creation of Unicef, the interest in adolescence is more recent, but continues to grow (Charbit 2018). Thus, the 45th sessions of the United Nations Commission on Population and Development has attached particular importance to adolescence and youth, while major international organizations, in particular Unicef, Unfpa, UNDP, Unesco, but also the World Bank, bilateral cooperations, major NGOs, such as the Population Council or the Guttmacher Institute, or finally *The Lancet* journal, have collected a considerable amount of information. Solid syntheses on several aspects of the current conditions of teenagers in developing countries and in particular in Africa are now available: health, nuptiality and fertility, and in particular early marriages and pregnancies, contraception, domestic violence, prostitution, gender-related inequalities, educational deficits, economic exploitation (either within the family or not), the incidence of poverty and last but not least, the impact of globalization. Added to this is the mass of academic research on countries and case studies of a more monographic nature. It is now accepted that predictions on the demographic transition and the demographic dividend, particularly in sub-Saharan Africa, will partly depend on the behavior of adolescents as a sociodemographic group. In addition, the development of this continent will condition the stabilization of the world population in the medium term. The importance of population and growth prospects are not to be neglected: in 2015, there were 43.7 million pre-teenagers (10–14 years) and 36.9 million adolescents (15–19 years) in Western Africa alone. And according to the United Nations average projection, these two age groups which are constitutive of adolescence will double between 2015 and 2050. The UNICEF *Generation 2030/AFRICA* report (Unicef 2014a) stresses that in 2100 half of children and adolescents under the age of 18 will live in Africa and, more than in any other region of the world, they will be "at the heart of the demographic and social transition". From this perspective, the fertility of teenage girls is a carefully monitored quantitative and social indicator. Indeed, the fertility of African adolescent girls aged 15–19 is twice the world average. This explains the interest in presenting the social, economic and cultural determinants of adolescence, which decisively shape their attitudes and behavior.

4.3.1. *The vulnerability of young married women*

Although the number of early marriages is declining worldwide, nearly 15 million girls are married every year before they reach the age of 18. These girls represent a highly vulnerable group: they are deprived of their childhood, their educational opportunities are limited and they often start to procreate while they are still too young. Those coming from the poorest households, as well as those living in rural areas, are at greater risk (Unicef 2014c)[1]. The frequency of child marriage within the poorest families has remained unchanged since 1990[2]. All over the world, these girls who are married while still being children are less likely to receive appropriate medical care during pregnancy than adult women. The lack of care and insufficient physical maturity expose them and their babies to obstetric risks. Complications during pregnancy and childbirth are the second leading cause of death among girls aged 15–19 (WHO 2014) and infants born to mothers under 20 are 1.5 times more likely to die in the first 28 days of life than those born to mothers between 20 and 40 (Unicef 2014). The study carried out by Unicef in Mozambique shows that more than 12% of girls between the ages of 15 and 24 were married before the age of 15. Data analysis reveals the importance of economic factors alongside geographic and religious factors. The probability of being married young decreases when the household is rich or enjoys land tenure. This probability also decreases with the age of the head of household, and in female-headed households (Unicef 2015).

The existing body of research agrees that marriage at an early age is unfavorable to the personal development of women, and it is still necessary to define what constitutes early marriage in a given society. This is the theoretical and methodological problem that must now be clarified. Behind epidemiological and demographic data, the sociocultural and economic reality is fundamental. We can oppose two nuptiality models, their alternative sociocultural foundations and the conclusions to be drawn about the effectiveness of the demographic policy to be adopted.

In the first demographic model where early marriage is universal in the society studied, it is clear that this type of behavior is strongly embedded in this society's values systems and standards. And, if this is so, it is because it must correspond to a major issue for society. A quick historical perspective suggests that nuptiality is a societal response to the problem of high infant mortality[3]. Without mentioning population growth, the simple renewal of populations has been jeopardized, because high fertility – made propitious through early and universal marriage – was somehow canceled out by high infant mortality, showing infant mortality probabilities of up to 200 per thousand, and infant and child mortality probabilities

1 Jensen and Thornton (2003) provide a global overview based on Demographic and Health Surveys (DHS) data.

2 We follow Unicef here, *A Profile of Child Marriage in Africa*, New York, 2015.

3 On the theory of Change and Response, see Charbit and Petit (2011).

of the order of 500 per thousand. This situation prevailed in Europe for centuries until the Pasteurian revolution (1880) and especially the generalization of the use of antibiotics after the Second World War.

Comparable mortality levels were observed in developing countries and particularly in Africa, certainly before colonization, and even after the independence of the 1960s, when the epidemiological context was not identical (disappearance of the plague and, conversely, frequency of infectious diseases which do not exist in Europe since they are related to the tropical and subtropical climate). In all these societies, early marriage, as close as possible to puberty (therefore before the age of 15), and at the same time universal (every girl should be married), helped to maximize the reproductive potential of women. Therefore, multiple pregnancies, especially in the absence of any contraception, were an effective means for ensuring group survival. In these conditions, the very concept of early marriage makes little sense, precisely because under no circumstances is there an example of a late marriage (except in cases of physical disability). One can then wonder about the merits and especially the effectiveness of a proactive policy aimed at pushing back marriage age, something which is strongly anchored in the overall functioning of this type of society.

In the second demographic model, only a fraction of women marry early. The problem is purely methodological. At what age should the researcher set the early marriage threshold? From the onset of menstruation and secondary sexual signs in girls (appearance of breasts, pubic hair), what is known as the nubile age? Or when the woman testifies to a real physical and physiological maturity, suggesting the capacity to conceive and to carry a pregnancy to term? Any marriage concluded before the age of 15 should therefore be defined as early. Unfortunately, demographic surveys do not provide sufficiently detailed data to decide between the two definitions for this early marriage threshold. Demographers offer a purely pragmatic statistical solution. They check at what age marriage frequency increases significantly. If many women marry after 15 years old, then one can no longer speak of early marriage after that age.

4.3.2. *The case of Benin*

In the context of Benin, as well as in Western Africa, female fertility is a central value. Indeed, the number of children a woman has is closely related to her status in the family and in society as a whole, hence the tendency toward early nuptiality and fertility. These are associated with a particular socioeconomic profile. One of the possible hypotheses is that these women constitute a population at risk, characterized by sociodemographic and socioeconomic handicaps, which hinders their autonomy. In concrete terms, this vulnerability is observed in data on marriage, pregnancy, pre- and post-natal care. Let us look at two examples.

In Benin, the Personal and Family Code established marriageable age at 18 years old, partly because early marriage and childbearing are the determining elements of high fertility and the primary risk factor for maternal death. In addition, marriage at a young age makes girls more likely to marry older men, who put them at greater risk of an HIV infection. The question that arises is whether the change in marriage age is specific to people with characteristics which are generally associated with modernization, namely urban residence, educational level and high well-being level, or whether it is common to adolescents regardless of their background. All the available variables (Charbit 2018) reveal deep differences, whether it is the department of residence, the place of residence, the level of education or the level of well-being. It follows, as has been shown and contrary to the Unicef strategy in Benin, that its population program should not target the adolescent as a global category without paying careful attention to the social determinants. The differences when entering into a union are notable: early marriages are three times more numerous in rural areas than in urban areas, eight times more numerous among the least educated teenagers compared to those with the most education, and finally, five times more numerous among the poorest compared to the richest. In addition, the WHO recommends at least four antenatal visits: the first one before the fourth month of pregnancy, the second one at 6 months of pregnancy, the third between the seventh and eighth months, and the last visit should be carried out at 8 months and half of pregnancy. In the latest MICS Unicef survey (1974) that we used, all the people consulted by the pregnant woman had been recorded. Only the most qualified person had been taken into account whenever several types of health staff members were mentioned. Adolescent girls, more often than other women, had no prenatal care, suggesting greater vulnerability.

4.4. Conclusion

This chapter examined in turn insularity, infant mortality, religion, contraception, population policies and land saturation. Many other avenues could also have been explored, but each would pose the same methodology problem, fertility being a complex fact, involving cultural, economic and social dimensions, which engages not only the woman, but also her spouse, and, in some African countries, her relatives and her ethnicity. How can one seriously believe that a single factor taken in isolation can account for the birth – or not – of a child? As for multifactorial explanations, the modernization theory of behavior is the most widespread, but it immediately raises an objection, that of the rationality of the large family, closer to the reality of developing countries, but which does not stand the test of facts.

Finally, the only reasonable conclusion that can be drawn from this scrutiny of the possible causes for fertility decline is that several different logics are likely to coexist within the same country and, *a fortiori*, the same continent. This outcome is entirely logical with regard to our initial postulate that a conceptualization as fine and rigorous as possible must prevail over so-called universalist syntheses.

In terms of demographic dynamics analysis, nuptiality is, along with contraception, one of the two major variables governing the evolution of fertility. Both are measured with fairly good accuracy, whereas the third mode of fertility limitation, abortion, poses serious problems of underreporting, precisely because it is socially repressed and punished by the law in numerous countries. As we have stressed in a chapter of another book (Charbit 2022), the sexuality of women remains largely controlled by men in developing countries, because they must contribute to the reproduction of the group, hence the social, cultural and even legal obstacles to the practice of contraception and, even more so, to the recourse to abortion.

Even more than these two major demographic variables, it is appropriate in the case of nuptiality, to go beyond the purely quantitative analysis of demographic dynamics, because the economic, social and cultural dimensions largely determine the behavior of populations. At variance with countries where women have acquired broad autonomy in the decision to marry and the choice of spouse, nuptiality in developing countries is not only the business of two individuals, but that of families and, in particular, their alliance strategies.

As has been discussed, it was impossible to deal with the whole question of nuptiality within the limits of this chapter, but there is one aspect where sociocultural factors are strongly intertwined with demographic dynamics: early nuptiality. The marriage of young girls is sometimes so early that some reports speak of "child marriage". It is the direct cause for pregnancies occurring in women barely of child-bearing age, for whom the negative consequences – both physical and psychological – have been widely emphasized. Despite some countries' awareness about the seriousness of this public health problem and the laws which have been adopted to define a minimum marriageable age, early nuptiality remains related to the status of the woman: nuptiality is all the more frequent when the woman is poor and little educated.

4.5. References

Bongaarts, J. and Casterline, J. (2013). Fertility transition: Is sub-Saharan Africa different? *Population and Development Review*, supplement 38, 153–168.

Carr, D.L. and Pan, W. (2002). Fertility determinants on the frontier: Longitudinal evidence from the Ecuadorian Amazon. *The 130th Annual Meeting of APHA*, Los Angeles.

Charbit, Y. (1975). *La population du monde et la Conférence de Bucarest*. La Documentation française, Paris.

Charbit, Y. (1987). *Famille et nuptialité dans la Caraïbe*. INED/PUF, Paris.

Charbit, Y. (2015). Le mystère de la baisse de la fécondité (1950–2010). In *La bombe démographique en question*, Charbit, Y., Gaimard, M. (eds). PUF, Paris.

Charbit, Y. (2018). *L'adolescence au Bénin*. L'Harmattan, Paris.

Charbit, Y. (ed.) (2022). *Population Issues and Development*. ISTE Ltd, London and John Wiley & Sons, New York.

Charbit, Y. and Léridon, H. (1980). *Transition démographique et modernisation en Guadeloupe et Martinique*. INED/PUF, Paris.

Charbit, Y. and Petit, V. (2011). Toward a comprehensive demography: Rethinking the research agenda on change and response. *Population and Development Review*, 37(2), 219–239.

Cleland, J. and Wilson, C. (1987). Demand theories of the fertility transition. An iconoclastic view. *Population Studies*, 41, 5–30.

Coale, A.J. (1973). The demographic transition reconsidered. *International Population Conference*, IUSSP, Liège, 53–73.

Coale, A.J. and Watkins Cotts, S. (1986). *The Decline of Fertility in Europe*. Princeton University Press, Princeton.

Cosio Zavala, M.E. (1992). Demographic transition and social development in low-income country. In *Population Growth and Demographic Structure, Proceedings of the United Nations Expert Group Meeting for Preparation of ICPD*, Paris, 16–20 November, 123–149.

Freedman, R. (1986). Theories of fertility decline. In *Fertility and Mortality, Theory, Methodology, and Empirical Issues*, Mahadevan, K. (ed). Sage Publications, New Delhi.

Jensen, R. and Thornton, R. (2003). Early female marriage in the developing world. *Gender and Development*, 11(2), 9–19.

Kenya National Bureau of Statistics (2010). Kenya demographic and health survey 2008–2009. Report, Kenya National Bureau of Statistics, Nairobi.

Ladier-Fouladi, M. (2009). *Iran, un monde de paradoxes*. L'Atalante, Nantes.

Mpyisi, E., Weber, M., Shingiro, E., Loveridge, S. (2004). Changements dans l'allocation des terres, la production et la taille des exploitations dans le secteur des petits exploitants rwandais sur la période 1984/1990 à 2002. Rwanda Food Security Research Project/MINAGRI, 6F.

Stycos, J.M. (1971). *Ideology, Faith and Family Planning in Latin America.* McGraw Hill, New York.

Szreter, S. (1993). The idea of demographic transition and the study of fertility change. A critical intellectual history. *Population and Development Review*, 19(4), 659–701.

UN DESA (2005). World Population Prospects, The 2004 Revision. Department of Economic and Social Affairs of the United Nations Secretariat, Population Division, New York.

UN DESA (2010). World Population Prospects, The 2010 Revision. Department of Economic and Social Affairs of the United Nations Secretariat, Population Division, New York.

UNFPA (2010). State of World Population. United Nations Population Fund, New York.

Unicef (2014a). Generation 2030|AFRICA. Child Demographics in Africa. New York.

Unicef (2014b). Committing to Child Survival: A Promise Renewed. Progress Report 2014, Unicef, New York.

Unicef (2014c). Ending Child Marriage: Progress and Prospects. Report, Unicef, New York.

Unicef (2015). Child Marriage and Adolescent Pregnancy in Mozambique: Causes and Impact. Report, Unicef, Maputo.

WHO (2014). Adolescent Pregnancy, Fact Sheet no. 364. World Health Organisation, Geneva.

5

Contraception and Reproductive Rights[1]

Aisha DASGUPTA
United Nations, Geneva, Switzerland

5.1. Introduction: population and the Sustainable Development Goals

In this chapter, I bring together work that I, together with colleagues and collaborators, have pursued recently to study the place of family planning and reproductive health in achieving sustainable development. I do that by studying the population–environment nexus. I start by looking at the role of population and the Sustainable Development Goals (SDGs). I review a decomposition of the demands we all make of the biosphere's goods and services that Ehrlich and Holdren (1971) made in their classic paper, and relate it to the biosphere's ability to meet those demands on a sustainable basis. Population was a factor in that decomposition. Thus, in the rest of this chapter I study a few salient features of and trends in reproductive behavior, and the role sexual and reproductive health care services can play in the world's poorest regions, including sub-Saharan Africa and Southern Asia. I discuss reproductive rights and comment on socially embedded preferences for childbearing. I conclude by comparing the case studies of Bangladesh and Pakistan. Although similar in many respects, these countries differ profoundly in

1 The views expressed in this chapter are entirely those of the author and do not necessarily reflect the views of the United Nations.

Demographic Dynamics and Development,
coordinated by Yves CHARBIT. © ISTE Ltd 2022.

their fertility dynamics. They demonstrate that we cannot underestimate the importance of national population policies.

The purpose of the 2030 Agenda for Sustainable Development is to provide a plan for achieving a better and more sustainable future for all (United Nations 2015). The SDGs of the 2030 Agenda are intended to integrate three dimensions of sustainable development: economic, social and environmental. They address global challenges related to poverty, inequality, climate change, environmental degradation, peace and justice.

Setting these goals was an important, even noble achievement, but the 2030 Agenda did not ask whether these goals – should they be achieved – are sustainable. For example, the SDGs are reticent about population, and yet it is difficult to regard them as sustainable unless they are studied in the context of global population and its distribution within and across countries. It has been argued that limiting the increase in mean global temperature to 2°C, relative to that of the pre-industrial revolution era, is unlikely to be met unless population growth is reduced substantially (O'Neill *et al.* 2010). However, even the recent Paris Agreement on climate change made no mention of population, nor of the lack of access to contraception and safe abortion services for many of the world's poorest women. Women's education is prominent in the SDGs and is regarded by development experts as the surest route to women's empowerment and the preference for smaller families. All governments insist on the importance of women's education for empowering women yet, even today, nearly 30% of young women between 15 and 24 years of age in low-income countries are illiterate (World Bank 2019). In contrast, family planning and reproductive health care programs are affordable for governments even in low-income countries. They provide "low hanging fruit" to governments for empowering women, yet they remain low on the development agenda: today less than 1% of international aid is devoted to family planning (Grollman *et al.* 2018). It is a paradox.

Ehrlich and Holdren (1971) introduced the equation I = PAT to trace humanity's *i*mpact on the biosphere to *p*opulation size, *a*ffluence (gross domestic product (GDP) per capita) and *t*echnology in use (including knowledge, institutions, social capital). Today, we know Ehrlich and Holdren's "impact" as "ecological footprint". The authors observed that Nature responds to the demands we make of it, not to rates of change in those demands. The declining growth rate of global population that has been observed in recent years is seen by development experts as a hopeful sign of a transition toward sustainable development (World Bank 2016).

The Ehrlich–Holdren decomposition instead indicates that the decline does not say much about the actual prospect of realizing sustainable development, for it is the size of our population that matters, other things remain equal.

A vast amount of recent literature in ecology and the Earth sciences has revealed that, over the past several decades, the annual global demand for the biosphere's flow of goods and services has exceeded the biosphere's ability to meet it on a sustainable basis (Wackernagel and Beyers 2019)[2]. This can be referred to as impact inequality. The idea underlying the concept of sustainable development is that impact inequality becomes impact equality. This conversion should therefore be the central SDG. The Ehrlich–Holdren decomposition shows that there are three (interrelated) ways the conversion can occur: (i) global population declines over time; (ii) per capita GDP declines; and (iii) the efficiency with which we convert the biosphere's goods and services into GDP increases. In this chapter, I discuss the role of family planning and reproductive health in this conversion.

The United Nations median projection of world population in the year 2100 is 10.9 billion, with a 95% uncertainty interval between 9.4 and 12.7 billion (United Nations 2019a). More than three quarters of the increase from today's 7.7 billion is expected to be in sub-Saharan Africa, where population in 2100 is projected to rise from today's ~1.1 billion to 3.8 billion (Figure 5.1). The 95% projection interval around this final value extends from 3.0 to 4.8 billion. Juma (2019) discusses the adverse impact on the region's ecology and thus on food and employment prospects in the face of such population growth. Made up of about 14% of the world's population, the region accounts for just over 3% of the world economy (World Bank 2019). Sub-Saharan Africa therefore cannot be held responsible for the global environmental problems that we face today. It is the future there that is problematic. Attempts to increase incomes in sub-Saharan Africa, even to the current global average income (~17,000 international dollars), in the face of a near 3 billion rise in numbers will require an increase in the region's annual output from 3.5 trillion international dollars to about 68 trillion international dollars at today's prices (Barrett *et al.* 2020). That rise, assuming that it is even possible, is likely to have negative consequences for the region's ecology, contributing to further societal conflicts there and greater attempts at population movements both within and outside the region (Juma 2019).

2 In a similar vein, Earth scientists now call our human-dominated era the Anthropocene.

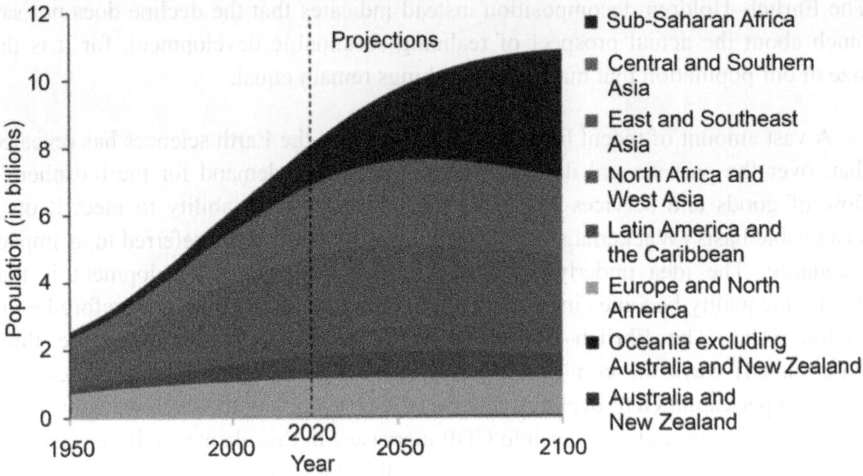

Figure 5.1. *Trends in total population by region, estimates and projections 1950–2100 (source: United Nations 2019a). For a color version of this figure, see www.iste.co.uk/charbit/demographic.zip*

Global population has risen sharply since the middle of the 20th century because the substantial reductions in the death rate were not matched by reductions in birth rate. But countries in East and Southeast Asia, as well as in Latin America and the Caribbean made rapid transitions to replacement level fertility, with some dipping below and some countries in Southern Asia moving closer to replacement level (Pakistan is an exception, which is explained later on in the chapter); fertility in sub-Saharan Africa remains much higher. Today, women in sub-Saharan Africa have around 4.6 births on average over the course of a lifetime, in contrast to a world average of 2.4. The total fertility rate in India has fallen to 2.2, while that in China (at 1.7) is well below replacement level (United Nations 2019a) (Figure 5.2). There are a number of reasons for the slow decline in fertility in sub-Saharan Africa, including inheritance rules, the prevalence of polygamy, lack of access to modern methods of contraception, low levels of education among women and kinship obligations (Bledsoe 1994; Bongaarts and Casterline 2013). I wish instead to explore a pathway that has been less discussed but that offers an explanation for why the desired number of children has remained substantially higher in sub-Saharan Africa than elsewhere.

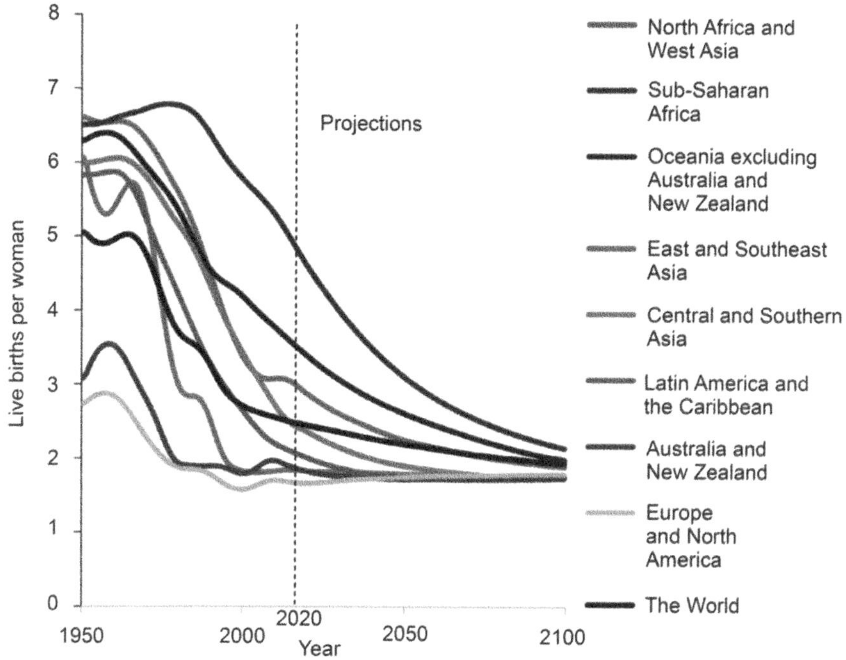

Figure 5.2. *Trends in total fertility rate by region, estimates and projections 1950–2100 (source: United Nations 2019a). For a color version of this figure, see www.iste.co.uk/charbit/demographic.zip*

5.2. Socially embedded preferences for childbearing[3]

Fertility and contraceptive behavior is driven by attitudes and preferences that are socially embedded. The term socially embedded preferences or "social preferences" for short is used to identify someone's behavior and practices that are influenced by the behavior of others. Anthropologists have argued that fertility practices, like other practices, are not only influenced by private desires and wants, they are also shaped by societal mores. People look to others when making their own choices (Douglas and Isherwood 1979, among many others). But anthropologists have reported that, unlike in East and Southeast Asia, Latin America and the Caribbean, and Central and Southern Asia, societal mores have remained powerful

3 The material in this section has been adapted from Dasgupta and Dasgupta (2017) and Barrett *et al.* (2020).

in sub-Saharan Africa, where women acknowledge that they are able to acquire social status through reproductive success (Bledsoe 1994). This attitude toward reproduction has been called "Children as wealth" (Guyer 1995). Using this as a template, it can be said that reproductive behavior is "conformist" when the family size that a household desires is positively related to the average family size in the community or, more broadly, in the world that households come into contact with. Conformism can thus give rise to multiple self-sustaining states of affairs. As long as all other households want small families, each will wish to restrict its fertility. On the other hand, if all the others want large families, no household will wish to deviate from the practice. A society can therefore be part of a self-sustaining pattern of behavior, characterized by high fertility and stagnant living standards, even when there is another pattern of potentially self-sustaining behavior that is characterized by low fertility and rising living standards, which would be beneficial to all (Dasgupta 1993; Dasgupta and Dasgupta 2017). A significant amount of demographic literature has sought to explain why fertility mores have been especially pertinent in sub-Saharan Africa. The role of family planning – particularly programs that encourage information, education and communication activities – in accelerating the demographic transition in the region becomes apparent.

Socially embedded preferences for children are illustrated in Figure 5.3. Curve ABCDE is a household's desired number of children plotted against the average number of children per household (the horizontal axis) in the community. The curve is upward sloping and intersects the identity line from 0 to F at three points (B, C, and D), each of which is a social equilibrium. B and D are stable, while C is unstable. In the figure, which is purely illustrative, every household desires d children if all other households have d children each, and b if each among all others have b. Imagine now that every household prefers the outcome in which all households have b children each to the one in which all have d children each. As having either b or d children is a stable equilibrium, a fertility rate of d would be just as stable as a fertility rate of b.

There is now growing evidence of conformist reproductive preferences. A study of contraceptive use in rural Kenya found that in communities with dense social networks and a poorly developed market economy, a woman would be unlikely to use contraceptive methods if contraception use in her network was low, whereas she would be likely to use such methods if contraception use in her network was high (Kohler *et al.* 2001). Further empirical evidence found that state-level fertility rates gradually declined following phased introduction of cable television across Indian states in the 1980s (Jensen and Oster 2009). Similarly, an analysis of mass media and reproductive behavior in six countries within sub-Saharan Africa suggested that modern ideas communicated via music, advertising, theatre, news or documentaries could play an important role in weakening traditional support for early marriage and high fertility (Westoff and Bankole 1997).

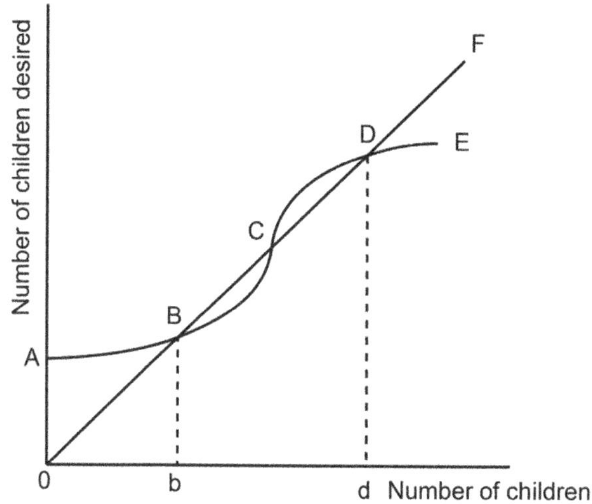

Figure 5.3. *Conformist preferences for childbearing (reproduced from Dasgupta and Dasgupta (2017); Barrett* et al. *(2020))*

Further support has been provided in an analysis of contraceptive uptake in Bangladesh (Munshi and Myaux 2016). The study concerned women living in the same community but belonging to different religious groups. After monitoring individual differences in education, age and wealth, the study found that a woman's choice to use contraception was strongly dependent on the predominant choice made by other women in her religious group and was unaffected by the predominant choice made by women belonging to the other group. It is also thought that the choice of contraceptive method is strongly influenced by the prevailing methods used in the community.

Persistent reproductive practices that go counter to present day interests may have had a rationale in the past. However, even when circumstances have changed, a society can remain stuck in a pattern of behavior characterized by high fertility (d) even when there is an alternative that is characterized by low fertility (b), which would be preferred by all. This suboptimal situation disappears when breaks with tradition (e.g. more educated women) pave the way for the move toward smaller families. Newspapers, radio, television and the Internet communicate information on other ways of life. The media can be a vehicle through which conformism becomes based on the behavior of a wider population than the local community, which disrupts existing practices. Community discussions about the benefits of a small family can encourage households to act on lowered fertility targets. Economic demographers have interpreted the persistence of high fertility in sub-Saharan Africa to a strong desire for children (Pritchett 1994). Conformist preferences point to a different interpretation. Behavior based on such preferences can be expected to have a strong positive correlation between fertility desires and fertility outcomes, but causality should not be attributed to the relationship. Conformist preferences tell us that it would be as true to say that fertility rates in a country are high because people there have a strong desire for children as it would be to say that people there have a strong desire to have children because fertility rates are high (Dasgupta and Dasgupta 2017).

Although conformist preferences supporting high fertility rates can amplify the impact we have on the biosphere, family planning appears in the environmental literature infrequently, perhaps because of concerns about state intervention in what are regarded as personal matters. The field of family planning has had a difficult history, with numerous examples of coercion. That led the international community to commit itself to reproductive rights at the 1994 International Conference on Population and Development. As a result, it is not easy to study conformist preferences over reproduction. The ICPD's reproductive rights are individualistic and thus reflect the view that reproduction is a purely private matter. However, social preferences reflect the fact that we do not regard our reproductive behavior as a purely personal matter. We acknowledge that we are influenced by what others do, and we know that others are influenced by what we do. Moreover, behavior based on such preferences can be shifted by social mechanisms that do not involve state directives but instead, bottom-up social mechanisms. The latter are likely to be better placed to bring about desirable changes. Conformist behavior can be shifted by changing expectations about others' fertility choices. Family planning programs can be designed so as to encourage members of communities to share information about modern methods of contraception and discuss the advantages of smaller families. As routes to fertility transition, investment in community-based family planning programs should be regarded as essential (Bongaarts 2011). By providing access to subsidized contraceptive commodities and services, family planning programs were successful in accelerating fertility declines in Asia and Latin America between the 1960s and 1980s. In the next section, we look at global and regional trends in family planning.

5.3. Trends in contraceptive use and unmet need for family planning

Every year, the United Nations Population Division publishes a comprehensive data set of family planning indicators for women of reproductive age. The most recent compilation includes 1,317 survey-based observations from 1950 to 2019, across 196 countries (United Nations 2020a). Historically, surveys reported estimates for married or in-union women but in more recent decades, surveys have expanded the population to include all women of reproductive age, regardless of marital status. This has gone hand in hand with developments in the international family planning field, which have refocused attention toward women. The recent initiatives of Family Planning 2020, which was established in 2012, and the SDGs established in 2015 have demanded monitoring of all women of reproductive age. These have been important developments in the measurement of progress in family planning.

Contraceptive prevalence (CP) is the proportion of women who report themselves or their partners as currently using at least one method of contraception at a point in time. The indicator is one of the most valuable and widely used in reproductive health research, and provides an indication of the progress made in family planning programs. Although the indicator could be calculated from Management and Information Systems or provider-recorded data (e.g. Dasgupta *et al.* (2015)), it is typically estimated from women's responses to questions in household surveys such as, "Are you currently doing something or using any method to delay or avoid getting pregnant?". If the response is "Yes", the respondent is then asked what method she or her partner is using. There is a long history of international survey programs using questions such as these, including Knowledge, Attitudes and Practices studies since the 1950s, World Fertility surveys established in 1972 to improve comparability of fertility at an international scale and Contraceptive Prevalence Surveys (as summarized in Kantorova *et al.* (2017)). In more recent decades, the United States Agency for International Development (USAID) funded Demographic and Health Surveys (DHS), Multiple Indicator Cluster Surveys of the United Nations Children's Fund, which pay particular attention to the health of women and children, and since 2013 the Performance Monitoring and Accountability 2020 surveys (which use mobile technology for quick and inexpensive annual surveys) have also addressed family planning needs and use, and the methodologies and indicators have become increasingly harmonized.

The availability of data on contraceptive use has increased significantly over time (Figure 5.4). The majority of observations come from the wealth of 511 independent National Surveys, followed by 320 from DHS. While DHS tends to be the most commonly used survey today, the historical surveys (including World Fertility Surveys, Reproductive Health Surveys and Contraceptive Prevalence Surveys) have been crucial for providing an understanding of longer term historical trends in contraceptive use worldwide.

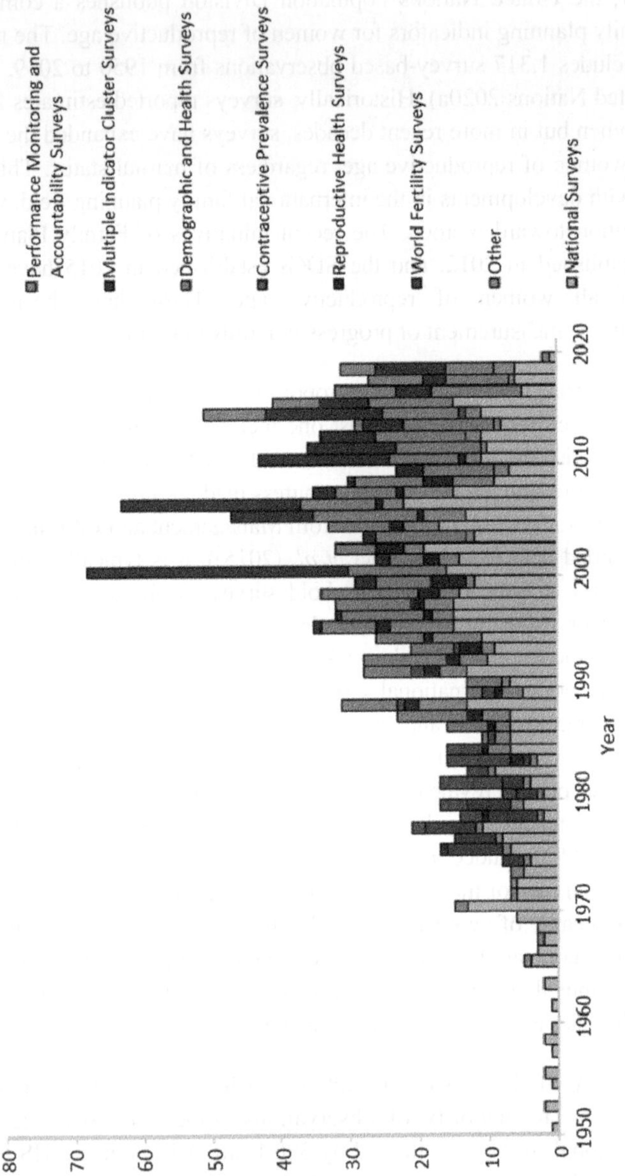

Figure 5.4. *Trends in the availability of survey data on contraceptive use by survey program and year (source: United Nations 2020a). For a color version of this figure, see www.iste.co.uk/charbit/demographic.zip*

Unmet need for family planning measures the gap between women's fertility intentions and contraceptive use. It is the percentage of women aged 15–49 who want to space out their births or limit the number of children they have, and who are not currently using contraception. Bradley and Casterline (2014) explain that it is the amount by which contraceptive use would need to increase if fertility intentions were fully realized by using a contraceptive method. The indicator is a population-level estimate and is not intended to identify individual women who are in need of contraception. In fact, the concept of "need" is constructed, and women do not use contraception for a range of reasons. The calculation of unmet need for family planning includes in the numerator women who are sexually active and fecund, and who report either wanting to delay the birth of their next child for at least 2 years or are undecided about the timing of the next birth, or who report not wanting any (more) children. The numerator includes pregnant women whose current pregnancy was unwanted or mistimed, and postpartum amenorrheic women who are not using contraception and whose last birth was unwanted or mistimed. The reason pregnant and postpartum amenorrheic women are included is because they might have had an unmet need at the time of conception. The calculation of unmet need for family planning uses more than 15 survey questions (Bradley *et al.* 2012). In the most recent data compilation, there were 566 observations of unmet need for family planning (United Nations 2020a).

For the calculation of unmet need, all women who are married or in a union are assumed to be sexually active. For unmarried women, it is necessary to determine the timing of their most recent sexual activity in order to identify those considered currently at risk of pregnancy. Unmarried women who are not pregnant or postpartum amenorrheic are considered at risk of pregnancy if they had intercourse in the 4 weeks prior to the survey interview.

The unmet need for family planning indicator can show whether or not there is progress towards meeting women's needs for contraception. However, it is also possible for unmet need for family planning to stagnate or even increase. This can occur when there are changes in fertility preferences with increasing numbers of women wanting to postpone or stop childbearing, and family planning services have not expanded fast enough to meet the increasing demand for contraception.

The compilation of observations of CP and unmet need for family planning are standardized where possible, updated annually by the United Nations Population Division and used to produce model-based national, regional and global estimates and projections of family planning indicators. The estimates for all women of reproductive age (15–49 years) are available for the period 1990 to 2030 (Alkema *et al.* 2013; Kantorova *et al.* 2020; United Nations 2020b) for 186 countries or areas that have a total population greater than 90,000 people and at least one observation of CP, and for aggregate regions. The model-based estimates are comparable across place and time. The medians and uncertainty intervals around the indicators are published. They have been used in recent years to monitor progress of Millennium Development Goal 5B ("Achieve, by 2015, universal access to reproductive health"), Sustainable Development Goal 3.7 ("By 2030, ensure universal access to sexual and reproductive health-care services, including for family planning, information and education, and the integration of reproductive health into national strategies and programs"), and contribute to the monitoring of key indicators for the partnership Family Planning 2020, whose goal was for 120 million additional women and girls to use modern methods of contraception between 2012–2020.

Contraceptive methods are often classified as either modern or traditional. Modern methods include female and male sterilization, the intrauterine device (IUD), the implant, injectables, oral contraceptive pills, male and female condoms, vaginal barrier methods (e.g. diaphragm, cervical cap and spermicidal foam, jelly, cream and sponge), the lactational amenorrhea method (LAM), emergency contraception and the contraceptive patch or vaginal ring. Traditional methods include rhythm (e.g. fertility awareness based methods and periodic abstinence) and withdrawal. Among contraceptive users globally, the vast majority use modern methods (91%), with a handful of countries in Europe, North Africa and West Asia, and sub-Saharan Africa that are the exception, in which a larger proportion of users rely on traditional methods. Unmet need for modern methods of family planning is the sum of women with unmet need for family planning and women using traditional methods. Because modern methods of contraception are generally more effective than traditional methods at preventing pregnancy (WHO/CCP 2018; Bradley *et al.* 2019), and because it is increases in the use of modern methods that has been the main driver of increases in contraceptive use in recent decades, I now focus on modern methods.

Globally, use of modern methods of contraception among women of reproductive age increased from 36% (475 million women) in 1990 to 45% (851 million women) in 2020, and is projected to stay around 45% (922 million women) at least until 2030 (Figure 5.5). The stagnation in the projected proportion of women using modern methods reflects underlying changes in the composition of women, with increasing numbers of women in countries with currently lower levels of use, and increasing shares of unmarried women among women of reproductive age[4].

4 The category 'unmarried women' includes women who are not sexually active and may have no need for contraception. It should be noted that generally a lower proportion of unmarried women use contraception, compared to married women.

By 1990, use of modern methods of contraception had already reached levels greater than 40% in Australia and New Zealand, East and Southeast Asia (driven predominantly by China), and Europe and North America. By 2020, modern CP in these regions reached 57%, 57% and 54%, respectively. Many of the contraceptive use transitions in countries of Central and Southern Asia, East and Southeast Asia, and Latin America and the Caribbean occurred prior to 1990 and thus only the end of the transitions in these regions are shown in Figure 5.5. In 1990, use of modern methods was low in sub-Saharan Africa (8%) and Oceania (excluding Australia and New Zealand) (15%), and today they are still the regions where the use of modern contraception is lowest (25% and 24%, respectively).

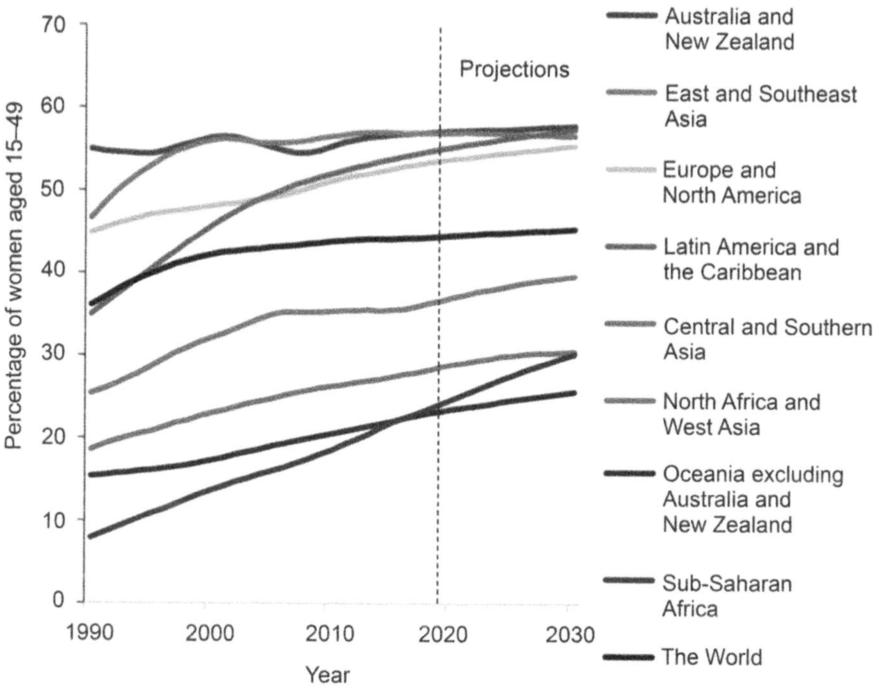

Figure 5.5. *Prevalence of modern contraceptive use among women aged 15–49 by region, estimates and projections 1990–2030 (source: United Nations 2020b). For a color version of this figure, see www.iste.co.uk/charbit/demographic.zip*

Among the countries that in 1990 had a modern CP of less than 5%, the countries experiencing the lowest increases in modern contraceptive use are Chad, Democratic Republic of the Congo, Eritrea, Guinea, Mauritania, Nigeria, Somalia, South Sudan and Sudan, each increasing fewer than 9 percentage points.

Nevertheless, there have recently been some rapid increases in contraceptive use among women of reproductive age in select countries of sub-Saharan Africa. Between 2000 and 2020, it is estimated that eight countries have experienced increases in modern contraceptive use greater than 20 percentage points, including Burkina Faso (from 7% in 2000 to 28% in 2020), Eswatini (from 27% to 53%), Ethiopia (from 5% to 28%), Kenya (from 24% to 45%), Lesotho (from 26% to 51%), Madagascar (from 10% to 35%), Malawi (from 20% to 47%) and Rwanda (from 4% to 30%). These success stories show that it is possible, to significantly increase contraceptive use in sub-Saharan Africa in a short space of time. Common themes that emerged from Ethiopia, Malawi and Rwanda included political commitment beyond the health sector, notable champions and partner collaboration, community provision of services and vision for scale-up, community engagement and the establishment of effective strategies and systems (USAID 2012).

There are a range of factors that determine the mix of methods in a population, including cost, effectiveness and side effects of the methods, together with women's short-term and long-term fertility intentions. Societal norms also influence which methods are acceptable. In terms of access and service provision, the frequency of stock-outs, provider biases and preference, provider training and local or national policies on family planning can also influence the method-mix. The IUD is the most common contraceptive method used in East and Southeast Asia (19%) followed by male condoms (17%). Female sterilization is the dominant method in Latin America and the Caribbean (16%) and Central and Southern Asia (22%). In Europe and North America, oral contraceptive pills (18%) and male condoms (15%) are the most commonly used methods. The common methods in North Africa and West Asia are the oral contraceptive pill (11%) and IUD (10%). The most common method in sub-Saharan Africa is injectables, with 10% of women using this method (United Nations 2019b). Once a method-mix is established in a population and there are social preferences for particular methods, it can take time to shift the method-mix toward a wider range of methods.

The rationale for expanding the content and reach of family planning programs is that 257 million women worldwide now want to stop or delay childbearing but are not using a modern method of contraception (United Nations 2020b) (Table 5.1). Although the proportion of women who want to postpone or stop childbearing but are not using modern contraception has decreased globally from 18% in 1990 to 14% today, the absolute number has increased from 232 million in 1990, in part due to population growth, particularly in countries with higher levels of unmet need. If the past trends continue, it is likely that there will still be around 260 million women globally with unmet need for modern methods in 2030.

Today the largest numbers of women with unmet need for modern methods of contraception are in Central and Southern Asia (77 million women), East and Southeast Asia (51 million) and sub-Saharan Africa (52 million). The high numbers of women with unmet need for modern methods in Central and Southern Asia, and East and Southeast Asia are driven by populous countries in these regions. The high number of women with unmet need for modern methods in sub-Saharan Africa is driven by the high proportion of women with unmet need for modern methods in this region (20%), which together with Oceania (excluding Australia and New Zealand) (22%) have the highest proportions of women who report wanting to stop or delay childbearing but are not using a modern method. The decline in the number and proportion of women with unmet need for modern methods of contraception in Europe and North America is predominantly due to declines in the proportion of women using traditional methods of contraception, which was 14% in 1990 and is 7% today.

	1990		2020		2030	
	Number (1000s)	%	Number (1000s)	%	Number (1000s)	%
Australia and New Zealand	572	10.6	696	9.9	708	9.5
Central and Southern Asia	61,115	21.1	76,661	14.6	77,713	13.6
East and Southeast Asia	54,432	11.3	51,140	9.1	46,237	8.7
Europe and North America	52,238	20.9	32,061	12.9	27,941	11.6
Latin America and the Caribbean	19,079	17	19,720	11.4	19,304	10.8
North Africa and West Asia	14,663	22.1	22,418	17.1	23,077	15.4
Oceania excluding Australia and New Zealand	358	23.8	625	21.6	688	19.9
Sub-Saharan Africa	28,472	25.9	52,031	19.8	62,632	18
World	232,251	17.6	257,311	13.5	260,722	12.8

Table 5.1. *Estimates and projections of the number and proportion of women of reproductive age with an unmet need for modern methods of contraception in 1990, 2020 and 2030 (source: United Nations 2020b)*

Among women experiencing unmet need for modern methods, some use traditional methods. Nevertheless, it should not be surprising that there were 121 million unintended pregnancies per year between 2015–2019[5], nor that an estimated 61% of all unintended pregnancies ended in abortion, a significant proportion of which were performed under unsafe conditions (Bearak *et al.* 2020).

In addition to reducing unintended pregnancies, contraceptive use enhances women's own health and that of her children by spacing out births and providing greater opportunity for education, women's empowerment and income (Koenig *et al.* 1992; Ahmed *et al.* 2012; Canning and Shultz 2012; Cleland *et al.* 2012; Sonfield *et al.* 2013).

A number of recent studies have aimed to make the economic case for the return on investment of family planning, and five in particular were assessed and summarized by Family Planning 2020 (2018). The five approaches were different in terms of timescale for measuring the benefits (short vs. long term), outcomes measured (health vs. other), benefits measured (US dollars saved vs. economic gains), scale (one country vs. developing countries) and estimated cost of contraception.

The Guttmacher Institute's Adding It Up (2017), and the Family Planning and Millennium Development Goals Scenarios (MDG) models estimated the short-term savings of meeting need for family planning. For every additional $1 invested in meeting the need for contraceptives, the Guttmacher Institute estimates that $2.20 is saved in maternal and newborn healthcare services by reducing the number of unintended pregnancies. The MDG Scenarios model estimated that for every $1 invested in contraception, this would save between $2 and $6 in meeting other MDG targets across the 16 countries studied. At the other extreme, the Copenhagen Consensus project compared the cost-effectiveness of different development interventions and concluded that every $1 invested in meeting unmet need would yield in the long-term $120 in accrued annual benefits.

The Demographic Dividend model demonstrated that in the long term, reduced fertility would lead to improved maternal and child health outcomes, and increased labor market productivity would result in increased GDP per capita. This made the case to policymakers outside the health sector that investments in family planning, education and the economy would increase per capita GDP. The family planning SDGs model has been applied to show that improvements in socioeconomic status, along with investments in family planning, maximize long-term progress toward reducing poverty and food insecurity, and increasing income growth.

5 Some unintended pregnancies are a result of contraceptive method failure.

Yet, family planning is a neglected feature of contemporary public policy; programs have been undervalued by national governments and international agencies and the benefits have been routinely underestimated. Developing countries relegate family planning expenditure to minor government departments. Despite evidence that family planning reduces poverty, the World Bank has given it low priority. Currently, less than 1% of overseas development assistance is awarded to it (Grollman *et al.* 2018).

5.4. Reproductive rights, fertility intentions and socially embedded preferences[6]

In response to target-driven and coercive programs, the 1994 International Conference on Population and Development reaffirmed the language of rights in the sphere of family planning and reproductive health. The Conference's conclusions in the Program of Action stated: "Reproductive rights [...] rest on the recognition of the basic right of all couples and individuals to decide freely and responsibly the number, spacing, and timing of their children, and to have information and means to do so, and the right to attain the highest standards of sexual and reproductive health" (UNFPA 1995, Chapter 7, Section 3).

The qualifier "responsibly" could be read as requiring couples to take into account the adverse environmental externalities[7] their reproductive decisions may give rise to but that would probably be a stretch. Certainly, writings affirming the Program of Action have interpreted the passage and its intent more narrowly. For example, the fundamental right of individuals "to decide freely and for themselves whether, when and how many children to have is central to the vision and goals of Family Planning 2020". It is also pivotal in the reproductive health indicators of the SDGs. There are rights to information and other services pertaining to family planning and reproductive health. There is also the right to choose one's family size.

But, to insist that the rights of individuals and couples to decide freely the number of children they have overrides all competing interests is to minimize the rights of all those (most especially, perhaps, future people) who suffer from the environmental externalities that accompany additions to the population. Additionally, the statement ignores the latent need among those who do not want

6 The material in this section has been adapted from Dasgupta and Dasgupta (2017).

7 Externalities are the unaccounted consequences for others, including future people, of actions taken by one or more persons.

family planning now but would want it if others among their peer group were using modern contraceptives.

Unmet need for family planning is calculated based on respondent's expressed fertility intentions to questions such as: "Now I have some questions about the future. Would you like to have a(nother) child or would you prefer not to have (any more) children?". This is followed by a question about how long the woman wants to wait, if she responded to the previous question that she does want a(nother) child. But there are dangers of biases in responses to the questions about fertility intentions. The questions do not ask women what her fertility intentions would be if the prevailing fertility practices of others were different. In fact, there is no mention of the prevailing fertility rate. Since respondents are not invited to disclose their conditional desires, it is most likely they disclose their fertility intentions on the assumption that fertility will remain at its prevailing rate.

A related measure of fertility intentions is desired family size, which is obtained from answers to the following question: "If you could go back to the time when you did not have any children and could choose exactly the number of children to have in your whole life, how many would that be?". A direct way to discover socially embedded preferences would be to reconstruct the questionnaire by asking a series of conditional questions, such as: "If you could go back to the time when you did not have any children and could choose exactly the number of children to have in your whole life, how many would that be, assuming everyone else in your community had *n* children over their whole life?". The questionnaire could pose a conditional question such as this in an ascending order of *n*, say from 0 to 10. The example in Figure 5.3 imagines that the answers to n = 2, 4, and 5 are, respectively, 2, 4, and 5. It also imagines that answers to the questions in which n = 0, 1, 3, 6–10, respectively, differ from 0, 1, 3, 6–10. No doubt responding to a string of conditional questions could be taxing on survey participants, but to not ask them is to misread fertility desires and thus to wrongly estimate unmet need and demand for family planning, satisfied by modern methods.

An indicator promoted more recently to reflect family planning's aim to satisfy individual's and couple's own choices regarding the number and timing of children, and to avoid contraceptive use targets, is the demand for family planning satisfied by modern methods (Fabic *et al.* 2014). This indicator is the ratio of modern contraceptive users to the total demand for family planning, which is the sum of contraceptive users and women with unmet need. If X is the number of women aged 15–49 who are users of modern contraception, Y is the number of women with unmet need, and Z is the total demand for modern contraception ($X + Y$), then the indicator demand for family planning satisfied by modern methods is calculated as *X/Z*. It is indicator 3.7.1 of the SDG target 3.7: "By 2030, ensure universal access to sexual and reproductive health-care services, including for family planning". The relationship between *X* and *Z* is illustrated in Figure 5.6.

Reproductive rights are at the heart of the demand for family planning satisfied by modern methods indicator, which is its attraction. The indicator reflects voluntarism, rights and equity, informed choice, and the imperative of satisfying individual's and couple's own choices regarding the timing and number of their children. Change in the demand for family planning satisfied by modern methods tends to be relatively slow. Regions with high levels of use of modern contraceptive methods tend also to have high levels of demand for family planning satisfied by modern methods; for example the highest levels are in East and Southeast Asia (86%), and Australia and New Zealand (85%) (Figure 5.6). But the indicator can be problematic when calculated for sub-groups, for example specific age groups, or among unmarried women when sexual activity among unmarried is rare and total demand (*Z*) is low.

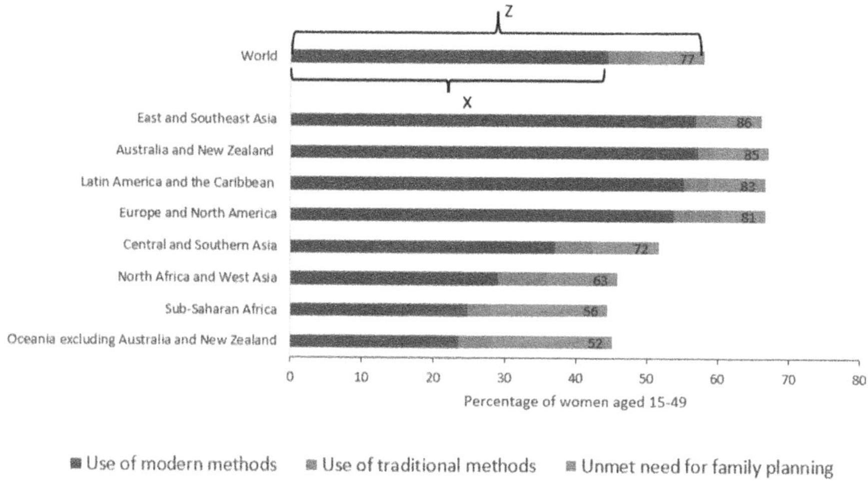

Figure 5.6. *Estimates of the proportion of women of reproductive age using contraception and having unmet need for family planning, as components of the demand for family planning satisfied by modern methods, in 2020. Note: The proportion of demand for family planning satisfied by modern methods (X/Z) is labeled at the end of the bars. (source: United Nations 2020b). For a color version of this figure, see www.iste.co.uk/charbit/demographic.zip*

There are additional problems. The use of the demand for family planning satisfied by modern methods indicator, as a measure of success, creates less desirable incentives among program managers. There is little incentive to generate demand for family planning, for example through community engagement or conversations about the benefits of spacing out or stopping childbearing. A program's performance could do well if fewer women want to space out or limit their childbearing. So long as women want many children, *Y* (unmet need) remains small and therefore *Z* (total demand) is only marginally greater than *X* (the number of modern contraceptive users). The program would score well on the demand for family planning satisfied by modern methods indicator, and appears not to need further family planning program effort. The apparent success could mask a situation where contraceptive use is low and stagnant and high fertility rates persist. But demand creation is an important component of family planning programs. The introduction of family planning-related media messages is credited for part of the rise in contraceptive use and demand in countries where such communication is active.

Additionally, fertility preferences, which contribute to the measurement of *Y*, are themselves influenced by the behavior of others. *Y* could therefore be small in a society that harbors another equilibrium in which *Y* is large. The basis on which women's expressed desires for children is elicited misestimates their desire and underestimates women's true need for family planning.

The concept of reproductive rights, as currently framed, undervalues family planning. There are collective benefits to be enjoyed if members of a community are enabled to alter their fertility preferences in a coordinated manner. Family planning can help to bring about changes in such social norms. This does not run counter to rights as part of family planning; it expands the sphere in which rights are acknowledged, protected and promoted.

5.5. The relationship between fertility, contraception and abortion

There is a negative relationship between modern contraceptive use and fertility (Figure 5.7). In countries where in 2020 there are higher proportions of women using modern methods of contraception, fertility tends to be lower. At every level of contraceptive use, countries in sub-Saharan Africa tend to have higher levels of fertility, compared to countries in other regions. Nevertheless, there are some countries that have reached relatively low levels of fertility despite still having relatively low levels of contraceptive use; while there are other countries that still have high levels of fertility hand in hand with relatively high levels of contraceptive use. Bongaarts' proximate determinants of fertility framework showed that there are other factors at play in addition to contraception (Bongaarts 1978). The length of postpartum insusceptibility from breastfeeding and sexual abstinence, sterility, patterns of marriage and sexual activity and abortion are all determinants of fertility. We now look at the role of abortion.

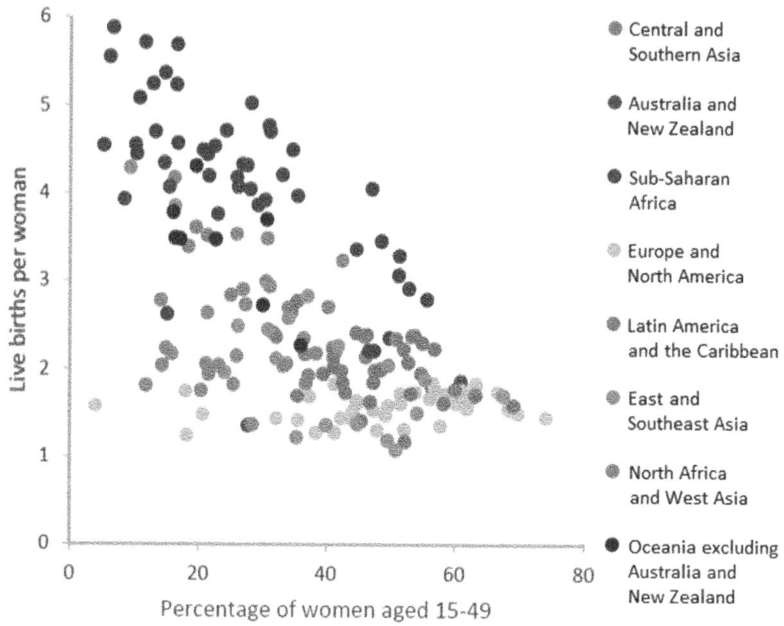

Figure 5.7. *Total fertility rate compared to modern contraceptive prevalence among women aged 15–49, 186 countries by region, 2020 (source: United Nations 2019, 2020b). For a color version of this figure, see www.iste.co.uk/charbit/demographic.zip*

Reliable data for the incidence of abortions are not consistently available across countries, especially in the developing world, but recent work led by the Guttmacher Institute and the Department of Reproductive Health and Research at the World Health Organization has produced model-based estimates of abortions (Sedgh *et al.* 2016; Bearak *et al.* 2020). Globally, it was estimated that there were around 40 abortions per 1,000 women each year between 1990–1994, which has declined slightly to 39 abortions per 1,000 women aged 15–49 between 2015–2019. The absolute number of abortions per year increased from an average of 55.0 million in the period 1990–1994 to 73.3 million in the period 2015–2019, due to growth in the population of women (Bearak *et al.* 2020).

The most substantial decline was in Europe and North America where the abortion rate declined from 46 abortions per 1,000 women in 1990–1994 to 17 in 2015–2019. Today, Australia and New Zealand has the lowest annual rate of abortions (15), followed by Europe and North America. In Eastern Europe, where abortion has been an important determinant of low fertility in the subregion, the rate fell from 107 abortions per 1,000 women in 1990–1994 to 31 in 2015–2019 (Bearak *et al.* 2020). This went hand in hand with an increase in the use of modern methods, from 30% in 1990 to 43% in 2020 in Eastern Europe, displacing the previously high levels of traditional method use (United Nations 2020b).

Bearak *et al.* (2020) found that unintended pregnancy rates were generally higher in settings where abortion was restricted than in settings where it is broadly legal. This is likely because the level of unmet need for family planning tends to be higher in countries with restrictive abortion laws. Where it is restricted, the abortion rate was 36 per 1,000 women, whereas for countries where abortion is broadly legal, excluding India and China, the abortion rate was 26. Some women in restrictive settings must take legal and physical risks to seek abortion care. When grouped by the legal status of abortion, Ganatra *et al.* (2017) found that the proportion of unsafe abortions was significantly higher in countries with highly restrictive abortion laws, than in those with less restrictive laws.

Advances in the provision of safe abortion have been important to enable more women to access services safely. For example, medical abortion (misoprostol alone or misoprostol with mifepristone) has become more widely available and used. Nevertheless, substantial numbers of women still undergo unsafe abortions which can put them at risk of physical harm, as a result of abortion restrictions or lack of access to safe services.

If the SDG target to ensure universal access to sexual and reproductive health care services were achieved, and all women who wanted to use contraception were able to, this would help many women to avoid unintended pregnancies and abortion. Nevertheless, there would still be a need for abortion since all contraceptive methods can fail, some with higher failure rates than others; some women would choose not to use contraception, and a woman might still want an abortion following an intended pregnancy. It is therefore important that women have access to a full range of contraceptive methods, as well as safe abortion services, as part of the comprehensive package of sexual and reproductive health care services.

5.6. Conclusion: the role of national policies in Bangladesh and Pakistan

Beyond the methodological considerations and analyses developed predominantly at the level of major regions of the world, the comparison of Bangladesh and Pakistan illustrates the importance of national policies. Bongaarts (2014) has shown that when two countries have similar social, religious, and economic characteristics, but one has implemented a family planning program while the other has not, it is possible to attribute differences in family planning indicators, in part, to the existence of the family planning program in the "experimental" country. I take this approach here.

From 1947 until 1971, Bangladesh and Pakistan were one nation and, as a result, there are a number of commonalities between the two countries. They both have predominantly Muslim populations and are at relatively similar levels of development. In 2018, Bangladesh ranked 135th in the Human Development Index at 0.61, and Pakistan ranked 152nd at 0.56, both falling within the category of medium human development (UNDP 2019).

Pakistan's family planning program has been weak, largely because of a lack of government commitment. In contrast, Bangladesh is known for having implemented one of the most effective voluntary family planning programs. This was informed by the lessons learned from a controlled experiment in the late 1970s in which the Matlab district of Bangladesh was divided into areas providing free family planning services with home visits, together with outreach to husbands and village leaders (the experimental group) versus the same minimal services as before (the control group). The impact of the improved services among the experimental group on increasing contraceptive use and lowering fertility was large (Cleland *et al.* 1994). A key feature of the Bangladesh family planning program is the staff of literate female workers who provide contraceptive supplies in the community, visiting women at their homes in order to overcome the barriers posed by purdah (Simmons *et al.* 1988). Additionally, there was an extensive government-led information, education and communication campaign to spread ideas concerning the benefits of contraception and smaller families. As an example, since the 1980s, an hour every day on the national station Radio Bangladesh was dedicated to family planning and population issues (Khuda *et al.* 2001).

According to the Family Planning Effort Index – a long-standing measure that quantifies the strength of national family planning programs on the dimensions of policies, services, evaluation and method access – the score for Bangladesh in 2014 was 67 as compared to Pakistan's 48 (a per cent of the maximum value) (Family Planning Effort Index no date). The score for Bangladesh has been consistently higher than for Pakistan for every survey since 1982. While the index may be biased by the responses of the key informants, the scores give an indication of the greater level of effort that has gone into the Bangladesh family planning program, and this is also reflected in reproductive behaviors.

In 1970, the proportion of married or in-union women who were using a modern method of contraception was low in both countries, estimated at around 4% in Bangladesh and 3% in Pakistan. The unmet need for modern methods of contraception among married or in-union women was high in both countries, above 30%, and the demand for family planning that was satisfied by modern methods was also similarly low for the two countries in 1970, at around 10%. However, by 2000 there were stark differences between the two countries according to these three family planning indicators. The use of modern methods among married or in-union women was more than double in Bangladesh in 2000 at 44% compared to 20% in Pakistan, and differences had appeared in the unmet need for modern methods and the demand for family planning satisfied by modern methods. In 2020, it is estimated that use of modern contraception is at 57% in Bangladesh while still only 27% in Pakistan. Unmet need for modern contraception declined to 19% in Bangladesh and 27% in Pakistan, and the demand for family planning satisfied by modern methods is 75% in Bangladesh and 51% in Pakistan (United Nations 2020b).

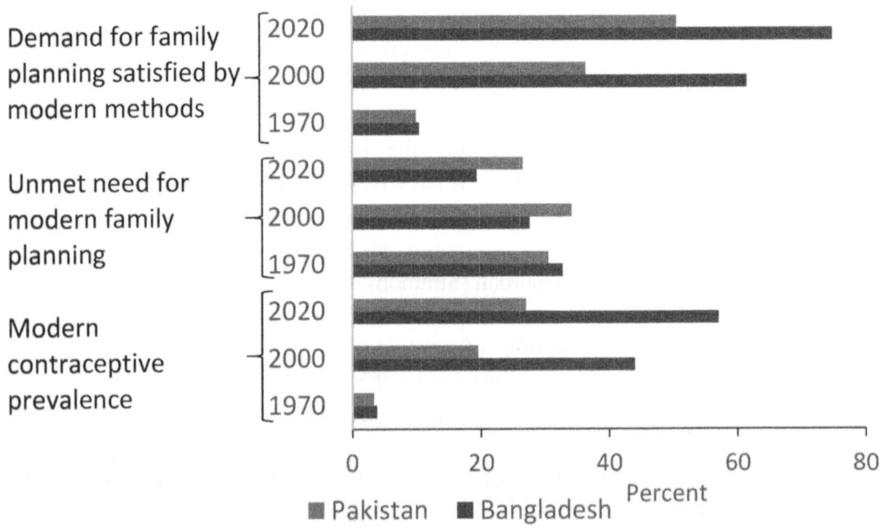

Figure 5.8. *Family planning indicators among married or in-union women in Bangladesh and Pakistan, 1970, 2000 and 2020 (source: United Nations 2020b). For a color version of this figure, see www.iste.co.uk/charbit/demographic.zip*

A similar trend is also seen in fertility outcomes. The total fertility rate in 1970 was high in both countries at 6.9 births per woman in Bangladesh and 6.6 in Pakistan. By 2000 the total fertility rate had dropped to 3.2 in Bangladesh but was still at 5.0 in Pakistan. Today, fertility is 2.0 in Bangladesh and 3.4 in Pakistan (United Nations 2019a).

The Human Development Index was slightly higher in Bangladesh compared to Pakistan, and it is of course possible that Bangladesh and Pakistan differed in other important respects not reported here. Nevertheless, the differences seen between the two countries, in terms of trends in family planning indicators and fertility, suggest that a well-organized family planning program, combined with information, education and communication activities, can have an impact on reproductive behavior. By making modern methods of contraception widely available, and removing barriers to their use, women who do not want to become pregnant are able to use contraception and control their own fertility. By increasing contraceptive use, this could reduce unmet need for family planning. Additionally, family planning programs, and communication activities around contraception, are also likely to raise the demand for contraception.

This brings me back to where I began: although family planning programs are a huge help in empowering women and enabling them to control their fertility, they remain low on the agenda of governments in the world's poorest regions, and they remain low in international aid. In this chapter, I have argued that because people's fertility preferences and contraceptive behavior is socially embedded, reductions in fertility in the world's poorest regions can be achieved without resorting to coercive measures. I have also argued that this neglected sphere of social investment is deeply related to the demands society ultimately makes of the biosphere. The idea of sustainable development means little without attention to population. This is why we should be puzzled that the United Nations SDGs did not place population more prominently on the agenda.

5.7. References

Ahmed, S., Li, Q., Liu, L., Tsui, A. (2012). Maternal deaths averted by contraceptive use: An analysis of 172 countries. *The Lancet*, 380(9837), 111–125.

Alkema, L., Kantorova, V., Menozzi, C., Biddlecom, A. (2013). National, regional, and global rates and trends in contraceptive prevalence and unmet need for family planning between 1990 and 2015: A systematic and comprehensive analysis. *The Lancet*, 381(9878), 1642–1652.

Barrett, S., Dasgupta, A., Dasgupta, P., Adger, W.N., Anderies, J., van den Bergh, J., Bledsoe, C., Bongaarts, J., Carpenter, S., Chapin III, F.S., Crepin, A.S., Daily, G., Ehrlich, P., Folke, C., Kautsky, N., Lambin, E.F., Levin, S.A., Maler, K.-G., Naylor, R., Nyborg, K., Polansky, S., Scheffer, M., Shogren, J., Jorgensen, P.S., Walker, B., Wilen, J. (2020). Social dimensions of fertility behavior and consumption patterns in the Anthropocene. *Proceedings of the National Academy of Sciences*, 117(12), 6300–6307.

Bearak, J., Popinchalk, A., Ganatra, B., Moller, A.B., Tuncalp, O., Beavin, C., Kwok, L., Alkema, L. (2020). Unintended pregnancy and abortion by income, region, and the legal status of abortion: Estimates from a comprehensive model for 1990–2019. *Lancet Global Health* [Online]. Available at: https://doi.org/10.1016/S2214-109X(20)30315-6.

Bledsoe, C. (1994). Children are like young bamboo trees: Potentiality and reproduction in sub-Saharan Africa. In *Population, Economic Development and the Environment*, Lindahl-Kiessling, K., Landberg, H. (eds). Oxford University Press, Oxford.

Bongaarts, J., (1978). A framework for analysing the proximate determinants of fertility. *Population and Development Review*, 4(1), 105–132.

Bongaarts, J. (2011). Can family planning programs reduce high desired family size in sub-Saharan Africa? *International Perspectives in Sexual and Reproductive Health*, 37, 209–216.

Bongaarts, J. (2014). The impact of family planning programmes on unmet need and demand for contraception. *Studies in Family Planning*, 45(2), 247–262.

Bongaarts, J. and Casterline, J. (2013). Fertility transition: Is sub-Saharan Africa different? *Population Development Review*, 38(supplement 1), 153–168.

Bradley, S.E.K. and Casterline, J.B. (2014). Understanding unmet need: History, theory and measurement. *Studies in Family Planning*, 45(2), 123–150.

Bradley, S.E.K., Croft, T.N., Fishel, J.D., Westoff, C.F. (2012). Revising unmet need for family planning. DHS Analytical Studies 25, ICF International, Calverton.

Bradley, S., Polis, C., Bankole, A., Croft, T. (2019). Global contraceptive failure rates: Who is most at risk? *Studies in Family Planning*, 50(1), 3–24.

Canning, D. and Schultz, P. (2012). The economic consequences of reproductive health and family planning, *The Lancet*, 380(9837), 165–171.

Cleland, J., Phillips, J.F., Amin, S., Kamal, G.M. (1994). *The Determinants of Reproductive Change in Bangladesh: Success in a Challenging Environment*. World Bank, Washington.

Cleland, J., Conde-Agudelo, A., Peterson, H., Ross, J., Tsui, A. (2012). Contraception and health. *The Lancet*, 380(9837), 149–156.

Dasgupta, P. (1993). *An Inquiry into Well-being and Destitution*. Clarendon Press, Oxford.

Dasgupta, A. and Dasgupta, P. (2017). Socially-embedded preferences, environmental externalities, and reproductive rights. *Population Development Review*, 43, 405–441.

Dasgupta, A., Zaba, B., Crampin, A. (2015). Contraceptive dynamics in rural Northern Malawi: A prospective longitudinal study. *International Perspectives in Sexual and Reproductive Health*, 41(3), 145–154.

Douglas, M. and Isherwood, B. (1979). *The World of Goods: Towards an Anthropology of Consumption*. Routledge, New York.

Ehrlich, P.R. and Holdren, J.P. (1971). Impact of population growth. *Science*, 171, 1212–1217.

Fabic, M.S., Choi, Y., Bongaarts, J., Darroch, J.E., Ross, J.A., Stover, J., Tsui, A.O., Upadhyay, J., Starbird, E. (2014). Meeting demand for family planning within a generation: The post-2015 agenda. *The Lancet*, 385(9981), 1928–1931.

Family Planning 2020 (2018). Family planning's return on investment. Washington [Online]. Available at: www.familyplanning2020.org/sites/default/files/Data-Hub/ROI/FP2020_ROI_OnePager_FINAL.pdf [Accessed 10 June 2020].

Family Planning Effort Index (n.d.). Family Planning Effort Index [Online]. Available at: http://www.track20.org/pages/data_analysis/policy/FPE.php [Accessed 26 September 2020].

Ganatra, B., Gerdts, C., Rossier, C., Johnson, B.R., Tuncalp, O., Assifi, A., Sedgh, G., Singh, S., Bankole, A., Popinchalk, A., Bearak, J., Kang, Z., Alkema, L. (2017). Global, regional, and subregional classification of abortions by safety, 2010–14: Estimates from a Bayesian hierarchical model. *Lancet* [Online]. Available at: https://doi.org/10.1016/S0140-6736(17)31794-4.

Grollman, C., Cavallero, F.L., Ducles, D., Bakare, V., Alvarez, M.M., Borghi, J. (2018). Donor funding for family planning levels and trends between 2003–2013. *Health Policy and Planning*, 33(4), 574–582.

Guttmacher Institute (2017). *Adding It Up: The Costs and Benefits of Investing in Sexual and Reproductive Health*. Guttmacher Institute, New York.

Guyer, J.L. and Eno Belinga, S.M. (1995). Wealth in people as wealth in knowledge: Accumulation and composition in equatorial Africa. *Journal of African History*, 36(1), 91–110.

Jensen, D.T. and Oster, E. (2009). The power of cable TV: Cable television and women's status in India. *Quarterly Journal of Economics*, 124(3), 1057–1094.

Juma, C. (2019). Game over? Drivers of biodiversity loss in Africa. In *Biological Extinction: New Perspectives*, Dasgupta, P., Raven, P.H., McIvor, A. (eds). Cambridge University Press, Cambridge.

Kantorová, V., Dasgupta, A.N.Z., Ueffing, P., Wheldon, M., Soerjanto, N. (2017). Who collects what on the current use of contraception? A review of survey data available for the estimation of contraceptive prevalence. Technical paper, Department of Economic and Social Affairs, Population Division, United Nations, New York.

Kantorová, V., Wheldon, M., Ueffing, P., Dasgupta, A.N.Z. (2020). Estimating progress towards meeting women's contraceptive needs in 185 countries: A Bayesian hierarchical modelling study. *PLoS Medicine*, 17(2), e1003026 [Online]. Available at: https://doi.org/10.1371/journal.pmed.1003026.

Khuda, B., Caldwell, J., Caldwell, B., Pieris, I., Caldwell, P., Ahmed, M. (2001). Determinants of the fertility transition in Bangladesh. In *Fertility Transition in South Asia*, Sathar, Z.A., Phillips, J.F. (eds). Oxford University Press, Oxford.

Koenig, M.A., Rob, U., Khan, M.A., Chakraborty, J., Fauveau, V. (1992). Contraceptive use in Matlab, Bangladesh in 1990: Levels, trends, and explanations. *Studies in Family Planning*, 23(6), 352–364.

Kohler, H.-P. and Behrman, J.R. (2014). Population and demography assessment paper: Benefits and costs of the population and demography targets for the post-2015 development agenda. Paper, Copenhagen Consensus Center, Lowell.

Kohler, H.-P., Behrman, J.R., Watkins, S.C. (2001). The density of social networks and fertility decisions: Evidence from South Nyanza district, Kenya. *Demography*, 38, 43–58.

Moreland, S. and Talbird, S. (2006). Achieving the Millennium Development Goals: The contribution of fulfilling the unmet need for family planning. Report, USAID, Washington.

Moreland, S., Madsen, E.L., Kuang, B., Hamilton, M., Jurczynska, K., Brodish, P. (2014). Modeling the demographic dividend: Technical guide to the DemDiv model. Technical guide, Futures Group/Health Policy Project, Washington.

Munshi, K. and Myaux, J. (2016). Social norms and the fertility transition. *Journal of Development Economics*, 80(1), 1–38.

O'Neill, B.C., Dalton, M., Fuchs, R., Jiang, L., Pachauri, S., Zigova, K. (2011). Global demographic trends and future carbon emissions. *Proceedings of the National Academy of Sciences*, 107, 17521–17526.

Phillips, J., Stinson, W., Bhatia, S., Rahman, M., Chakraborty, J. (1982). The demographic impact of the family planning health services project in Matlab, Bangladesh. *Studies in Family Planning*, 13(5), 131–140.

Pritchett, L.H. (1994). Desired fertility and the impact of population policies. *Population Development Review*, 20(1), 1–55.

Sedgh, G., Bearak, J., Singh, S., Bankole, A., Popinchalk, A., Ganatra, B., Rossier, C., Gerdts, C., Tunçalp, Ö., Johnson Jr, B.R., Johnston, H.B., Alkema, L. (2016). Abortion incidence between 1990 and 2014: Global, regional, and subregional levels and trends. *The Lancet*, 388, 258–67.

Simmons, R., Baqee, L., Koenig, M.A., Phillips, J.F. (1988). Beyond supply: The importance of female family planning workers in rural Bangladesh. *Studies in Family Planning,* 19(1), 29–38.

Sonfield, A., Hasstedt, K., Kavanaugh, M.L., Anderson, R. (2013). *The Social and Economic Benefits of Women's Ability to Determine Whether and When to Have Children.* Guttmacher Institute, New York.

United Nations (2015). Transforming our world: The 2030 agenda for sustainable development – A/RES/70/1. Report, United Nations, New York.

United Nations (2019a). World population prospects: 2019 revision. Report, Department of Economic and Social Affairs, Population Division, United Nations, New York.

United Nations (2019b). Contraceptive use by method 2019: Data booklet. Report, Department of Economic and Social Affairs, Population Division, United Nations, New York.

United Nations (2020a). World contraceptive use 2020. Report, Department of Economic and Social Affairs, Population Division, United Nations, New York.

United Nations (2020b). Estimates and projections of family planning indicators 2020. Report, Department of Economic and Social Affairs, Population Division, United Nations, New York.

UNDP (2019). Human Development Report 2019. Beyond income, beyond averages, beyond today: Inequalities in human development in the 21st century. Report, United Nations Development Programme, New York.

UNFPA (1995). Programme of Action of the International Conference on Population and Development. Report, United Nations Population Fund, New York.

USAID (2012). Three successful sub-Saharan Africa family planning programs: Lessons for meeting the millennium development goals. Report, United States Agency for International Development, Washington.

Wackernagel, M. and Beyers, B. (2019). *Ecological Footprint: Managing Our Biocapacity Budget*. New Society, Gabriola Island.

Westoff, C.F. and Bankole, A. (1997). Mass media and reproductive behaviour in Africa. DHS Analytical Reports No. 2, Macro International Inc., Calverton.

WHO/CCP (2018). Family planning: A global handbook for providers. Report, World Health Organization, Department of Reproductive Health and Research and Johns Hopkins Bloomberg School of Public Health Center for Communication Programs, Baltimore/Geneva.

World Bank (2016). Development goals in an era of demographic change. Report, World Bank, Washington.

World Bank (2019). World development indicators. Report, World Bank, Washington.

6

Mortality and Health, the Factors Involved in Population Dynamics

Maryse GAIMARD

LIR3S Laboratory, University of Burgundy, Dijon, France

6.1. Introduction

The evolution of mortality is one of the main components of population dynamics. In fact, its downward trend is generally considered to be the driving force of the demographic transition[1]. The level of mortality, especially infant mortality, influences fertility/birth rates. Different populations in the world have experienced a similar evolution, reaching these changes at different moments. The demographic transition, which began at the end of the 18th century in Europe, will extend to all countries in the world. However, since the mid-20th century, the evolution of the population has seriously diverged between northern and southern countries. The demographic transition, much later in southern countries, did not reach its full extent until the 1950s, with sub-Saharan Africa being the last region to enter this process. Demographic changes are not independent from socioeconomic, cultural and political contexts. While mortality has reached very low levels in developed countries, the trend remains much more hesitant in developing countries.

---

1 The demographic transition describes the evolution by which populations move from a high equilibrium regime, with high birth and mortality rates, to a low equilibrium regime, characterized by low birth and mortality rates.

Demographic Dynamics and Development,
coordinated by Yves CHARBIT.

The level of mortality is closely related to the population's health conditions and progressing within the epidemiologic transition, which is the model that theorizes long-term changes in death causes. The decrease in mortality is accompanied by a change in the population's health profile. Infectious diseases are gradually being replaced by degenerative ones, or diseases related to stress and modern lifestyle. These changes lead to a radical transformation in the age at death, shifting from infancy to childhood, from youth to older age, resulting in an increase in life expectancy. Profound changes in the disease panorama are part of the demographic process: the demographic transition and the epidemiologic transition are interdependent (Gaimard 2017). While most countries around the world have already started this epidemiologic transition, their level of involvement varies considerably. These processes, observed from the 18th and 19th centuries in developed countries, take place later in developing regions. While the relationship between mortality and health has weakened in developed countries, this is not the case in the developing world. Death is still very often the outcome of the disease process.

The health status of a population is therefore a key factor in the evolution of mortality and the demographic dynamics of a country. In addition, health is an essential component of human development and societies (Tizio 2004). It is both an end and a means for development; it can act as a lever for economic growth (Tizio 2004; Couderc *et al.* 2006; Moatti and Ventelou 2009). Thus, worldwide differences in health closely follow development gaps between northern and southern countries. The pathologies that predominate in the north are not found in the south with the same intensity as chronic diseases and traffic accidents (please note that chronic diseases have also been called "civilization diseases", and include cardiovascular disorders, cancer and obesity). In southern countries communicable diseases prevail, either due to infectious agents or parasites. With the rapid development of means of communication, as well as industrialization and urbanization in the south, globalization tends to transform this pattern: so-called civilization diseases spread their devastation in the south. The epidemiologic transition model observed in developed countries is not identically reproduced in developing countries, which are subject to a "double burden of disease" weighing on mortality rates (Gaimard 2011). Thus, the evolution of mortality and that of health conditions reveal a sharp contrast depending on social, economic, cultural and geographical contexts (section 6.2).

In southern countries, and more particularly in Asia and sub-Saharan Africa, the level of mortality and its evolution appear to be strongly dependent on the mortality of children and women, both of which are abnormally high. The health, socioeconomic and environmental conditions, in which children are born and grow up and women carry out their pregnancies and deliveries, are still the source of a great vulnerability to mortality. The large number of premature deaths is a worrying public health problem and an important issue for the increase in life expectancy. The serious character of these questions can be appreciated in the importance given to children's and women's health, which rank high on the international agenda. Two of the eight Millennium Development Goals (MDGs)[2] were oriented in this direction: to reduce the mortality rate of children under five by two-thirds between 1990 and 2015 (MDG 4), and to reduce the maternal mortality rate by three quarters between 1990 and 2015 (MDG 5). Launched in 2015, the Sustainable Development Program for 2030[3] also dedicates particular attention to health improvement, in particular to infant and maternal health (MDG 3). Health, and more particularly that of children and women, appears to be one of the major demographic challenges that southern countries will have to meet in order to accelerate their decline in mortality (section 6.3).

The evolution of mortality and its corollary, the health of populations, as well as the disparities observed between developed and developing countries – and even within different regions and continents – are much less subject to interpretation than in the case of other phenomena (nuptiality, fertility and mobility), and are more factual. These aspects will be analyzed below on the basis of the data provided by the World Health Organization and the United Nations, as part of the monitoring of Millennium Development Goals and Sustainable Development Goals.

6.2. Mortality around the world: deep inequalities

Mortality has declined all over the world. This movement began at the end of the 18th century in Europe, after which it gradually spread elsewhere. For the most part, it was after the Second World War that all southern countries benefited from the decline in mortality, but their degree of involvement in this process varies greatly. Until the 1970s, it was believed that the least developed countries, where progress was faster, would catch up and that the life expectancy of different countries across the world would converge toward an insurmountable limit. In recent decades, this

2 The Millennium Development Goals include eight targets adopted in 2000 in New York at the United Nations headquarters on the occasion of the Millenary Summit. They constitute a development plan for 2015, approved by all of the countries in the world and all of the major global development institutions.

3 The 17-Goal Program adopted by the world's leaders in September 2015, at a historic United Nations Summit. They build on the success of the Millennium Development Goals (MDGs) and aim to go further, striving to end all forms of poverty. They meet a range of social needs, including education, health, social protection and employment opportunities, while fighting climate change and protecting the environment.

convergence has been called into question. As a matter of fact, in developing countries, mostly located in sub-Saharan Africa, life expectancy has increased more slowly, leaving them on the margins of health progress. Along with the still significant burden of communicable diseases (malaria, AIDS, nutritional diseases) in the health landscape of the developing world, non-communicable diseases are growing rapidly; these represent almost half of the morbidity burden in these regions. Thus, developing countries face a double burden of disease.

6.2.1. *The decrease in mortality*

To appreciate the decrease in mortality, life expectancy at birth is the most relevant indicator, since it eliminates the influence of the population's age structure. At the global level, expectancy at birth currently stands at nearly 73 years old (71 years old for men and 75 years old for women[4]) compared to 25 years old two centuries ago (Figure 6.1).

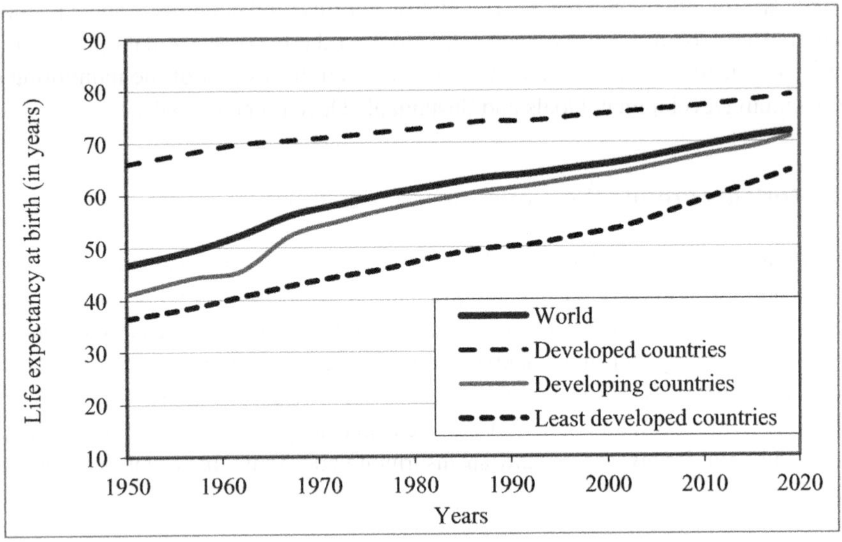

Figure 6.1. *The evolution of life expectancy at birth depending on development levels (source: UN 2019)*

Over the past 70 years, the average lifespan has increased by more than 25 years worldwide, from 47.7 years old in 1950–1955 to 72.3 years old in 2015–2020. This

4 Data drawn from (UN 2019).

lengthening of the lifespan is related to economic development and the improvement in food quantity and quality, major hygiene and public health policies, making it possible to significantly reduce infant mortality. The average increase in recent decades has been higher in developing countries than in developed countries. The average increase was 14 years in developed countries (Europe, North America, Australia, Japan and New Zealand) and 29 years in developing countries.

The most notable progress has occurred in the countries in transition, where economic development and health improvements have been most recent. Thus, in China, the average life expectancy rose from 68 years old in 1990 to 77 years old in 2019, in India from 58 to 70 years old, and in Morocco from 65 to 77 years old. Growth has also been strong in Latin American countries and the Caribbean region (Figure 6.2). In Africa, progress has taken place later and has been much slower than in Asia, despite the fact that these two regions had reached almost the same level in the 1950s.

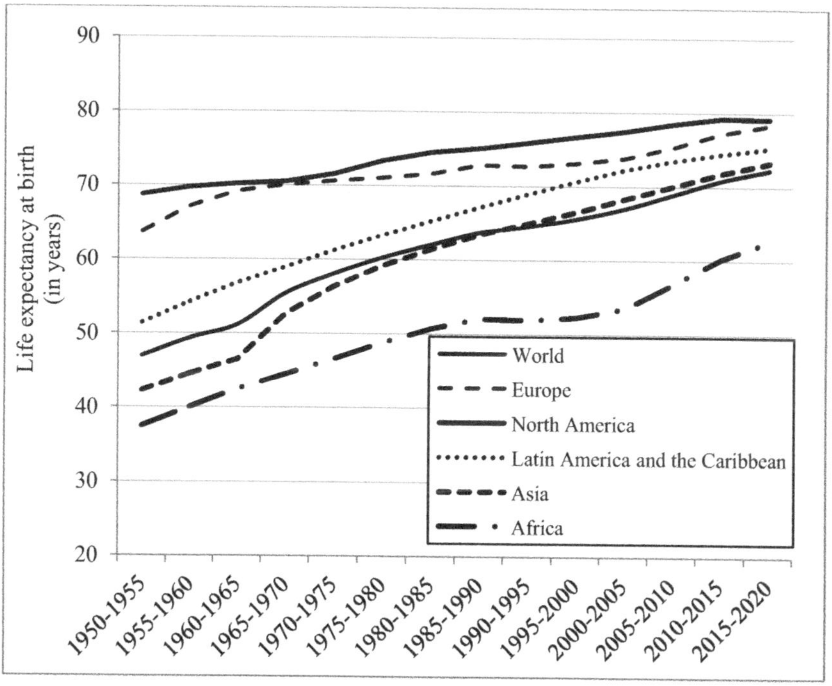

Figure 6.2. *Evolution of life expectancy at birth by major world region (source: UN 2019)*

This context of overall increase in life expectancy locally conceals stagnation scenarios, or even declining situations, especially in countries affected by the AIDS epidemic or involved in conflict. In sub-Saharan Africa, the rapid progress until the end of the 1980s then came to a halt. In Southern Africa, life expectancy, which was the highest on the African continent until the 1990s, fell from 61 years old in 1990 to 51 years old in 2010.

In those countries most affected by AIDS, life expectancy decreased by 20 years between 1990 and 2006. Over 15 years, it fell from 63 to 51 in South Africa, from 60 to 42 in Swaziland, from 62 to 41 in Zimbabwe and from 61 to 42 in Lesotho. Since the 2000s, the average lifespan has started to increase again in these countries (Figure 6.3).

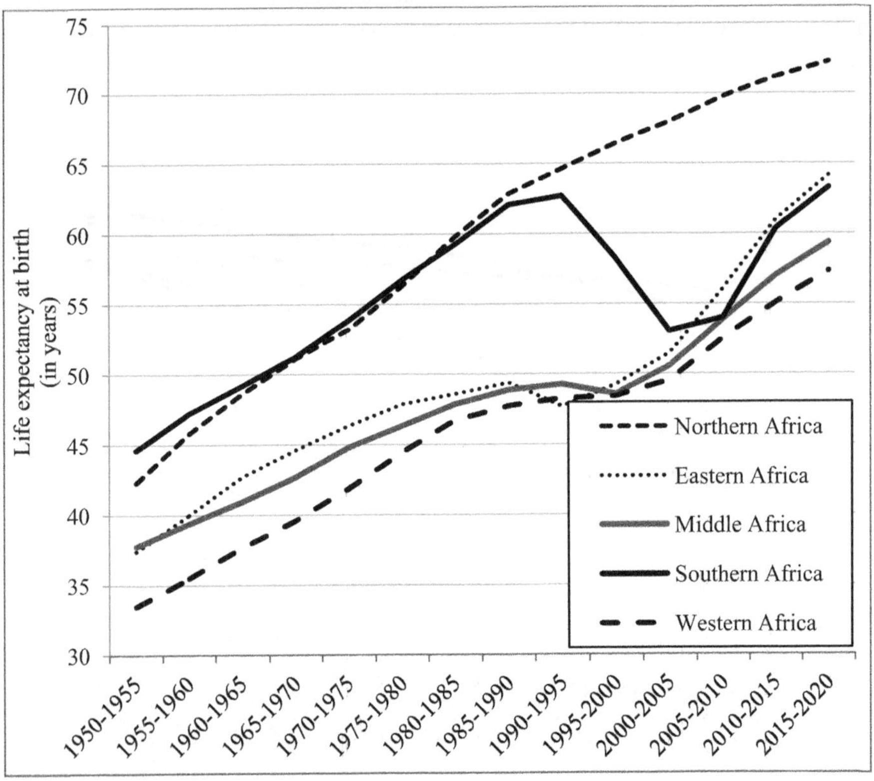

Figure 6.3. *Evolution of life expectancy at birth in Africa (source: UN 2019)*

6.2.2. *Current disparities*

Nowadays, situations are highly contrasting depending on development levels, as well as changeable from region to region. Inequalities are strong, not only between developed countries and the rest of the world (Figure 6.4), but also within developing countries, where disparities are particularly large.

In developed regions, life expectancy at birth is on average 79 years old, whereas in developing regions it is on average between 71 and 69 years old, excluding China, and 64 years old in the least developed countries, a category which includes the least socioeconomically developed countries on the planet, which are located, for the most part, in sub-Saharan Africa[5].

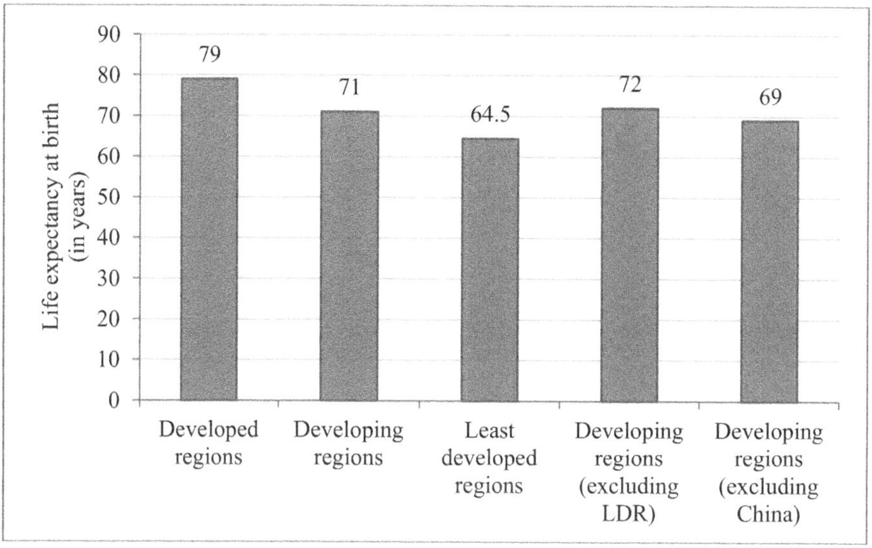

Figure 6.4. *Life expectancy at birth in 2018, depending on economic development levels (source: UN 2018)*

5 The Least Developed Countries (LDC) are a category of countries created in 1971 by the United Nations (UN), bringing together the least socioeconomically developed countries on the planet. They have the lowest Human Development Indexes (HDI). Since 2011, there have been 49 LDCs: 34 in sub-Saharan Africa (Angola, Benin, Burkina Faso, Burundi, Djibouti, Guinea, Lesotho, Mali, Niger, etc.), nine in Asia (including Afghanistan and Bangladesh), five in Oceania and one in Antilles (Haiti).

At the regional level (Figure 6.5), life expectancy at birth is 79 years old in North America, 78.5 years old in Europe and 76 years old in Latin America and the Caribbean. It also reaches a high level of 72.5 years old in Asia (71 years old excluding China), but it drops to 62.5 years old in Africa.

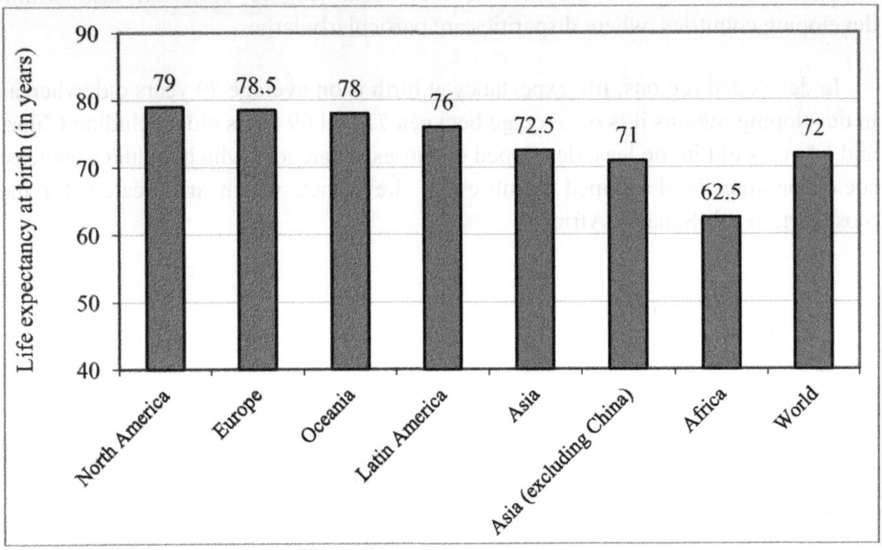

Figure 6.5. *Life expectancy at birth in 2018 by continent (source: UN 2018)*

Disparities are not only regional, they are even found within a region (Figure 6.6). In Africa, the gap is large between Northern Africa (72.5 years old) and sub-Saharan Africa (60 years old). On average, life expectancy only reaches 58 years old in Middle Africa, 57 years old in Western Africa, 64 years old in Eastern Africa and 64 years old in Southern Africa. In these sub-regions, men and women live, on average, 20 years less than in Western Europe or Japan. The differences between regions appear to be smaller in Asia.

Nowadays, the life expectancy of women is higher than that of men everywhere in the world, but the difference is only one or two years in the countries with the highest mortality, against five to six years on average in developed countries. In developing countries, excess mortality among females compensates for excess mortality among males (section 6.3.2.1). The differences observed in the evolution of mortality as well as the current disparities are not only due to the country's socioeconomic and political context, but also to sanitary conditions and the health condition of populations.

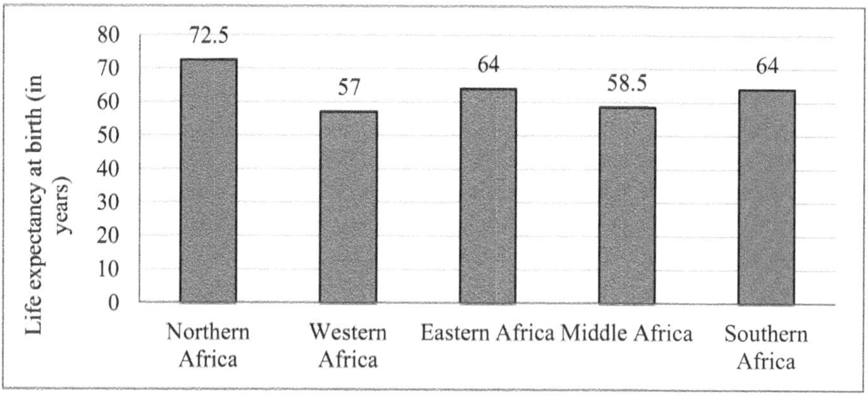

a) Africa

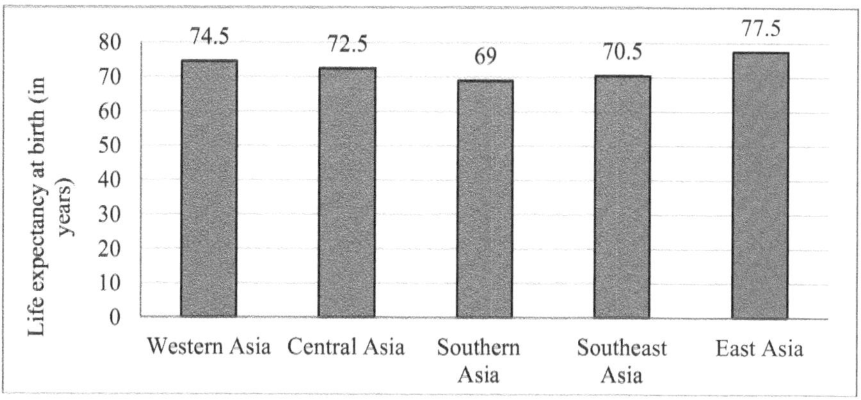

b) Asia

Figure 6.6. *Life expectancy at birth in Africa and in Asia (source: UN 2018)*

6.2.3. *The health of populations: a double burden of disease in developing countries*

The decrease in mortality is accompanied by a change in the population's health profile, characterized as an "epidemiologic transition" (Omran 2005). The epidemiologic transition model defines three ages through which any society presumably went through during modernization. At an early stage, "The Age of Pestilence and Famine", mortality was high under the influence of infectious diseases. Then, during the "The Age of Receding Pandemics", life expectancy increased above the age of 50, because of a decrease in infant mortality. Finally, the third was “The Age of Degenerative and Man-Made Diseases”, where the decline in mortality slowed down, and infectious diseases were replaced by chronic diseases. These changes led to a radical transformation in the age at death, shifting from infancy to childhood, from youth to older ages, thus provoking an increase in life expectancy. Observed since the 18th and 19th centuries in developed countries, these processes have been slower in developing regions where evolution has disrupted the model featuring modernization; there is still a clear predominance of infectious and parasitic diseases which particularly affect the early stages in life. Unlike rich countries, developing countries, particularly those in sub-Saharan Africa, accumulate all types of pathologies: alongside the still significant burden of communicable diseases, chronic diseases are also growing rapidly, leading to a double burden of disease.

6.2.3.1. *The burden of infectious diseases*

Almost all of the morbidity burden related to communicable diseases is caused by diarrheal infections, malaria, tuberculosis, measles, pneumonia and HIV/AIDS, to which many other parasitic and viral infections are added.

Malaria is still the main parasitic disease transmitted by the bites of infected Anopheles mosquitoes. In particular, it triggers high fever attacks which, if left untreated, can lead to death. The geographical area of malaria has shrunk considerably over the past 50 years, but due to the emergence of resistance to drugs and pesticides, there has been some resurgence in recent years. Despite the development of preventive measures, the number of cases[6] increased in sub-Saharan Africa, which is currently still the most exposed region, accounting for 95% of deaths in 2015. Endemics are unstable in Asia and Latin America, and some epidemics can also occur in Southern Asia and parts of the Middle East. There are several reasons for the higher risks in sub-Saharan Africa: disease transmission is more intense, the most lethal form of the parasite is more abundant there and the region has less efficient health care providers. Malaria is a poverty-related disease, and cases and deaths tend to concentrate in the least developed countries. In addition to deaths, especially among children and women, the consequences of the disease are also economic. The economic burden is heavy not only for families, but also for the public authorities, due to the loss of productivity, school and professional absenteeism and the high cost of care.

> Malaria-related expenses can represent up to 40% of public health expenditure, 30 to 50% of hospitalizations and up to 60% of outpatient consultations. Over several years, this loss has widened substantial

6 A total of 216 million cases worldwide in 2016.

> gaps in GDP between malarious and non-malarious countries (Vaillant and Salem 2008, p. 34).

Since 2000, international funding for malaria has increased significantly, granting access to prevention and treatment, namely through the use of insecticide-treated mosquito nets in households. Access to rapid diagnosis has also increased noticeably since 2000, thus contributing to a more rational use of anti-malaria drugs. However, only nearly 20% of children with fever in sub-Saharan Africa have been tested for malaria, according to the surveys carried out in households from 2012 to 2014.

> Sustained political commitment, predictable financing and strategic investment in health systems, disease surveillance and new tools are necessary to reduce resurgences and the malaria disease burden in the years ahead (UN 2015, p. 48).

Tuberculosis, deemed definitively defeated, reappeared in connection with the AIDS epidemic. Most of the time, it is a curable disease. It is often associated with a state of malnutrition and poor housing conditions. Tuberculosis strikes the most productive age groups, that is to say, adults. Estimates on the prevalence of the disease are highly uncertain, but the number of people living with the disease was estimated at 11 million in 2015. Almost nine million patients were newly diagnosed in 2013, and 1.1 million died from it. India, China, Indonesia, South Africa and Nigeria have the highest number of cases. The infection tends to affect men more than women (1.8 ratio) due to biological factors at certain ages and differences in the risk from exposure, as well as access to care. Social roles, which are different for men and women, could have an impact on the risk from exposure to tuberculosis and access to care. The tuberculosis incidence rate has been falling in all regions since 2000, declining by about 1.5% per year on average. However, the slow decline is due in part to lack of effective strategies (such as a post-exposure vaccine or treatment for latent tuberculosis infection) to prevent the reactivation of disease in the more than two billion people who are estimated to have been infected by *Mycobacterium tuberculosis*.

Sexually transmitted diseases (STDs), which are poorly reported in most countries, are a serious public health concern and are becoming increasingly common in developing countries. AIDS occupies a special place among STDs due to severity and its rapid spread. In the regions where it is most prevalent, and in particular in some of the poorest countries on the planet, it has helped to reverse the gains in life expectancy obtained during the last decades of the 20th century. The heaviest morbidity burden is borne by the African continent, where the spread of the pandemic is accelerating under the influence of several factors, in particular poverty, gender inequality and the weakening of health systems. The United Nations have estimated that 35 million people are living with AIDS worldwide, 70% of whom are in sub-Saharan Africa. However, since 1996, the annual number of new infections has been decreasing, as well as AIDS-related mortality. These positive trends are, in large part, due to the decline in the annual number of new infections in some countries and increased access to antiretrovirals in the poorest countries. The decline was faster in Southern Asia and Southern Africa, while it was slower in Latin America and Southeast Asia; in Northern Africa, East Asia and Western Asia, estimates suggest an increase. People infected with the virus survive longer, which explains the increase in the number of people living with AIDS, despite a decline in new infections (UNAIDS 2013). Deaths from AIDS have not declined among adolescents aged 10–19, and AIDS is still the leading cause of death among teenagers in sub-Saharan Africa. This may be due to a lack of access to screening and treatment for this age group. A growing number of married women are infected, as well as many girls and young women, representing nearly 60% of infected individuals in sub-Saharan Africa[7]. Women are more exposed to HIV for physiological reasons and because they lack authority in sexual relations, often finding themselves in a state of inferiority and forced to accept unprotected sexual intercourse. Thus, the unequal power relations between men and women have tilted toward a feminization of the epidemic. The unspoken social acceptance of violence against women only worsens the problem.

The impact of AIDS is considerable. The most notable effects are visible on adult mortality. The spread of the epidemic has been so rapid and of such magnitude that, in many African countries, advances in life expectancy have been reduced to nothing. In sub-Saharan Africa as a whole, life expectancy stagnated between 1985 and 2005, as it did in Eastern Africa. Among the most affected populations, AIDS wreaks greater havoc on the social fabric than the suffering caused by the disease. Thousands of children are orphaned, communities shattered, health services depleted and entire countries struggle against famine and economic collapse. AIDS is changing the very structure of the population. The proportion of dependents is increasing in many African countries with fewer working-age adults to ensure the subsistence of children and the elderly.

In addition to these great epidemics, southern countries and sub-Saharan Africa in particular, suffer from chronic intestinal parasitoses (Schistosomiasis or Bilharziosis, Leishmaniasis, Filariasis, Onchocerciasis, human Trypanosomiasis).

7 In sub-Saharan Africa, the HIV incidence rate among women of childbearing potential is 10 times higher than the global average (UN 2018).

Although rarely a direct cause of death, these conditions have negative consequences on the growth of children. The fight against these intestinal parasitoses requires environmental sanitation, sanitary education and systematic deworming within the framework of health systems.

Pathologies related to malnutrition are responsible for many deaths, especially among the youngest. The nutritional status is often used for describing the health condition of populations. A significant height–age delay and/or a weight–height delay provide information about the environmental and social context, eating habits and access to preventive and curative care. Local situations are complex. It has been found that high prevalence of thinness and stunted growth in children or low weight women are found more particularly in sub-Saharan Africa, but in some countries (Liberia, Namibia and Mozambique), the burden related to the nutritional status is threefold: underweight children, obesity in children and obesity in adults. The proportion of undernourished people is highest in sub-Saharan Africa, reaching 26% of the population.

6.2.3.2. *The rise of chronic diseases*

The adoption of "modern" lifestyles and habits in developing countries leads to the diffusion of so-called new "civilization" risks as countries progress along the path of demographic and epidemiologic transitions. In the long term, the health of individuals also deteriorates under the effect of chronic diseases, sensory and mental disorders, and violence. Non-communicable diseases have long been regarded as diseases from industrialized countries, or western-world diseases, due to lifestyles which are completely different from those prevalent in the most of Africa, Asia and many other developing regions. Now, contrary to popular belief, chronic diseases are no longer necessarily related to development and wealth. In Africa, they are largely related to changes in lifestyle, especially urbanization, which profoundly affect behavior. Sedentarization, the reduction of physical activity, a diet rich in sugar and in fat, apart from excesses in alcohol and tobacco, as well as the city's stress all contribute to the development of chronic diseases (Khlat and Le Cœur 2002).

In developing countries, mortality from cardiovascular diseases represents 20% of general mortality, and the prevalence of coronary heart disease and stroke is similar to that of infectious and nutritional diseases. Deaths from cardiovascular diseases are actually twice as numerous in developing countries than in developed countries, and these diseases rank third in the morbidity burden (behind traumatic conditions and neuropsychiatric disorders). The relatively young age at which people in developing countries succumb to these diseases, compared to those in developed regions, is particularly alarming. In India, one in two deaths from cardiovascular disease occurs before the age of 70, whereas the proportion in countries with better developed economies is one in five. The main risk factors are hypertension and hypercholesterolemia. The globalization of trade and the rise of marketing continue to encourage nutrition based on diets rich in saturated fat, sugar and salt. Combined with smoking and the lack of physical exercise, this diet develops atherosclerosis in the general population and leads to the wide distribution of cardiovascular diseases. The brutality of these changes makes being overweight and obesity coexist with malnutrition, sometimes within the same social environment, and even within the same family. In sub-Saharan Africa, 30% of the adult population is considered hypertensive. The burden of cardiovascular disease is set to increase in the years to come, together with population aging.

Different types of cancer are another and no less important morbidity factor in developing countries. More than 70% of the 7.6 million cancer deaths occur in developing countries. However, tumors are only responsible for 10% of deaths compared to more than 20% in developed countries. People in developing countries are just as much at risk as anyone else, but due to the shorter life expectancy and latency time of many types of cancer, they often die from a different pathology before they develop cancer.

Among the harmful practices related to modernization, smoking is already responsible for high mortality and morbidity, in some cases attaining nearly 50% of male smokers. Prospective studies anticipate an extension of consumption in these countries in the years to come. Despite the adoption of the Framework Convention on Tobacco Control (FCTC) by the WHO in 2003, few countries have taken all the necessary measures to significantly reduce their consumption. Most of them cannot afford it. They have neither the infrastructure nor the human resources needed to maintain a minimum tobacco control program. Moreover, in most countries, public opinion has not yet been mobilized around this issue.

Mortality and disability resulting from road traffic accidents are expected to rise in southern countries, in relation to the increase in the vehicle fleet, unless the road network is improved and provided that safety measures are imposed on drivers. The toll is particularly heavy, especially in sub-Saharan Africa and Southeast Asia. The WHO estimates that between 2010 and 2020 the number of road deaths will have increased by 92% in China, 147% in India and 80% on average in many other developing countries (WHO 2010). However, road accidents are largely preventable.

Although there are many economically affordable interventions to prevent accidents and save lives, until now their effectiveness has mostly only been studied in developed countries. In the poorest countries, universal access to security means will require international assistance for the local development of infrastructure and human resources. In addition to injuries and deaths, the increase in the number of vehicles has other serious health consequences. In some countries, air pollution from motor vehicles kills even more than traffic accidents. This type of morbidity is still receiving little attention in relation to the main communicable and non-communicable diseases.

The challenge is major in developing countries: not only do they have to cope with the rise of new pathologies ("the diseases of abundance"), but they also have to deal with old infectious pathologies that have not yet been eradicated. The situation is all the more serious insofar as the health system is already under-resourced. The decline in mortality will only accelerate under this condition. In this context of mortality and morbidity, there are population categories that are more vulnerable and more affected than others: children and women.

6.3. Children's and female mortality

The mortality of children and women is still disproportionately high in developing countries. The large number of premature deaths is a worrying public health problem, especially affecting children under five and women of childbearing potential.

6.3.1. *Infant and child mortality and health: a diversified evolution*

Over the past quarter century, child mortality has considerably declined. The number of preventable deaths in children under five fell from 12.7 million in 1990 to 9.9 million in 2000 and to 5.6 million in 2016 (UN 2018). Thus, the mortality rate declined by more than half, dropping from 90 to 43 deaths per 1,000 live births between 1990 and 2015. However, this decline does not suffice to meet the Millennium Development Goals' target, which was to "reduce the under five mortality rate by two-thirds, between 1990 and 2015"[8]. Of the 5.6 million child deaths worldwide, 98% occur in developing countries, half in Africa and 47% in Asia.

8 Goals adopted in September 2000 by political leaders from all over the world gathered at the United Nations Headquarters in New York for the Millennium Summit.

While child mortality has declined in all of the regions of the world, the decline has not been simultaneous or identical from one region to another (Figure 6.7).

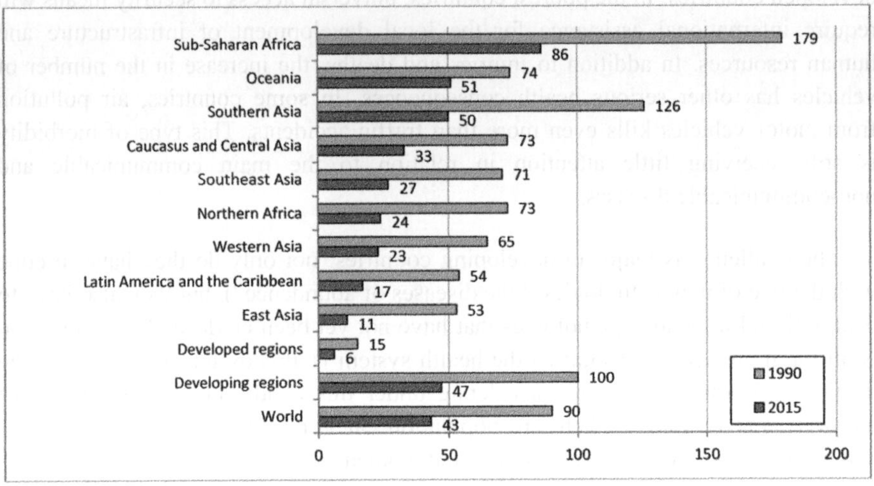

Figure 6.7. *Infant and child mortality rate in 1990 and 2015 (per 1,000 live births) (source: UN 2015)*

The most significant progress was made in developing countries where infant and child mortality was already low (in Northern Africa, East Asia, Western Asia, Latin America and the Caribbean). Economic growth, the improvement of nutrition and the generalization of health care have greatly favored the survival of children. However, sub-Saharan Africa is still the region in the world displaying the highest death rate. Middle Africa has the highest levels (126 out of 1,000 children die before their fifth birthday), followed by Western Africa (11 deaths per 1,000). The highest rates are observed, among others, in Angola (156 per thousand), Chad (155 per thousand), Mali (122 per thousand), Nigeria (122 per thousand), Cameroon (115 per thousand) and the Central African Republic (115 per thousand) (UN 2015). For a child born in Sierra Leone, the probability of dying before their fifth birthday is three and a half times higher than for a child born in India, and over 100 times higher than for a child born in Iceland or Singapore. AIDS (transmitted from mother to child), war and poverty explain these high mortality levels. Sub-Saharan Africa is the only region where, despite the progress made as a result of the increase in the number of live births, the number of child deaths is expected to increase in the coming years, unless progress in reducing the under five mortality rate is enough to outpace population growth.

Around the world, child mortality is closely related to poverty. Significant disparities, depending on the socioeconomic status, currently persist. The most obvious increase in child survival has been observed in the richest households, or in urban areas, or in children whose mothers have been educated. It seems that the poor populations have stayed away from the health measures taken in recent decades. On average, child and infant mortality rates are almost twice as high for children in the poorest households as for children in the richest. Mortality is also higher among children in rural areas. These children are about 1.7 times more likely to die before their fifth birthday than those in urban areas. Mother's education remains the most powerful determinant of inequality in survival. Children of mothers with no education have a mortality rate 1.5 times higher than children of mothers with primary education, and 2.7 times higher than children of mothers with secondary or higher education.

The first day, week and month of life are the most critical for the survival of children following preterm birth complications, complications during labor and delivery and sepsis. Many deaths are also caused by infectious diseases that can be prevented (such as pneumonia, malaria or AIDS), and to diarrheal diseases caused by poor hygiene, the lack of access to safe water and contaminated food. Undernourishment and malnutrition further increase the risk of death and are responsible for a third of child deaths. Undernutrition among children under five remains widespread, not only due to the lack of food, but also to its poor quality, as well as the lack of services in the safe water, sanitation and health sectors, and less than optimal health and nutrition practices. Despite an improvement in the situation since 1990, in 2017 worldwide, 151 million children under five were stunted (inadequate height for age), 51 million were emaciated (underweight for height) and 38 million were overweight.

Southern Asia has the highest prevalence of children being underweight, with around one in three children affected in 2015, while it has seen the largest absolute decrease since 1990, a decrease of 22 percentage points. The backwardness of Southern Asia (28% of children suffering from being underweight) often appears to be the consequence of bad food habits and frequent shortages in good quality food. In addition, nearly two-thirds of the population are lacking in improved sanitation, leading to repeated episodes of diarrhea in children. More than a quarter of babies are underweight at birth and many of them never succeed in catching up with their nutritional status. In sub-Saharan Africa, although the rate has fallen by one-third since 1990, the number of malnourished children has actually risen 1990 due to the region's growing population. Stunting, more common than being underweight, affects approximately one in four children under five. This chronic form of undernutrition puts these children at risk of diminished cognitive and physical development. The number of stunted children has fallen in all regions except sub-Saharan Africa, where the numbers increased by about one-third between 1990 and 2013. The lack of breastfeeding, and especially exclusive breastfeeding during the first months of life, is a major risk factor for morbidity and mortality for infants and children in developing countries, mainly due to diarrheal disease and infections of the acute respiratory tract. Malnutrition is more the result of infections, namely intestinal infections (provoking diarrhea and leading to weight loss and stunted growth), than the consequence of a poor diet.

Vaccination is one of the simplest and most effective means for preventing diseases and reducing infant and child mortality. In 2013, 84% of children under two had been vaccinated in developing countries, compared to 70% in 2000. The most significant progress has been made in sub-Saharan Africa, where immunization coverage increased from 53% in 2000 to 74% in 2013. In the most backward countries like Chad, Equatorial Guinea or Gabon, only half of the children are vaccinated; about 60% are in Benin, Côte d'Ivoire, Liberia, Nigeria, Central African Republic and Sierra Leone, compared to 95% in developing countries, where the supply in basic care has made great strides in recent times, such as in North Africa, the Middle East and Latin America. Vaccination is a good indicator of the quality and access to basic health services among children under five. Intensive measles control programs contribute to the development of health services infrastructure for routine immunization and other health-related services. In addition, vaccination campaigns are a means for facilitating the distribution of other life-saving methods, such as mosquito nets against malaria, deworming drugs or vitamin A.

In developing countries with high mortality, the infant and child mortality system is fundamentally different from the one in developed countries. Levels may differ, as well as timing, the structure of death causes, how these are measured, the search for determinants and the identification of priorities for action.

6.3.2. *Maternal mortality: too high in the developing world*

Far too many women are still victims of premature mortality, corresponding to an epidemiologic transition which has barely started, or due to discriminating behavior toward women. Pregnancy, complications during labor and delivery and their consequences are still the main causes of death, disease and disabilities among women of childbearing potential in developing countries. Maternal mortality is one of the indicators that reveals the widest gap between the rich and the poor.

In 2015 worldwide, 303,000 women (nearly 800 per day) died during pregnancy or following delivery. Most of these deaths take place in developing regions, where the maternal mortality ratio (230 female deaths per 100,000 live births) is 14 times that of developed countries (16 deaths per 100,000 live births) (UN 2015). Sub-Saharan Africa (56%) and Southern Asia (30%) account for 86% of the global burden with a maternal mortality ratio of 510 and 190 deaths per 100,000 live births, respectively (Figure 6.8). Although the maternal mortality ratio has halved since 1990, the targets of the Cairo Conference are still out of reach. Back in 1994, the Conference on Population and Development asked the most backward countries to reduce this rate to less than 125 deaths per 100,000 births by 2005, and to less than 75 deaths per 100,000 births by 2015.

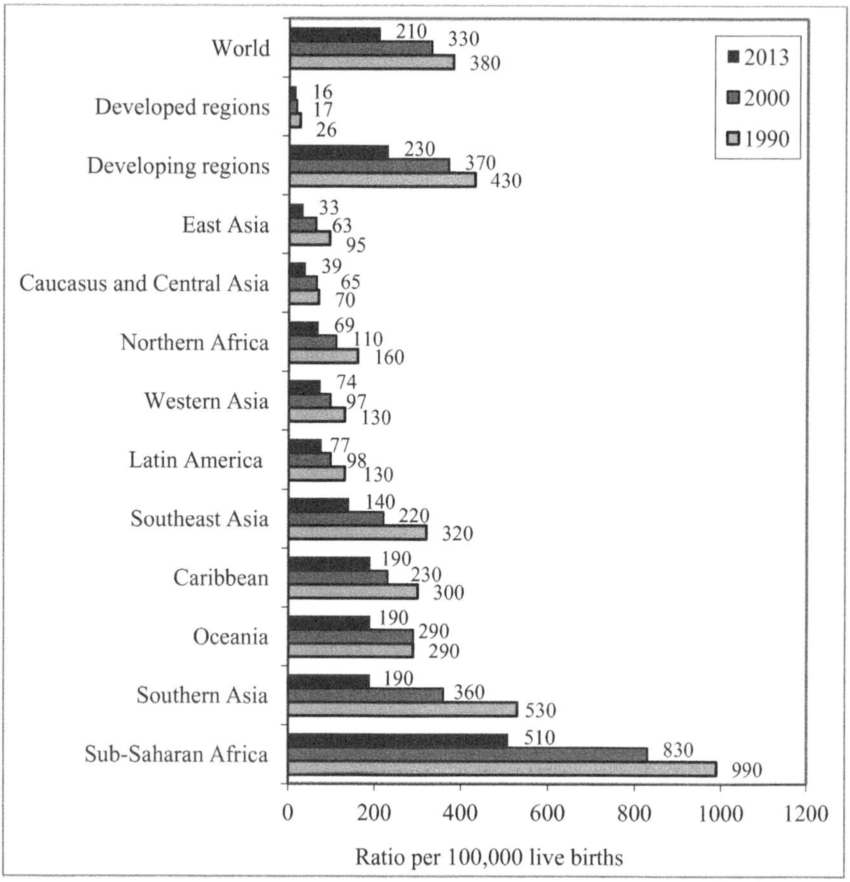

Figure 6.8. *Maternal Mortality Report (deaths per 100,000 live births) (source: UN 2015)*

In countries where women have many children and where health supervision is weak, the risks of pregnancy accumulate to the point that one young woman in 10 will succumb to maternal death one day, while the same risk is one in 7,300 in developed countries. In sub-Saharan Africa, a woman's risk of dying from such complications is one in 16. Maternal deaths underestimate women's health problems related to motherhood. Thus, for every woman who dies of complications during her reproductive life, another 30 end their pregnancies with a disease, injury or painful handicap, sometimes related to genital mutilation.

Most of these deaths can be prevented. The majority of them occur during delivery itself or during the postpartum period. Based on data from 2003 to 2009[9], hemorrhage was the cause of the greatest number of maternal deaths: it accounted for more than 27% of maternal deaths in the developing regions and approximately 16% in the developed regions. It is the promptness with which care is provided that determines the proportion of deaths. The second most common cause of death is sepsis, which is the cause for most deaths occurring toward the end of the postpartum period. While in developed countries this threat has almost disappeared, in the developing world, one woman out of 20 who give birth will contract an infection which, if left untreated, can lead to death or sequelae. Teenage pregnancies, in girls aged 15–19, are an aggravating cause of maternal mortality. Girls who give birth before the age of 15 are five times more likely to die from labor complications than women in their 20s (UN 2012). The teenage birth rate was 44 per thousand (number of births per 1,000 women aged 15–19) in developing regions in 2018, compared to 15 per thousand in developed countries. Sub-Saharan Africa has the highest rate (101 births per 1,000 adolescent women) and little progress has been made since 1990 (123 per 1,000). Poverty and the lack of education perpetuate the high rates of teenage births.

The risks surrounding pregnancy are lower than those related to delivery. Nevertheless, they should not be neglected. Despite highly fragmented data, the WHO has estimated that the proportion of deaths occurring during pregnancy can be as high as a quarter of maternal deaths. In addition to the complications of unsafe abortion, three major health problems can arise during pregnancy: complications related to pregnancy itself, an unforeseen disease in the woman (which may be aggravated by pregnancy or not), and the negative effects of unhealthy lifestyles on pregnancy to arrive to term. Indirect causes, such as anemia, malaria and HIV/AIDS (which worsen in pregnant women), account for 18% of maternal deaths. There are many societies where women and girls eat the leftovers of men and boys, or may not even eat at all. Pregnant women can also suffer from traditional dietary restrictions that weaken them. As a result, anemia is very common among women, affecting

9 The availability of data on maternal health is uneven across regions. Globally, only 51% of countries have such data. More than 90% of countries in Latin America have national data addressing the causes of maternal mortality, compared to less than 20% of countries in sub-Saharan Africa.

one-third of them during their reproductive life, and half of them during their pregnancy. The highest rates are found in Southern Asia where 75% of women may suffer from anemia during pregnancy.

In developing countries, more than 15 million unintended pregnancies end in abortions practiced by people who do not have the necessary skills, performed in unsanitary conditions, to such an extent that pregnant women are in serious danger. The WHO estimates that nearly 100,000 maternal deaths could be prevented each year if women who do not want children were to use contraception effectively. Unsafe abortion is a problem, especially among younger women. If women wish to terminate their pregnancy at all costs in circumstances where abortion is dangerous, illegal, or both, it is vital for them to have the power to control their fertility by means of a better diffusion of contraception, something which could also prevent closely spaced pregnancies and teenage pregnancies. While the use of contraceptives has increased in many developing regions since 1990, unmet needs are nonetheless still important in some countries. In 2015, 64% of women aged 15 to 49 (as compared to 55% in 1990), either married or in union, used some form of contraception, but in sub-Saharan Africa this proportion fell to 28% (13% in 1990), and to 59% (39% in 1990) in Southern Asia. Apart from these women using contraceptive methods, 12% of women in the world do not have access to any kind of contraception, even when they wish they could avoid or delay pregnancy. This level rises up to 24% in sub-Saharan Africa, and has remained almost unchanged since 1990.

The vast majority of deaths in women can be prevented by appropriate medical interventions such as prenatal care, the presence of trained staff during delivery, or postnatal care in the weeks that follow delivery. However, serious deficiencies exist in these areas in developing countries. Labor and delivery are still considered a woman's affair and a natural event, so no medical expenses are contemplated. Hospitals and clinics are in no measure to grant access to delivery within an institutional framework for all women. However, it is essential for delivery to be assisted by qualified health staff, trained to detect problems as quickly as possible and effectively provide emergency obstetric care, or refer the women concerned to adequate care, if necessary. In 2014, 71% of women in the world gave birth with professional assistance (59% in 1990). This proportion drops to 52% in sub-Saharan Africa and Southern Asia, regions with the highest maternal and neonatal mortality rates.

Access to prenatal care is also an essential component of maternal health services. They are not only meant to identify women at risk of having a difficult delivery, but to help women cope with possible health problems during pregnancy.

These women can receive services such as tetanus vaccination, screening and treatment for infections, as well as vital information on some of the warning signs during pregnancy. Only half of the women (52%) in developing regions receive the four antenatal care visits recommended by the WHO in 2014. Progress has been slow in recent decades and Southern Asia and sub-Saharan Africa still lag behind, with 36% and 49% of pregnant women, respectively, receiving four antenatal care visits, whereas in other world regions, these proportions oscillate between 90% and 100%. In rural areas, the monitoring of pregnant women is considerably reduced and only reaches 25–30% of women.

The gap between those who have access to health care and those who are excluded is increasingly stark. The inequalities that this entails in terms of survival are even stronger for women. When a woman dies giving birth to a child, it is generally following a series of disruptions in the interactions with the health system: delay in seeking treatment, inability to follow the doctor‘s advice and, finally, the inability of the health system to deliver timely, quality care. These failures are most likely to arise and combine in a catastrophic way in deteriorating macroeconomic and social contexts. Risk management caused by pregnancy and delivery is inextricably related to the woman's status in society. Wherever women are denied their right to decide for themselves in terms of reproductive health, they find it difficult to access family planning services, thus becoming powerless to space births, protect their health and even their lives. Maternal health is, therefore, at the heart of the development process. In the most backward countries, the reduction in maternal mortality appears to be a key factor for the survival and development of children until adolescence. Investing in human resources is, therefore, an integral part of a healthy development policy.

6.4. Conclusion

Mortality, one of the two main driving phenomena of demographic dynamics, raises many questions. Despite the continued decline in mortality and, consequently, the increase in life expectancy at birth all over the world, deep inequalities exist between developed countries and southern countries, and even within the developing world. The situation remains critical in sub-Saharan Africa.

In developing countries, the level of mortality is a good indicator of the health of populations. The epidemiological transition which, during its course, is translated as a decrease in the risk of dying is lagging behind in southern countries, particularly in Asia and in sub-Saharan Africa. Developing countries are far from having eradicated the old infectious and parasitic pathologies whose importance has been accelerated by rapid population growth in most areas, despite the efforts to control the spread of epidemics. While these old pathologies still strike, the epidemic of non-communicable diseases already affects many developing countries. The "diseases of abundance" (cardiovascular diseases, digestive diseases and cancers) are no longer the prerogatives of development and wealth; they are on their way to becoming major causes of morbidity and mortality, even in the poorest countries on the planet. The brutality of these changes make being overweight and obesity coexist with malnutrition, sometimes within the same social environment, and even within the same family. Cardiovascular diseases have made their appearance in almost all of the poorest countries and their weight is set to increase in the coming years, as a consequence of population aging, which is expected to persist in developing countries. The spread of chronic diseases in the poorest countries is a manifestation of the so-called "double burden" of epidemiological transition, whereby the group of non-communicable diseases is added to prevailing communicable diseases. In developing countries, the main problem for public health policy makers is to cope with this double burden of disease. The task is even more difficult when health services systems are seriously lacking in resources, all the more so as this double burden, increasingly heavy, risks compromising the socioeconomic development of these countries.

Thus, highly different mortality rates systems coexist in the world, generally associated with the macrosocietal level, in terms of economic and social development levels. An increasingly large gap is deepening between regions, between countries, but also within states; this is largely explained by the context in which health systems have been developed. This association is so systematic that the level of infant mortality has become one of the indicators of a country's development level. At the individual level, the extent of inequalities in terms of infant mortality could also be used as an indicator of a country's fair distribution of resources. The urgency is all the greater since, as the situation is improving less quickly than expected, the gain made in terms of deaths avoided is partly wiped out by the swift demographic growth. The number of premature deaths of mothers may well be on the rise because, although rates are falling, the number of mothers and births continues to rise. Most of this increase will take place in sub-Saharan Africa and parts of Asia, regions where delivery is most risky and where mortality from unsafe abortions is the highest.

In part, the future evolution of mortality will depend on the proper functioning of accessible health systems (WHO 2008). This involves significant expenditure and viable financing mechanisms. Nevertheless, while health expenditure has increased in the world in recent decades, the poorest countries have been marginalized from this movement. The lack of qualified health workers affects developing countries most strongly, while this is where needs remain the most crucial. "In developing countries, the varying degrees of staff and equipment shortages overshadow all other issues, such as the establishment of social protection for the poorest" (UN 2015, p. 43).

Improving the health of populations is also achieved through primary or secondary prevention, whether this relates to the medical field, such as vaccination, or to behavior and lifestyles, such as eating a balanced diet or limiting the consumption tobacco and alcohol. For these goals to be achievable, the best investment is the development of policies that promote healthy lifestyles, encouraging a balanced diet and regular physical activity, limiting the consumption of tobacco and alcoholic beverages, prompting the use of condoms during sexual intercourse and reducing the use of illicit drugs. Education is a determining factor in behavioral changes. The education of women and girls also contributes to the decline in fertility, the diffusion of contraception and the consequent reduction of maternal mortality. The health of women is affected by their social and family status, and education is a means for promoting gender equality, thus contributing to health improvements and the reduction of female and infant mortality.

The socioeconomic and political contexts play an essential role in promoting the health of populations by mobilizing additional resources and targeting public investment toward disadvantaged populations, who are indeed the most vulnerable. The decrease in mortality following a better health condition in the population requires concrete measures aimed at making basic services more accessible: access to essential medicines, food self-sufficiency, drinking water supply, sanitation of the living environment, habitat health and health education programs. It is, therefore, essential to implement policies in these different areas. Much is still to be done, and more can be achieved if all of the parties involved live up to their commitments. Progress is still achievable.

6.5. References

Couderc, N., Drouhin, N., Ventelou, B. (2006). Sida et croissance économique : le risque d'une "trappe épidémiologique". *Revue d'économie politique*, 116(5), 697–715.

Gaimard, M. (2011). *Population et santé dans les pays en développement*. L'Harmattan, Paris.

Gaimard, M. (2017). Démographie et santé en Afrique subsaharienne. In *Développement et environnement en Afrique*, Ferréol, G. (ed.). EME Editions, Louvain-la-Neuve.

Khlat, M. and Le Cœur, S. (2002). La santé : anciennes et nouvelles maladies. In *La Population du monde*, Chasteland, J.-C., Chesnais, J.-C. (eds). INED, Paris.

Moatti, J.-P. and Ventelou, B. (2009). Économie de la santé dans les pays en développement, des paradigmes en mutation. *Revue économique*, 60, 241–256.

Omran, A. (2005). The epidemiological transition. A theory of the epidemiology of population change. *The Milbank Quarterly*, 83(4), 731–757.

Tizio, S. (2004). État de santé et systèmes de soins dans les pays en développement : la contribution des politiques de santé au développement durable. *Mondes en développement*, 127, 101–117.

UN (2015). Objectifs du millénaire pour le développement. Report, United Nations, New York.

UN (2018). Rapport sur les objectifs du développement durable 2018. Report, United Nations, New York.

UN (2019). World Population Prospects 2019. Department of Economic and Social Affairs, Population Division, New York [Online]. Available at: https://population.un.org/wpp/DataQuery/ [Accessed 15 December 2019].

UNAIDS (2013). How Africa turned aids around. Africa Union Summit [Online]. Available at: www.unaids.org [Accessed 26 November 2019].

Vaillant, Z. and Salem, G. (2008). *Atlas mondial de la santé*. Autrement, Paris.

WHO (2008). The world health report 2008 : primary health care now more than ever, World Health Organisation, Geneva.

WHO (2010). World Health Statistics 2010, Report, World Health Organisation, Geneva.

7

Dynamics of Migration History in Western Europe

Leslie Page MOCH
Department of History, Michigan State University, East Lansing, USA

7.1. Introduction

This chapter analyzes the dynamic relationship between migration patterns and economic development in Western Europe since the mid-17th century. It is based on changing factors that determine migration: patterns of land ownership, deployment of capital, places of employment locations and demographic regimes. This scaffolding alone is insufficient; I therefore also recognize that individual characteristics determined who was likely to leave home, for example lifecycle stage, class and gender. Finally, because mobility is largely a social phenomenon, it is important to understand the role of family, locale and migration system as well, because migration decisions were often family decisions, consistent with the customs of the region.

Of the large-scale elements shaping migration, land ownership is fundamental; this history begins in the countryside, where the vast majority of Europeans resided in the 17th and 18th centuries. Free peasants were bound to their land by ownership, yet it also sent them and their children out to earn the means to buy further parcels of land or, increasingly, to pay taxes. As many sold or lost their land subsequently, they became rural proletarians without that tie to the land and joined the more mobile proletariat.

Demographic Dynamics and Development,
coordinated by Yves CHARBIT. © ISTE Ltd 2022.

Rural work also determined who could stay at home. In the 17th century, rural areas largely produced their own clothing and tools, supporting armies of artisans such as smithies, weavers, spinsters, tailors and shoe makers. From the end of the 17th century, and increasingly in the 18th century, rural industry expanded and supplied larger markets. More and more rural folk in such regions could earn a living at home, and they were more likely to be proletarians. With the advent of factory industry in the 19th century, the market for handcrafted goods collapsed, creating spectacular crises for rural producers.

The migration systems in which Europeans moved provide the framework for this chapter, as they expanded, contracted and changed according to circumstance. Such systems can be characterized by how far people travel from home and the degree to which home connections survive (Tilly 1978). *Local migration systems* moved people within their home market – whether to marry or buy land – but this did not remove people from their home contacts. Women who married and moved to a nearby parish, and peasants who bought land in a nearby village moved in such systems. *Circular migration systems* returned people to their home; these provided important contingents of harvest workers from upland villages in the 18th century and Italian workers to the grain fields in Argentina in the 19th century, as well as seasonal construction workers in urban areas. Some of these systems evolved into *systems of chain migration* that brought people from a particular location to stay, helped to settle by compatriots who had already done so. It was throughy such connections that young women who worked as urban domestics or construction workers stayed in the city that they had originally intended to leave. *Career migration systems* are distinct because the institution rather than local custom has the greatest influence over where and when people moved – be they bishops, state bureaucrats or schoolteachers. Systems of *coerced migration* that intentionally fractured ties with home and *military migration* played a minor role on the continent of Europe before the 20th century (Moch 2003; Siegelbaum and Moch 2014).

Data measuring historical migrations are problematic. No single body of data measures human mobility, so scholars have depended on a host of local, regional and national sources: census lists, developed in the 1880s by British pioneer Arthur Ravenstein (1976), parish records (Souden 1984), registers of specific groups such as citizens (*Bürgerbucher*; Hochstadt 1983) and the occasional government inquiry such as the French Imperial survey of temporary migration in 1811 (Lucassen 1987). Such sources force the researcher to infer migration behavior from information about one point in time and reveal little about the actual volume of movement. Prussian migration statistics, recorded for a specific period and place, offer unique insights into high levels of mobility (Hochstadt and Jackson 1984). Finally, population registers for Belgium, Italy and Holland trace individuals after 1840 and allow a more nuanced view (Hogan and Kertzer 1985; Gribaudi 1987). Fortunately, these many sources provide the basis for interpreting migration patterns in Europe since the 17th century. Available data and classic case studies reveal comprehensive changes in patterns of migration as Western Europe moved from a sparsely populated, largely rural society to the highly urbanized society of the early 21st century.

Rural population patterns led to a more crowded countryside over time. In the 17th century, marriage was far from universal and came late in most regions, limiting fertility. Moreover, crises of disease and famine kept the population in check. With the disappearance of the bubonic plague and a reduction in famines in the 18th century, crisis mortality dropped. At the same time, industrial villages attracted workers who married younger than their forebears and produced more babies who were healthier. This created a full countryside by 1850.

Rural patterns of landholding, work and population manifest the distribution of capital. Outside the important centers of world trade such as Amsterdam and London, capital was scarce and diffused in the 17th century. With the expansion of rural industry, capital increasingly came to the countryside in the form of raw materials and the pennies paid to laborers. The rise of factory production and trade after 1790 precipitated a long-term movement of capital from agriculture to industry and countryside to city. This shift and concentration of capital was, in the end, the power that terminated the vacillation of people between rural and urban work, pulling them into full-time employment in the factory, the mine, the urban workshop and the office.

7.2. Migrations in preindustrial times (1650–1750)

7.2.1. *The character of the age*

This was a period of peace that followed religious wars in France (1562–1593) and the Revolt of the Netherlands against Spain (1572–1581) that made possible the rise and commercial expansion of the Netherlands. The Thirty Years' War decimated German territories (1615–1648), and civil war beset England, 1642–1660.

Economic stagnation struck small and medium-sized cities, which were actually in decline (Hohenberg and Lees 1985) while only Atlantic ports and very large cities expanded; London, Paris and Amsterdam dominated while the cities of Italy were losing population. In this essentially rural world, most people lived in villages or small towns and only one in nine lived in a town of 5,000 or more. Even the great cities were not large: in 1650, 450,000 resided in Paris, 400,000 in London and 175,000 in Amsterdam.

The population slumped, brought on by plagues, low marriage rates, high rates of infant and child mortality and hunger as a result of poor harvests in the late 17th and early 18th centuries. For example, the winter of 1693–1694 brought a great famine to northern Europe; one in 10 French perished, and only half the usual number of children was born (Goubert 1966).

Migration at this time is of great interest precisely because the eras of population growth and urban expansion that would fuel highly visible migration lay in the future. Rural areas were relatively self-sufficient and peasant landholding, which tied people to their home village, was near its peak in many parts of Europe. In this so-called "traditional world", who were the migrants?

7.2.2. *Migration in the preindustrial countryside*

Migration was integral to rural routine, to the rhythm of the seasons, the lifecycle and family life. The four migration systems described above animated the countryside: in addition to considerable local mobility, circular migration engaged both harvesters and temporary urban workers. The largest circular systems developed systems of chain migration, and career migration relocated church and government officials. Evidence from across southern England between 1660–1730 indicates that a clear majority of rural men (69%) and women (76%) left the parish of their birth, although relatively few (15% and 16%, respectively) left their home county (Clark 1979).

Most mobile young people worked as what French call *valets de ferme*, Germans *Gesinde*, the English servants in husbandry and Americans farmhands. They lived away from home and customarily changed jobs annually. Although elusive to the historical record, they were ubiquitous in England and northwestern Europe. In the 63 available English parish lists dating from 1547 to 1821, servants comprised 60% of the population aged 15–24. The ratio of male to female servants in these records is 121:100 (Kusssmaul 1981). Women milked cows, cared for the barnyard animals and prepared food; men handled the draught animals and sheep, performed the heavy labor of plowing and carting; everyone worked the harvest. Marriage migration also took women, especially, from their home village. Extant evidence suggests that this was local movement and that most people found a mate within 10 km of home (Sabean 1970). Between service work and marriage, women in peasant societies were more likely than men to leave home in local migration systems.

If one desired or was forced by circumstance to leave home, local knowledge provided the itineraries and destination, be it a nearby market town or regional capital. In the case of Germans in Westphalia, the booming Netherlands and especially Amsterdam called; for the south of France, it was labor-hungry Spain. Large systems of circular migration animated the countryside: harvest teams from the north of England came to East Anglia to harvest the grain that fed London; harvesters from West of Paris came to the large farms of the Ile-de-France; smaller groups from France's central highlands harvested wheat and grapes on the Mediterranean plain.

7.2.3. *Migration to the preindustrial city*

Every kind of city in preindustrial Europe – large and small, trading and manufacturing – depended on newcomers to function. The demographic fact of urban natural deficit meant that cities could not survive without a substantial proportion of newcomers and this labor-intensive age demanded armies of young, strong newcomers. The citizenship lists of towns and cities from Danzig and Berlin, south to Marseille, and west to Cornwall show that the respectable portion of city dwellers came from the region and beyond. German *Bürgerbucher* from before 1800 show that about half the citizens were migrants. Less prosperous citizens were even more mobile: for example, in Frankfurt am Main, about half the citizens were born outside the town in 1700, but two-thirds of noncitizens were migrants (Hochstadt 1983). Typically, high turnover, intense local migration and long-distance movement of the very poor and elites, as well as circular and career systems appear common to cities of this era.

But not all cities were alike. The most successful were capitals and port cities that grew between 1600 and 1750; here, Amsterdam is the quintessential city of the age. Center of the Dutch Republic, Amsterdam was a gateway to an imperial network as well. New construction expanded the city to 200,000 in 1700 and it attracted not only burghers from Antwerp and the Spanish Netherlands but also from abroad: Flanders to the south, German territories and Scandinavia. Foreign immigrants were especially important to this city. Among the seamen who married in the 1650s, very nearly half were German, and as chain migration brought people to stay, over 19,000 German women married there (Hart 1974). The number of people attracted to Amsterdam is much greater than city statistics suggest, since many departed under the auspices of the Dutch East India Company to die at sea or abroad.

The small and much less dynamic textile town is more typical of this age, such as Beauvais, northwest of Paris. Hard times hit its woolen market and the population remained at about 13,000 from 1680 to 1730. Only about one in 10 marriage partners came from outside the urban parishes surveyed and in 1700 nearly all came from within 20 km, one indication that this town was part of a low-mobility regime. Yet people of all social stations were on the road: women and men en route to market, beggars, wool workers and church personnel. Even in this depressed period before the 18th century, some 1000 villagers worked in Beauvais's industry, 640 as weavers, 240 as combers and 227 as cloth finishers. A host of other outsiders were employed by the church because the town supported a bishop and his staff, 17 churches and 10 religious houses within the 1 km^2 enclosed by its walls. The rural and urban worlds lived side by side, as one-tenth of its population had rural occupations in 1696, as agricultural laborers, vineyard keepers, coopers and smithies. Even in this sedentary period, people moved by the day or the season, for their life's work, marriage and career (Goubert 1960).

7.3. Migration in the age of early industry (1750–1815)

The balance among various systems of migration – local, circular, chain and career migration – as well as rates of migration, changed in the later 18th century with economic developments and demographic change. Circular and chain migration became more important in some regions, while those with flourishing rural industry would become more sedentary. Chances to earn cash in rural areas increased as merchant capital came into the countryside, expanding industrial production which allowed more village people to marry, to marry earlier and to decrease infant and child mortality. This same economic trend worked to decrease peasant holdings and land ownership itself.

Older patterns persisted. Rural service away from home continued to be the means by which young people became trained; systems of seasonal migration thrived; at marriage, most brides continued to relocate in their husband's parish; peasant families remained in one place more than rural proletarians. For cities, little was new: about half the enumerated *burghers* continued to be migrants along with a third to half of marriage partners, and turnover was high. The fundamental changes to migration patterns after about 1750 are rooted in the substantial increase in population and rural employment outside agriculture.

7.3.1. *Character of the age*

Western Europe remained essentially rural in this period; more than nine in 10 people lived in villages or small towns into the 19th century. Most of them lived in peace, because after the War of Spanish Succession ended in 1713, deadly upheavals were nearly at an end and most armed conflicts took place in North America, where France and Britain struggled for hegemony in the Seven Years' War (1756–1763), and England contested the independence of some colonies (1775–1783). The great famines waned after the 1730s and there would be no armed conflict until the wars of the French Republic and Napoleonic Empire began in 1792. This was a period of expansion.

Some took the form of long-distance colonizing migration. Germans moved into Eastern Prussia at the invitation of Frederick the Great, into southeastern Europe and Russia, as well as North America. A surge of settlers from Britain moved to British North America at the end of the Seven Years' War, approximately 221,000 in 15 years (Fenske 1980; Bailyn 1986). As important as these settlers would be to their destinations, their departure had little impact at home because after 1750, the population of Europe expanded substantially and irreversibly. Between 1750 and 1800, for example, the number of Germans increased by 33%, the number of English by 50% (see Table 7.1).

Country	Population around 1750 (in millions)	Population around 1800 (in millions)
Norway	0.7	0.9
Sweden	1.8	2.3
Finland	0.5	1.0
Germany	18.4	24.5
The Netherlands	1.9	2.1
Belgium	2.2	2.8
Switzerland	1.4	1.7
France	24.5	29.0
Scotland	1.3	1.6
Wales	0.3	0.6
England	5.8	8.7
Ireland	2.4	5.2

Table 7.1. *Population in Northwestern Europe, 1750–1800 (in millions) (source: Anderson 1988)*

This dramatic increase in population resulted from a decrease in mortality and an increase in fertility that came with earlier and more widespread marriage. Although the mechanics varied from place to place, the drop in mortality crises was widespread. With the exception of the plague in Marseille in 1720, the bubonic plague nearly disappeared. Especially in the years of good harvest between 1740 and 1786, relief from the hunger that made people susceptible to disease, killed children and cut marriages short seemed to have supported population growth. And there were more children. This trend was most apparent in England, where a greater proportion of people married, and married younger: age at marriage fell from about 26 to 23 between 1680–1820, and the proportion who remained single was halved – from 15 to 7.5% (Wrigley 1983). The great power of earlier marriage to increase population is the key to population increase in areas of early industry.

Proletarians were on the increase at the expense of the peasantry after 1750 – a fundamental shift in landholding that would have important consequences for the history of migration. The decline of the peasantry occurred from England east to Saxony and from Scandinavia to southern France. More and more peasant holdings decreased, so that fewer peasants could support families without supplemental wage work; moreover, there were more *de facto* proletarians, cotters and renters who did not own any land to speak of. For example, in the Leicestershire village of Wigston Magna, peasants owned 40% of the land in 1765 and large capitalist farms held the rest. With enclosure 3 years later and a shift from farming to livestock pasturage, peasants were reduced by one-third as they sold out or rented out their holdings; by 1831, the peasant economy had disappeared entirely. Peasant ownership was much stronger in France, where an estimated 40% of the rural population was proletarian or semi-proletarian by 1790, and a visible minority of rural proletarians were found even in peasant strongholds in the Pyrenees (30–40%). The best general study concluded that the proletariat expanded in cities as well. Here Strasbourg is typical, where the proportion of wage laborers expanded from 27% in 1699 to 45% in 1784 (Soboul 1970; Lis and Soly 1979).

Rural industry, population increase and proletarianization worked together to create a more economically vulnerable population. This translated differently in the political systems of England and France. In England, untrammeled enclosure meant a rapid decline in the peasantry and soaring agricultural output. In France, the peasantry remained in place and the landholding nobility was held in check by an absolutist regime, but it could burden peasants and sharecroppers with feudal dues and taxes. The English were burdened by dependence on wage labor, and the French by taxes and fees. Both were impoverished as mountains spilled over with people, cities grew and plains became more crowded.

7.3.2. *Early industry and migration*

Rural industry had a distinct and complex effect on mobility. It enabled people to earn a living while remaining in the countryside and working outside agriculture; second, it expanded manufacturing villages that attracted and retained newcomers. Finally, it reduced the geographic and economic distance between town and country. The production of thread, cloth and products such as nails in the countryside was not ubiquitous, but it was widespread enough that per-capita levels of industrial output for 1750 were about the same for Britain, Belgium and France, and these were only slightly greater than figures for Germany, then Italy and Switzerland (Bairoch 1982).

Manufacturing villages were most attractive early in their development when they established a labor force whose prolific marriages subsequently supplied workers. In a comparison of 16 English villages, those with industry had high levels of inward migration and relative permanency. By contrast, married people often departed villages that lacked manufacturing work (Souden 1984). The French village of Auffay, between Rouen and the sea, provides a vivid example of the dynamic connection between early industry and patterns of migration. During the heyday of cotton spinning (1751–1786) high birth rates, low death rates and immigration expanded the population. The number of households, and the population increased by 65% in 39 years. Women brought a spinning wheel as part of their dowry at marriage, and men wove in the winter and otherwise worked as laborers on the rich farms nearby. Those who did move headed for the villages on the outskirts of Rouen, virtual industrial suburbs. City and countryside, as a unit, were dependent on the vagaries of the international market for cotton (Gullickson 1986).

7.3.3. *The expansion of circular and chain migration*

Between 1750 and 1800, seasonal and circular migration systems expanded. Population increased in areas without rural industry as well, albeit less dramatically. This underwrote an expansion of extant systems of circular and chain migration. Seasonal and temporary migration became more crucial to highland areas where strong traditions had developed from high elevation climates, practices of livestock grazing and trading needs. From the Pyrenees, villagers would descend to Spain, the city of Bordeaux and the plains of Languedoc. Savoyards came out of the mountains in winter to work as chimney sweeps, take odd jobs in the city and tutor. The central highlands of France would send an army of men to Spain in the winter, as well as to the cities and plains of southern France and Paris. Lowland rural people, pressed by high rents, took to the road in search of work as harvesters or petty artisans – among these were the Westphalians who harvested hay and cut peat in Holland.

Seven massive systems of temporary migration engaged at least 20,000 people by 1800, most of them men. In the north, the largest drew at least 60,000 French to the Paris basin for harvest work in the Ile-de-France and seasonal urban employment. The North Sea system to Holland was the second most important, perhaps reaching 30,000 by 1790, who came primarily from German territories but also from Belgian and French territory. The third system in the north drew some 20,000 people to London, the home counties and East Anglia. Working in harvests and in the city, they came from western Ireland, the Scottish highlands and Wales. The largest system in the south drew at least 100,000 to Corsica, Rome and Italy's central plain from mountainous Abruzzi and the Apennines, as well as from Umbria, north of Rome. Some 50,000 people from the Alps and northern Apennines came to work in the Po Valley, Turin and Milan. The Iberian peninsula – Madrid and Castile, specifically – drew about 60,000 harvest workers and navvies from Galicia in northwest Spain, the Pyrenees and the Auvergne in the French highlands. Finally, the Mediterranean coastal plain from Catalonia through southern Languedoc to Provence attracted 35,000 workers to its fields, vineyards and the cities of Barcelona and Marseille (Lucassen 1987).

7.3.4. *Migration to 18th-century towns and cities*

This was the era of the smaller provincial center rather than that of the great city. The 17th-century pattern of large city growth faded, while midsize cities and capitals of rural industry prospered. After 1700, it was towns of 5,000–9,900 that were most likely to grow. Urbanization concentrated in 3,000–4,000 centers of production, marketing and administration (de Vries 1984). Migration to cities in this age was marked by an intense rhythmic interdependence between town and country. For industrial centers, this meant an expansion of surrounding villages marked by trade and production cycles; for capital and port cities, it meant waves of temporary migrants and chain migration systems that operated at all economic levels, from servant girls to members of the bourgeoisie.

The most careful studies of each kind of city reveal an impressive turnover of population; even when towns grew very little their stable population masked the comings and goings of many people. Young single people were the most mobile and hard to find in any record. For example the Norman city of Caen grew by only 3,000 people between 1753 and 1795 to reach 35,000, but this small net growth masks the entry of 20,842 people and the exit of 20,153, while it counted some 47,000 baptisms (Perrot 1975).

The expansion of a major city like Bordeaux shows how seasonal, permanent, long distance and local migration together supplied an urban area. This city grew from 45,000 in 1700 to 60,000 in mid-century, then 111,000 by 1790. While peasant holdings declined and rural rents rose, higher urban salaries attracted people, most immediately, from the surrounding dozen cantons (where a quarter of the city's brides were born), and then from settlements along the rivers that fed Bordeaux. Thousands of seasonal workers came from the uplands, including sawyers to provided lumber to build the city, laborers who laid its streets and masons who constructed the buildings. A minority of newcomers came from other large cities, and an elite group of merchants were particularly important to the national and international commerce that underwrote city growth.

Women dominated the temporary and circular migration systems from nearby, the majority coming to work as servants, dressmakers, seamstresses and market women; they were two-thirds of the migrants from Bordeaux's *département* of the Gironde, two-thirds of those who married in Bordeaux were from the three nearest departments. The farther newcomers traveled, the more likely they were to be men. The systems of circular, temporary migration to Bordeaux from the uplands were entirely masculine. Not until the 19th century would these groups include women, and women would signal the shift from circular to chain migration that in turn signaled permanent settlement. In the 18th century, demands for labor were extremely seasonal in this port city: construction took place in the summer, trade on the high seas began in September and the wine trade began its season in October. When grapes were ripe in the early fall, urban people would join men and women from the vineyards and farther afield in a massive, collective effort to achieve a timely harvest (Poussou 1983).

By 1820, several trends were emerging in the diverse locales of Western Europe: the land supported many more people than before, many of whom left home at a steady rate; a smaller proportion were land-owning peasants, and those working in rural industry relied on international markets over which they had no control. Patterns of land ownership, labor, demographic expansion and deployment of capital had created a vulnerable population.

7.4. Migration in an age of urbanization and industrialization (1815–1914)

The 19th century produced an urban society. Urbanization, the growth in the proportion of city dwellers, was a central phenomenon of this period. Over half the population of Britain lived in cities of over 20,000 by 1900; likewise a quarter of the people of Belgium and the Netherlands, and a fifth of Germans and French. Moreover, cities became larger than any time in history. Greater London reached 6.5 million and Paris 2.5 million. Suburbs expanded at unprecedented rates and new factory cities appeared.

Despite the temptation to focus on the dazzling lights of the city and the call of the factory, careful research reveals that the great growth of cities was founded in rural insecurity and multiple moves. The full countrysides of 1815 were vulnerable to the multiple crises of the following century: crop failures, the collapse of longstanding practices of rural work and the restructuring of markets for goods and labor that came with the railroad. German data sources reveal what others can only suggest, that people moved to and from the city as their lifecycle and employment dictated, and they moved often (Hochstadt 1999). Technological innovation must share center stage with the movement of capital and labor as the engine of industrialization.

This was an age of international and long-distance migration. The end of serfdom in Prussia (1807), Austria (1848) and Russia (1861) mobilized the Central European labor force and brought Poles especially into German territory. Although Europeans had settled and colonized other continents for 300 years, the 19th century saw the departure of millions for the Americas and beyond, to Australia and New Zealand. Many would be settlers, but circular migration systems also developed which carried men and women back and forth as part of the global labor force, because of the innovation of the steamship and relatively cheap transoceanic fares.

The issues of rural decline, urbanization/industrialization and transoceanic migration made for a complex series of changes, but we must keep in mind that they overlay existing patterns of mobility. Local migration systems maintained a certain importance as other kinds of mobility grew. Teams of harvest workers and construction workers that moved seasonally built the cities and supplied them with food. Simultaneously, chain migration systems expanded as more people sought urban work where their kin and compatriots had gone before. Finally, career migration expanded as the growth of postal and educational systems, the bureaucratization of government functions and the creation of the nation states of Germany and Italy meant that unprecedented numbers of officials, clerks and school teachers were assigned to posts by the state. And every kind of migration system included more women than before.

7.4.1. *The character of the age*

International conflicts, state restrictions and laissez-faire policies all influenced migration in the period between 1815–1914. It was preceded by a decade of revolution in France that stretched into 25 years of conflict. France's civil wars, international wars and divisions sent some 200,000 French people out of the country as *émigrés*, largely in 1793–1794. The revolutionary decade took a toll on France's cities, whose population declined as the demand declined for luxury goods, servants and construction workers; for example, Paris lost 12% of its population between 1790 and 1806. France's general call-up (*levée en masse*) in 1793 ushered in a period of mass armies across the continent that would take young men – the most likely of migrants – out of the labor force and into battle from Moscow to Spain. As the Napoleonic wars raged, the continental blockade against British goods devastated the merchant marine of the Atlantic coast and took the fortunes of Amsterdam and its migrant workers with it. Fortunately, it would be 100 years before Europe would see this scale of disruption and hostilities.

In terms of military and demographic disaster, the 1815–1914 period was much better than the 17th or 18th centuries. Military interventions and revolutions punctuated the century, but even the widespread revolutions of 1848 – so important politically – killed and exiled many fewer people than the French Revolution; and no conflict had the disastrous impact of the Thirty Years' War or the mobilizations of the Napoleonic wars.

The population increased as never before, surpassing the 1750–1800 period when the increase was 34%. The population that was 187 million in 1800 grew to 266 million in 1850, then 468 million by 1913, an increase of 42% in the first half of the century and another 76% by World War I. The number of people more than tripled in Denmark, Finland and Great Britain and more than doubled in Belgium, the Netherlands, Germany and Austria-Hungary (see Table 7.2).

Improvements in the production and distribution of food underwrote this great expansion. Among these was the expansion of fodder crops and the potato, which enabled people to survive on smaller acreage. With the exception of the "hungry forties" which brought on poor harvests, high grain prices and the potato famine, food production increased. In England, food production tripled between 1700 and 1870. A fall in mortality also provides a key to population increase. Not only were there few mortality crises apart from the 1840s, but also ordinary mortality declined for adults, for children, and finally, for infants. Importantly, this meant that more people would survive to reach reproductive age and bear their own children. For example, in France only 62% of women survived to the age of 20, 1805–1807, but 76% reached their childbearing years in 1900–1902 (Armengaud 1976).

	Around 1800	Around 1850	Around 1900	Around 1910
Norway	0.9	1.5	2.2	2.4
Sweden	2.3	3.5	5.1	5.5
Finland	1.0	1.6	2.7	3.1
Denmark	0.9	1.6	2.6	2.9
Germany	24.5	31.7	50.6	58.5
The Netherlands	2.2	3.1	5.1	5.9
Belgium	3.0	4.3	6.7	7.4
Switzerland	1.8	2.4	3.3	3.8
France	26.9	36.5	40.7	41.5
Great Britain	10.9	20.9	36.9	40.8
Ireland	5.0	6.6	4.5	4.4
Spain	11.5	15.5	18.6	19.9
Portugal	3.1	4.2	5.4	6.0
Italy	18.1	23.9	33.9	36.2

Table 7.2. *Estimated population growth in Western Europe, 1800–1910 (in millions) (source: Armenagaud 1976)*

The increased number of adult survivors shared finite resources and, as a result, the proportion of proletarians in rural areas increased. This was a long process in Britain and a less drastic one in France, where the peasantry remained strong. In eastern German territories, however, the transition from serf to laborer was swift and dramatic. In many instances, serfs were freed only to become farm servants or cottagers, then landless laborers with a small potato patch (Perkins 1981).

Population growth and proletarianization had clear implications for migration. Even without crises, the countryside was unable to support its doubled or tripled population (or even the 50% increase in France). Rural livelihoods became less stable, above all because the expansion of large capitalist farms meant fewer farmhands would be hired year-round, replaced by seasonal workers. Crop failures like the widespread potato crisis, the phylloxera that struck vineyards and the disease that plagued silkworms all threw rural economies into crisis. The demise of rural industry, unable to compete with machine production, put whole villages out of work.

7.4.2. *Changing patterns of circular migration*

In the long run, shifts in land ownership and the movement of capital to urban areas would produce a metropolitan world, but in the short run, the changes described above inflated seasonal work, economic insecurity and temporary movement. By 1841, at least 50,000 Irish worked in England between planting their potatoes in February and digging them up in November. At the same time, 264,000 men and 98,200 women moved in seasonal agricultural circuits in France while nearly 526,500 men and 352,000 women worked in the short intense work of the grape harvest (Chatelain 1977; Harris 1989). Other systems faded, as when the French were no longer welcome in Spain or the decline of the Netherlands would diminish demand for German workers.

Importantly, large systems of temporary migration emerged to serve the harvests of central Europe with the end of serfdom in the Baltic territories, German territories east of the Elbe and western Russia. No industrial crop needed more concentrated power over such extensive regions or grew so quickly as the sugar beet, feeding a demand for animal fodder and alcohol, as well as for sugar itself. By 1900, Germany produced half the world's sugar; central and eastern German territories and northern France were the most important arenas of sugar production. Sugar beet migrations began with *Sachengängerei* – workers going to Saxony – in the 1840s. They went by the same name as sugar production spread east of the Elbe and drew 119,000 international workers in 1900 and an estimated 433,000 by 1914. These were primarily Russian and Austrian Poles but also Italians, Scandinavians, White Russians and Ruthenians. To the west, 50,000 Belgians came to France's sugar beet fields (Chatelain 1977; Perkins 1981). Over half the Poles were women, favored by employers because they were skilled at working on root crops, accepted low wages and were perceived as docile workers. The German government regulated the Poles who entered the Reich from Austrian and Russian Poland. Because dreams of a resurrected Polish state (uniting the Poles of eastern Germany, Austria and Russia) threatened German's eastern border, repressing Polish nationalism guided policy (Bade 1987). Foreign Poles could only work as temporary labor and were only allowed in the eastern provinces of the German Reich. They were neither allowed to bring dependent family members nor to settle; rather they were required to depart German territory before December 20 of each year and to stay away until February.

Poles from Germany who worked in the western industrial provinces were also regulated.

The situation of Polish workers in prewar Germany forecast that of 20th-century migrant workers because restrictions on them foreshadowed state regulations that would attempt to control foreign labor in the future. State regulation and widespread importation of proletarian labor would become hallmarks of migration on the continent in the coming century.

7.4.3. *Migration and urbanization (1815–1915)*

Capital cities became spectacular metropolises in this period and cities of over 100,000 proliferated, increasing from 23 to 135 by 1900. Great factory cities provided the most striking new feature, sprawling from small manufacturing centers or market towns. Crises of the late 1840s put an end to rural industry in many areas, then boom years in the 1850s through 1870s expanded the urban demand for labor, while agricultural prices dropped in many regions, endangering subsistence agriculture. At the same time, heavy industry grew from the Ruhr Valley in northwestern Germany, south to the French coal and iron basin. The momentum behind industrialization and migration became especially strong in the 40 years before World War I.

The migration that fed European cities was primarily regional. Over half the migrations within France, Switzerland, the Netherlands and Norway were within the home *département*, province or canton (Weber 1958). This is surprising because the presence of long-distance and foreign workers like the Irish in Manchester was so striking to contemporaries. Nonetheless, the most reliable migration data (from the Ruhr to England to southern France) indicate that most urban newcomers came from the next town, village or neighboring county. Some international moves, like those from Belgium to France, were nonetheless short distance.

Moreover, itineraries of employment and the insecurities of the age meant that much migration was temporary. Although few historical data sources measure temporary migration, Prussian data measure the volume of arrivals and departures from cities. They reveal that from about 20% to over 54% of a given Rhine-Ruhr city's total urban population arrived and departed in a given year, depending on the local economy, and migration rates became especially high after 1850 (Jackson 1982; Hochstadt and Jackson 1984). Much urban work was seasonal, like that in water-powered mills and even dressmaking, which changed with the fashion season. Crucially, seasonal labor built the cities: housing, commercial spaces, public facilities and infrastructure, such as sewer systems. Like the "swallows" from

Spanish Galicia and northern Portugal who built Madrid, masons from the Limousin built Paris and Lyon. Such seasonal work complemented and even aided families with landholdings to survive in rural areas. Insecurity kept many people on the road, especially single men.

Patterns of circular migration became chain migration systems as people whose regions had a practice of temporary migration were drawn to permanent residence in the city. The classic example is that of the urban construction worker like the masons of the Limousin. They had spent summers in Paris since the 18th century, numbering 30,000 by 1848. With the building boom of the 1850s and 1860s agricultural work became less attractive, the women also wanted to leave, and the railroad facilitated family moves. By 1880, 2,000 wives lived in Paris along with 3,000 single women who worked as servants from the *département* of the Creuse within the Limousin. By 1900, over 24,000 men and women born in the Creuse lived in Paris (Chatelain 1977).

Case studies of Roubaix, France reveal migration patterns characteristic of the industrial city. Just south of the Belgian border, Roubaix served as a growing wool-finishing center for rural production in the eighteenth century, housing 8,000 people by its end. The demise of rural production and innovations such as the machine loom gave rise to an industrial boomtown of 30,000 in 1851 that was at 124,000 by 1900. Most migrants came from nearby, and by 1886 the majority were Belgians. In addition, an estimated 40,000 Belgians lived at the border and commuted to Roubaix, taking advantage of Belgium's low cost of living and France's relatively high wages. Foreign origins do not set Roubaix apart, rather it resembles Manchester with its Irish population, and the industrial Ruhr valley with its Poles, Dutch and eastern Germans and the regions of France, Switzerland and Germany served by Italian workers; an international labor force animated industrializing Europe. The extraordinary growth of this city masks high turnover and seasonal movement with a textile dead season, summer construction work, strikes and layoffs (Alter 1988; Blanchard 1906; Franchomme 1969).

7.4.4. *Transoceanic migrations (1815–1914)*

Transoceanic emigration streams grew and diffused in this period to become the greatest transfer of people to date, expanding significantly on previous practices. Although some 1.5 million people had emigrated from Britain in the 18th century and at least 140,000 Germans had settled in North America, this was just the beginning. Crop failures and economic dislocations after the Napoleonic wars increased the number of Europeans heading to the Western hemisphere to 30,000–40,000 annually. The 1840s heralded 80 years of mass migrations: each year in the 1840s, 200,000–300,000 Europeans departed every year. Between 1840 and 1880, an estimated 13 million embarked and another 13 million in the last 20 years of the century. About 52 million Europeans in all departed between 1860 and 1914, of whom roughly 37 million (72%) traveled to North America and 11 million (21%) to Latin America. Others – some 3.5 million, primarily British – departed for Australia and New Zealand (Morner and Sims 1985). The first groups knew little about their destination and could not easily return home, but as migration streams developed and steam ship companies facilitated transportation, the men and women who crossed the oceans knew more about what awaited them and were more able and more likely to return home. Two trends explain this massive migration. The demand for labor increased in the farms and cities of North America and in the sugar and coffee plantations of Latin America, partly because the slave trade, then slavery itself, was abolished. Moreover, Europe's "hungry forties", the potato famine and political struggles exacerbated suffering and unemployment on a continent whose population was greater than ever before (Moch 2003).

7.5. European migration in the 20th century

World War I proved to be a death knell not only for millions of Europeans, but for free migration as well. The previous century of relatively free mobility gave way to a time in which states directly sponsored, regulated and forced migration. The status of foreigners became more salient. In wartime, neither armies nor civilians moved by choice. State control between the wars and after World War II allowed workers to cross borders in great numbers in response to labor shortages, and often in response to recruiting efforts and bilateral government agreements.

The history of worker migrations in the 20th century is sharply divided into two periods. A so-called "second thirty years' war" decimated the population and minimized the movement of free labor, 1914–1945. International labor migration was controlled by hostilities until 1919; post-war rebuilding took the energies of surviving workers; transatlantic migration was squelched when the United States dramatically narrowed immigration quotas in the 1920s; the international depression of the 1930s so reduced the demand for labor that some nations closed their borders to foreign workers. There were massive displacements at the end of each war, but the scale was fundamentally different from that of the 18th and 19th centuries.

In the decade after World War II, a familiar migration scenario appeared. Men and women came to European cities to perform menial tasks that would allow them to retain or upgrade their family landholdings. In some cases, newcomers sent for their wives or married a compatriot. They visited home and talked to others about making the trip. Circular migrations became the chain migration systems that are so important to history. Yet two important distinctions separate these migrants from the past. The newcomers crossed borders from countries of southern Europe, the Mediterranean basin (North Africa, Yugoslavia, Greece, Turkey), sub-Saharan Africa and far-flung colonies of Europe. Also, the states of Western Europe took an active part, if not as recruiters then as agencies that attempted to control the volume and direction of migration. By 1981, over 11 million foreign nationals from southern Europe, North Africa and the British New Commonwealth lived in the United Kingdom and northwestern Europe (Rogers 1985). These international migrations occurred against a background of internal migrations that depleted the countryside, inflated urban populations and raised concerns about what came to be called the rural exodus or *Landflucht*. Native-born young people became more educated and more likely to take on white-collar work, inflating the ranks of career migrants and moving at the behest of the bank, the business or the educational system.

Demographics, labor force demands and movements of capital underwrote these patterns. As European fertility dropped to its lowest levels, the continent needed to import labor and sent fewer emigrants abroad. Non-farm capital attracted workers to cities, so wages, not land ownership, provided a living for most Europeans. Thus, three distinct tales dominate the 20th century: wartime migrations, urbanward migration and international labor in the post-war period.

7.5.1. *The character of the age*

Europe's 20th century has been viewed as a disaster by historians, most famously judged as "the worst century that has ever been" (Ignatieff 1998). For Westerners, the persecutions and wars produced by fascism and communism in the 1930s and 1940s mark the nadir of the continent. For the rest of the world, the failure of Europe lies in the destructive relations of European states with colonial and other developing countries. Western Europe is implicated both in the tale of internal ethical failure and the more global tale of exploitation, and these are reflected in patterns of migration. Colonization and the conflicts of decolonization are key explanations for the reversal of migration trends that brought Africans, Asians and South Americans to the shores of Europe. On the other hand, the great need for labor and the "*Trente glorieuses*" – the decades of economic growth after World War II – provided rising standards of living for Europeans and employment for newcomers from abroad.

7.5.2. *Wartime and interwar migrations*

The great discontinuities of wartime migrations in Europe do not fit into a normal economic or demographic framework for migration. When war began in the summer of 1914, migrations abroad nearly ceased. The flow of emigrants from Britain to North America and beyond, which had been 200,000 people per year, reversed when 20,000 returned home in 1915. Emigration from Germany and France, which had been minimal, dwindled. Within Europe, the majority of Germans and Austrians working in France quickly departed for home. At the outset of war, over 1.5 million refugees fled northern France to the west and south. Some foreign workers could not return home: in the interests of the German state, over 300,000 Russian Polish seasonal workers were kept on to prevent them from joining enemy armies; Austrian Poles were released to their home army (Dupâquier 1988; Herbert 1990).

War economies demand an intensive, functioning labor force; with men absent at war, women were recruited to work but more or less voluntary methods brought in foreign workers. Germany found workers in Belgians who were forcibly recruited in 1916–1917; in all, over 2 million volunteers, civilian prisoners and prisoners of war were at its disposal. France added prisoners of war and contract labor. Its hastily created Ministry of Armaments brought in over 80,000 workers from Greece, Portugal, Spain and Italy; the Ministry of Agriculture brought in 113,00 workers from Spain and Portugal, along with 35,000 women and children. Rougher recruitment garnered Algerians, other North African colonials, Indochinese and Chinese to the French labor force (Cross 1983; Herbert 1993; Stovall 1993).

When hostilities ceased in November 1919, a vast movement began as surviving soldiers and wartime workers went home, yet many people were permanently displaced. The war, then revolution in Russia and civil war in central Europe from 1914 to 1923 yielded a stream of refugees and exiles into Germany (500,000), France (400,000), Poland (70,000) and other newly-formed central European nation states. The war years had decimated Polish territories and scattered its people. In the reassignment of Alsace-Lorraine to France, 120,000 Germans left for the Rhineland and 50,000 French moved in. The brutality of the First World War not only cost some 20 millions of lives but it also set off the first refugee crisis of the 20th century (Stovall 1983; Zolberg *et al.* 1989; Herbert 1990; Gatrell 2013).

State policy and vacillations of the interwar economies created distinct patterns of migration within Europe. France was liberal in its immigration policies and in great need of labor after the war to replace its war dead and to rebuild damaged areas, so it sponsored the entry of over a million foreigners between 1919 and 1924.

Poles and Belgians came to work in the north, Italians and Spanish in the south in the 1920s, when France had a higher proportion of foreign-born than any other nation, 1.6 million foreign workers. The depression of the 1930s put an end to this influx of foreigners, although a bedrock of 2.2 million foreign residents remained, reflecting France's wartime losses and longstanding low birth rates. Unlike France, Germany suffered from inflation and unemployment in the 1920s, so it continued to regulate entries, but employed fewer workers, and many Germans went to work in the Netherlands, as in the 17th century. With the depression Germany closed its doors to new foreign workers and Germans went to the Netherlands once again, until the Third Reich managed to stimulate employment after 1933 (Cross 1983; Ogden 1989).

Between the wars of the 20th century, patterns of internal migration changed fundamentally for two reasons: first, birth rates which had declined earlier in France began to decline everywhere between 1890 and 1920, then dropped sharply between 1900 and 1930 (Coale and Treadway 1986). Infant and child mortality decreased as well and so the population grew, but it did so more slowly than before. Less population pressure in the countryside slowed emigration. Second, mechanization, low agriculture prices and a lack of rural jobs meant that employment and capital – in short, a future – lay in urban areas. Concern over the "rural exodus" reached a peak as scholars and journalists expressed their fears that rural life was in decline. They seized upon a grain of truth, that rural life was perceived as untenable and undesirable; this was especially true of young women who, in most areas, were more likely than men to leave the village (Tugault 1973; Ogden 1980).

A second wave of refugees grew between the wars, crossing borders after fascist victories ousted political enemies and persecuted ethnic groups. After Mussolini's victory, most of the 10,000 leftists who departed Italy joined the Italian communities in France. For Jews and Communists fleeing Germany and Spain, France was also the most frequent destination. Some 450,000 Spanish republicans sought refuge in France with Franco's victory, where there were an estimated 40,000 Jewish refugees. On the eve of World War II, there were about 8,000 Jewish refugees in Switzerland and many of the 40,000 refugees in the UK. Despite restrictions and anti-Semitism, many Jews and other refugees from throughout Europe found refuge in Palestine and North America during the war (Marrus 1985).

As many refugees experienced hardship and dislocation, millions more suffered during World War II. When Germany invaded the Low Countries, then France, in 1940, Dutch Belgians, Luxemburgers and French fled. A year after the invasion, one million French people remained uprooted, including 100,000 pushed from

Alsace-Lorraine when Germany repossessed its former territory. Displacements were most significant and brutal on Germany's eastern front where Poles were displaced to the General Government zone to be used as labor, Germans were moved in from abroad to join the Reich and Soviet forces evacuated people to the East (Kulischer 1948; Marrus 1985; Siegelbaum and Moch 2014). As in World War I, war economies demanded a vital labor force. Germany drew on over 7 million foreigner laborers, including 2.7 Soviet citizens, 1.7 million Poles, 1.25 million French as well as Italians, Belgians and Dutch (Herbert 1990). Alltogether, 30 million people were displaced in the 1939–1945 war. Approximately 44 million Europeans lost their lives – and this estimate does not include the North Americans, Asians and Africans who fought in Europe.

With the collapse of the Third Reich in 1945 came a fundamental reversal in patterns of European migration. Germans in Central and Eastern Europe who had been so favored under the Third Reich were now expelled to the west, reversing a centuries-old pattern of Germans moving to the East. By 1950, 12 million had reached occupied Germany. They were part of the second refugee crisis of the century, compounded by the efforts of surviving forced laborers and prisoners of war to return home.

7.5.3. *Post-war urbanization and international migration*

Rural and agricultural work declined precipitously after the war. Between 1950 and 1972, the agricultural labor force in Italy and France declined by more than half, and that of West Germany and Belgium by two-thirds. By 1970, the great majority of Europeans lived in cities and towns: 91% of the British, 87% of Swedes, 85% of West Germans, 78% of the French and 69% of Italians lived in urban areas (Ogden 1984).

Two patterns marked interregional migrations in the 1960s. Firstly, intense exchanges among prosperous urban regions were overlaid by net flows of migrants from declining rural or industrial areas. In Italy, people moved from the south to the northern industrial regions; in Spain to Madrid, Barcelona and the Mediterranean coast; in Britain, from Scotland, northern England and Wales to the south; in France, from the central highlands and northeast to the Paris basin and the Midi (Wood 1976).

Despite this internal migration to growing urban areas, there were not enough workers for these prosperous times. Wartime deaths, a lower birthrate and the tendency for native-born workers to spend more years in school depleted the numbers of people ready to work. Longstanding patterns of international migration (such as the Irish in London and Italians in Paris) had resumed, but the most visible change was the arrival of unprecedented numbers of foreign laborers and their families in the 1960s. By the mid-1970s, over 8 million foreign men, women and children resided in northwestern Europe. One in seven manual laborers was a foreigner in Germany and Britain; one in four industrial workers in France, Switzerland and Belgium was an immigrant. They came primarily from nine countries in southern Europe and North Africa: Portugal, Spain, Italy, Yugoslavia, Greece, Turkey, Tunisia, Morocco and Algeria. Over one million more people from the worldwide British Commonwealth resided in Britain than in 1961 (Rogers 1985).

These new immigrant workers echoed longstanding patterns and processes. Newcomers entered a labor force decimated by deaths and low birthrates that had created a demographic lacuna as they had in the 17th century, and they would bring demographic vitality to their new homes. The overwhelming demand for labor would not last beyond 1973, however. With the oil crisis and subsequent downturn of Western European economies, the demand for labor would decline.

Secondly, many migration streams that began with adult males came to be a chain migration system that included women and children who would settle permanently, as in centuries past. Such systems transformed overwhelmingly male migration streams into the settlement of families who were "guests come to stay", as labor migration settlements became long-term immigrant communities raising new generations in Europe (Rogers 1985).

Yet these post-war migration patterns also diverged from the past on two counts. First, most migrants moved within a state-negotiated context that had been relatively rare before 1914. Bilateral treaties negotiated the terms of movement between nations. And relations between nations were fraught in some cases, caught in violent struggles around decolonization. For example, among newcomers to France around 1962 were some 80,000 Algerian *harkis*, loyal to the French colonial administration, and 20,000 Asian Ugandans who arrived in Britain in 1972, both significant minorities of colonial citizens (Zolberg *et al.* 1989). When European states attempted to limit immigration after the 1970s, specific policies were set in place. In Britain, this meant the passing of laws that made foreigners out of Commonwealth citizens who had full rights until the Immigration Act 1971 and the British Nationality Act 1981. The Schengen Agreement of 1985 established free movement between nations of the then European Economic Community, but it also shifted controls to the exterior borders of the EEC in an attempt to fortify Europe against illegal entries. This pattern continued with many more entries from the east as of

1989, the formation of the European Union in 1992 and its expansion to 27 members by 2007, including Baltic and Central and East European countries.

Perhaps more significantly, post-war migrants made Europe more ethnically, culturally and religiously diverse. Those from Muslim and Arab countries brought languages, gender relations, cultural habits, religious worship and reproductive patterns that set them apart from mainstream Western Europeans. The hostility and racism faced by some immigrants echoed the well-documented historical hostility of Germans to Poles, English to Irish and French to Italians. Yet the racialization of immigrants is bound up with the colonial histories of European nations, particularly in the case of France and Britain, whose immigrants included many former colonials. By 1981, 810,000 Algerians lived in France and the Indians, Pakistanis and West Indians in Britain outnumbered all other immigrants, except the Irish (Castles *et al.* 1984). Islam was a salient feature of some immigrant groups because Western Europeans thought of themselves as non-Muslims, whose ancestors had expelled Islam from the continent in key battles of Early Modern times. Islam was perceived to be more crucial, and more negative with the departure of the Ayatollah Khomeini from France to lead the Islamic revolution in 1979, the arrival of conservative imams to serve the Muslim faithful, and terrorist attacks of the next century, from the 9/11 attacks on New York in 2001 to the Bataclan and Saint-Denis attacks at the end of 2015.

At the end of the 20th century, the nations of Western Europe were in a defensive posture vis à vis non-European immigrants. To a greater or lesser degree, each enacted programs to integrate newcomers or gave them the cold shoulder. With the political and economic crises in the Middle East and Africa, many more refugees sought entry into Europe only to be faced with increasingly exclusionary policies and politics as the 21st century entered its second decade.

7.6. References

Alter, G. (1988). *Family and the Female Life Course: The Women of Verviers, Belgium, 1849–1880*. Wisconsin United Press, Madison.

Anderson, M. (1988). *Population Change in North-Western Europe, 1750–1850*. Macmillan, London.

Armengaud, A. (1976). Population in Europe, 1700–1914. In *The Fontana Economic History of Europe* 3: *The Industrial Revolution, 1700–1914*, Cipolla, C. (ed.). Harvester Press, Hemel Hempstead.

Bailyn, B. (1986). *Voyagers to the West: A Passage in the Peopling of America on the Eve of the Revolution*. Knopf, New York.

Bairoch, P. (1982). International industrialization levels from 1750 to 1980. *Journal of European Economic History*, 11, 269–333.

Blanchard, R. (1906). *La Flandre : étude géographique de la plaine flamande en France, Belgique et Hollande.* Danel, Lille.

Castles, S., Booth, H., Wallace, T. (1984). *Here for Good: Western Europe's New Ethnic Minorities*. Pluto, London.

Chatelain, A. (1977). *Les migrants temporaires en France de 1800 à 1914.* Publications de l'Université de Lille, Lille.

Clark, P. (1979). Migration in England during the late seventeenth and early eighteenth centuries. *Past and Present*, 83, 57–90.

Cross, G. (1983). *Immigrant Workers in Industrial France: The Making of a New Laboring Class.* Temple University Press, Philadelphia.

Coale, A. and Treadway, R. (1986). A summary of the changing distribution of overall fertility, marital fertility, and the proportion married in the provinces of Europe. In *The Decline of Fertility in Europe*, Coale, A., Watkins, S.C. (eds). Princeton University Press, Princeton.

Dupâquier, J. (1988). *Histoire de la population française.* PUF, Paris.

De Vries, J. (1984). *European Urbanization, 1500–1800.* Harvard University Press, Cambridge.

Fenske, H. (1980). International migration: Germany in the eighteenth century. *Central European History*, 13, 332–347.

Franchomme, G. (1969). L'évolution démographique et économique de Roubaix dans le dernier tiers du XIXe siècle. *Revue du Nord,* 51, 201–247.

Gatrell, P. (2013). *The Making of the Modern Refugee.* Oxford University Press, Oxford.

Goubert, P. (1960). *Beauvais et les Beauvaisis de 1600 à 1730.* SEVPEN, Paris.

Gribaudi, M. (1987). *Itinéraires ouvriers : espaces et groupes sociaux à Turin au début du XXe siècle.* EHHSS, Paris.

Gullickson, G. (1986). *Spinners and Weavers of Auffay: Rural Industry and the Sexual Division of Labor in a French Village, 1750–1850.* Cambridge University Press, Cambridge.

Harris, R.-A.M. (1989). Seasonal migration between Ireland and England prior to the famine. *Canadian Papers in Rural History*, 7, 363–386.

Hart, S. (1974). Gens de mer à Amsterdam au XVIII siècle. *Annales de démographie historique*, 145–163.

Herbert, U. (1990). *A History of Foreign Labor in Germany, 1880–1980.* Michigan University Press, Ann Arbor.

Hochstadt, S. (1983). Migration in preindustrial Germany. *Central European History*, 16, 195–224.

Hochstadt, S. (1999). *Mobility and Modernity: Migration in Germany, 1820–1989.* Michigan University Press, Ann Arbor.

Hochstadt, S. and Jackson, J. (1984). "New" sources for the study of migration in early nineteenth-century Germany. *Historical Social Research/Historische Sozialforschung*, 31, 85–92.

Hogan, D. and Kertzer, D. (1985). Longitudinal methods for historical migration research. *Historical Methods*, 18, 20–30.

Hohenberg, P. and Lees, L.H. (1985). *The Making of Urban Europe, 1000–1950.* Harvard University Press, Cambridge.

Ignatieff, M. (1998). *Isaiah Berlin: A Life.* Metropolitan Books, New York.

Jackson, J. (1982). Migration in Duisburg, 1867–1890: Occupational and familial contexts. *Journal of Urban History*, 8, 235–270.

Kussmaul, A. (1981). *Servants in Husbandry in Early Modern England.* Cambridge University Press, Cambridge.

Lis, C. and Soly, H. (1979). *Poverty and Capitalism in Pre-industrial Europe.* Humanities Press, Atlantic Highlands.

Lucassen, J. (1987). *Migrant Labour in Europe, 1600–1900.* Croom Helm, London.

Marrus, M. (1985). *The Unwanted: European Refugees in the Twentieth Century.* Oxford University Press, New York.

Moch, L.P. (2003). *Moving Europeans: Migration in Western Europe since 1650.* Indiana University Press, Bloomington.

Mörner, M. and Sims, H. (1985). *Adventurers and Proletarians: The Story of Migrants in Latin America.* UNESCO, Paris.

Ogden, P. (1980). Migration, marriage and the collapse of traditional peasant society in France. In *The Geographical Impact of Migration*, White, P., Woods, R. (eds). Longman, London.

Ogden, P. (1984). *Migration and Geographical Change.* Cambridge University Press, Cambridge.

Ogden, P. (1989). International migration in the nineteenth and twentieth centuries. In *Migrants in Modern France: Population Mobility in the Later Nineteenth and Twentieth Centuries*, Ogden, P., White, P. (eds). Unwin Hyman, London.

Perkins, J.A. (1981). The agricultural revolution in Germany, 1850–1914. *Journal of European Economic History,* 10(1), 71–118.

Perrot, J.-C. (1975). *Genèse d'une ville moderne : Caen au XVIIIe siècle.* Mouton, Paris.

Poussou, J.-P. (1983). *Bordeaux et le sud-ouest au XVIIIe siècle.* EHHSS, Paris.

Ravenstein, E. (1976). *The Laws of Migration.* Arno, New York.

Rogers, R. (1985). Post-World War II European labor migration. In *Guests Come to Stay: The Effects of European Labor Migration on Sending and Receiving Countries*, Rogers, R. (ed.). Westview, Boulder.

Sabean, D. (1970). Household formation and geographical mobility: A family register study for a Württemberg village, 1760–1900. *Annales de démographie historique*, 275–290.

Siegelbaum, L.H. and Moch, L.P. (2014). *Broad is My Native Land: Repertoires and Regimes of Migration in Russia's Twentieth Century.* Cornell University Press, Ithaca.

Soboul, A. (1970). *La civilisation et la Révolution française.* Arthaud, Paris.

Souden, D. (1984). Movers and stayers in family reconstitution populations, 1660–1780. *Local Population Studies*, 33(1), 11–28.

Stovall, T. (1993). Colour-blind France? Colonial workers during the First World War. *Race and Class*, 35(1), 35–55.

Tilly, C. (1978). Migration in modern European history. In *Human Migration: Patterns and Policies*, McNeill, W., Adams, R. (eds). Indiana University Press, Bloomington.

Tugault, Y. (1973). *La mesure de la mobilité : cinq études sur les migrations internes.* INED, Paris.

Weber, A. (1965). *The Growth of Cities in the Nineteenth Century.* Cornell University Press, Ithaca

Wood, P. (1976). Inter-regional migration in Western Europe: A reappraisal. In *Migration in Post-war Europe: Geographical Essays*, Salt, J., Clout, H. (eds). Oxford University Press, London.

Wrigley, E.A. (1983). The growth of population in eighteenth-century England: A conundrum resolved. *Past and Present*, 98, 121–150.

Zolberg, A., Suhrke, A., Aguago, S. (1989). *Escape from Violence: Conflict and the Refugee Crisis in the Developing World.* Oxford University Pressa, New York.

8

Current International Migrations[1]

Serge FELD
University of Liège, Belgium

8.1. Introduction

According to the definition used in all UN documents, an international migrant is someone who lives in a country other than their country of birth. Over the past 30 years, international migration stocks have recorded an unprecedented growth of 91.2 million migrants. According to the latest estimates, these amounts have risen from 152.6 million in 1990 to reach 258 million, representing a 70% increase. This increase in the total number of migrants is almost twice as high as that of the total population, and the result of a great diversity of situations and factors, both in the major regions and in the individual countries. The nature and structure of international migrations have experienced remarkable changes in recent years: changes in the proportions of permanent, temporary and circular migrations, and significant variations in the respective weight of economic, political and environmental factors, which have influenced the growth in the proportion of illegal migrants and refugees. The first part of this chapter provides a long-term assessment, as well as an analysis of short-term changes. Three types of data provide a general overview of migratory movements: first, international migration stock estimates, then the evolution of net migration flows and their distribution by origin and destination and finally the most

---

1 Much of the data have been drawn from my French book *Les migrations internationales et le développement* (Feld 2019), updated in 2021. I would like to thank Yves Charbit who offered invaluable help for writing this chapter.

recent changes that have marked the main flows. We mainly use data from the United Nations Population Division. The definition of groups of countries and regions is the one adopted in the United Nations nomenclature.

The second part of this chapter introduces the most recent trends in the flow of Highly Qualified (hereafter HQ) migrants, and then the 30 main countries of HQ emigration toward OECD countries. For a more accurate assessment of the phenomenon, we define a "HQ emigration rate". The concerns raised by the large-scale emigration from people in developing countries have prompted development actors and researchers to compile accurate and harmonized data for the largest number of countries beyond a few *ad hoc* fragmentary of monographs. In the beginning, the definition of HQ personnel focused on specific professions, such as doctors, engineers, professors and so on. Very quickly, for data standardization purposes, it was agreed to include all individuals holding a higher education degree in this category. Over the years, several studies have produced the most reliable data possible on HQ migration flows, which served as a reference for almost all subsequent analyses.

Carrington and Detragiache (1998) were the first to present estimates of emigration rates from 61 developing countries to OECD countries for three educational categories. These were constructed using 1990 U.S. Census data. Using more recent data, Docquier and Marfouk (2006, pp. 151–200) then completed and deepened the assessment of migration stocks by country of origin and by education attainment across 192 countries and territories over the period 1990–2000. The first large-scale standardized database was produced by the OECD and covered 227 countries of origin and 29 host countries based on the censuses of the 2000s (Dumont and Lemaitre 2005). Beine *et al.* (2007) continued to develop this database by collecting information concerning the age of migrants on arrival in the host country in order to determine in which country they had obtained their higher education. Later on, the best critical synthesis of the research of the last 40 years was proposed by Docquier and Rapoport (2012) who considered the economic consequences of HQ migrations as manifestations of the globalization process. They presented the data available at the beginning of the 2000s regarding flow volume and intensity, and analyzed the determinants and main consequences of the brain drain. Of course, the most relevant approach to measure all the aspects of this phenomenon would be to compare the annual HQ emigration flows from each country against the number of higher level graduates educated each year. If these data were available, they would make it possible to calculate a "depletion rate" that emigration induces each year by taking a number from each cohort of HQ graduates. It would then be possible to measure the additional cost this entails for national budgets, a cost which should therefore be allocated to the higher education of each new graduate who decides to stay in the country of origin.

8.2. Migration flows and migration stocks

8.2.1. *Review of the last 25 years*

The annual growth rate of the global migration stock fell 2.8% between 2005 and 2010 and reached 2.2% in 2019 (UN 2019). This trend has been subject to exogenous shocks such as natural disasters and epidemics of international scope. In 2017, of the 258 million international migrants, 165 million (64%) lived in developed countries, whereas 93 million (36%) lived in developing countries.

Destination	Origin					
	Africa	Asia	Europe	Latin and Central America	North America	Oceania
Africa	16.4	1.2	1.0	0.0	0.1	0.0
Asia	4.1	59.4	6.9	0.4	0.5	0.1
Europe	9.2	20.2	39.9	4.6	1.0	0.4
Latin and Central America	0.1	0.3	1.3	5.9	1.3	0.0
North America	2.3	15.5	7.5	24.6	1.2	0.3
Oceania	0.5	3.0	3.0	0.2	0.2	1.1

Table 8.1. *Number of international migrants by continent of origin and destination in 2015 (in millions) (source: UN 2015a)*

This proportion has slightly changed since 2000. It increased by 6% in favor of developed countries. Within the group of developed countries, 61% come from developing countries and 39% from developed countries. In contrast, in the case of developing countries, 87% come from other countries in this group, whereas only 13% have moved from developed countries. Over the past 25 years, two regions – Asia and Europe – have received two-thirds of the total migrants.

The volume and movement are almost similar for these two regions, with around 48 million migrants having arrived in 1990, and 75 and 76 million in 2015.

These two regions have experienced an annual increase of 1.1 million migrants. In third place, they are followed by North America, with 54.5 million migrants. During this same period, the global number of migrants increased at an annual rate of 3.6%. Two-thirds of this growth went to developed countries and one-third to developing countries. Asia, North America and Europe have recently experienced the same 1.1% annual growth rate. On the other hand, the rates are almost zero for Africa, Oceania and Latin America.

It was during the decade 2000–2010 that international migrations recorded the highest growth, with a rate of 4.9%. Europe experienced an annual peak of 1.8% during these years, which doubles the rate of the previous period and the rate of the period following 2010. This considerable variation in the number of migrants was the result of several factors, mainly the fall of the Iron Curtain, which led to an increase in intracontinental immigration, mainly from the countries of Central and Eastern Europe. It can also be largely explained by a sort of "methodological artifact" resulting from the official definition of international migration stocks which, in this case, produces a bias in the assessment of migratory movements. In point of fact, it counts all the people who were born in a different country from the one where they reside. However, with the dismantling of the former USSR and the former Yugoslavia, more than 27 million people found themselves "born abroad", in new countries, without ever having crossed any border. Paradoxically, one can argue that the more there are new countries (by separation or split), the more there are "foreigners" who have never immigrated in their lifetime.

More than two-thirds of international migrants live in just 20 countries. With 50 million migrants, the United States is the first host country, followed by Germany, Russia and Saudi Arabia, each with 12 million migrants. Next come the United Kingdom with 10 million migrants and the United Arab Emirates with 8 million migrants, followed by France and Canada, with 8 million migrants each. The origins and qualifications of these migrants are certainly different depending on the host country (section 8.3). However, the magnitude of these flows should not mask the fact that, contrary to a widely held opinion, migrants currently represent only 3.4% of the world population, and this fraction has increased little during the last 25 years (2.9% in 1995). These figures at the global level hide a significant portion of the differences which exist at the level of large regions (developed and developing countries). Table 8.2 shows that this proportion remained at the same level (1.7%) for all developing countries throughout the period, whereas for developed countries it increased from 7.2% to 11.2%.

	Migration stock and % of total population			
	1990 (millions)	2015 (millions)	1990 (%)	2015 (%)
World	152.6	243.7	2.9	3.3
Developed countries	82.4	140.5	7.2	11.2
Developing countries	70.2	103.2	1.7	1.7
Africa	15.7	20.6	2.5	1.7
Asia	48.1	75.1	1.5	1.7
Europe	49.2	76.1	6.8	10.3
Latin and Central America	7.2	9.2	1.6	1.5
North America	27.6	54.5	9.8	15.2
Oceania	4.7	8.1	17.5	20.6
	Migration stocks growth rate			
	1990–2000	2000–2010	2010–2015	1990–2015
World	2.0	4.9	4.4	3.6
Developed countries	2.1	2.9	1.6	2.3
Developing countries	–0.1	2.0	2.8	1.3
Africa	0.1	0.2	0.8	0.2
Asia	0.1	1.7	1.8	1.1
Europe	0.7	1.6	0.8	1.1
Latin and Central America	0.1	0.2	0.2	0.1

Table 8.2. *Number of migrants (millions) in destination countries as a percentage of the total population (1990 and 2015) and migration stocks growth rate between 1990–2015 (source: UN 2015a)*

This increase in the share of migrants as a percentage of the total population is very significant in North America (15.2%) and in Europe, where 10.3% of the population is made up of immigrants. It results from the combination of increased migratory flows and near demographic stagnation in most of these countries. On the other hand, in Africa, Asia and Latin America, the situation is very different, where the total number of migrants represents only 1.5% of the total population. These data mask considerable national differences (section 8.2.3).

8.2.2. *Origins and destinations of major migration flows*

The distribution of migrants by country of origin presents diverse situations in the major continents of immigration. In Asia, for example, 90% of the 27 million new migrants in the period 1990–2015 were born in an Asian country different from their country of residence. On the other hand, in Europe and in North America, the situations are more varied. In Europe, 45% of migrants were born in another European country and 25% in Asia. In North America, 54% of migrants come from Latin America and 35% come from Asia. A widely held opinion maintains the illusion that international migratory movements are mainly fueled by flows from the "South" to the "North". It is not a geographical definition, but rather a classification depending on global development indicators. The North tends to group high-income countries (GNP of more than US$ 12,476), and the South tends to group low-income (less than US$ 1025) and middle-income countries (lower bracket between US$ 1025 and US$ 4030, and upper bracket between US$ 4030 and US$ 12,476) (World Bank 2017). The reality is quite different (Figure 8.1).

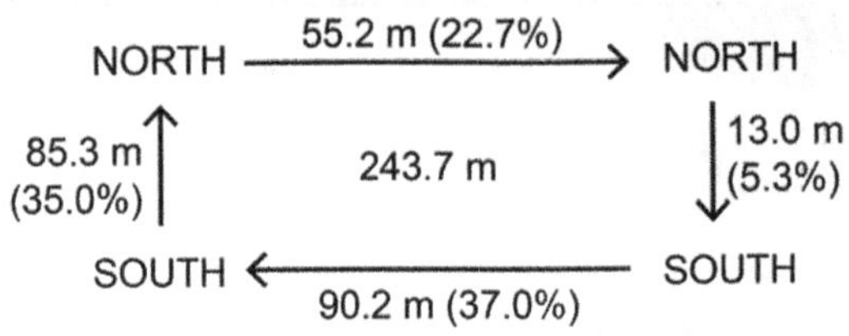

Figure 8.1. *Distribution of migratory movements between "North" and "South" countries, in 2015 (in millions and %) (source: UN 2015b)*

In 2015, for 244 million migrants globally, that is to say, people living outside their country of birth, South → North (35%) and South → South (37%) flows are practically of the same volume. They are followed by North → North flows (22.7%) and, in a very small proportion, North → South flows (5.3%). Between 1990 and 2015, "Northern" countries experienced the strongest international migration stocks growth from Southern country flows (76%), but since 2010 growth has clearly been strong within the group of "Southern" countries. On average, the increase in migration stocks has been 2.9% per year. More than 90% of it is attributable to flows coming from the South.

Recent trends also reflect the considerable increase in the number of refugees, which has reached its highest level since the end of the Second World War[2]. In 2015, it amounted to more than 21 million people, or 8% of the total migrant population. In recent years, several countries in southern Europe and Germany have faced massive arrivals of refugees, but overall it is the "Southern" countries which have received 86% of the refugee world total. Among these, the group of least developed countries received 25% of refugees. More than half of them come from three countries which have suffered the most violent armed conflicts: Syria with 3.9 million refugees, Afghanistan with 2.6 million and Somalia with 1.1 million refugees.

Over the same period (1990–2015), with the exception of North America – where they amounted to only 27% of the total – *intracontinental* migrations have represented a large majority practically everywhere. This proportion corresponds to 52% for Africa, 60% for Asia, 66% for Europe, 71% for Latin America and 59% for Oceania. Migrants from African countries chose Europe as a second option (27%) and North America, in a very small proportion (7%). The African continent is still highly unattractive for migrants from other regions. In Asia, nearly 60 million people have migrated to another country on the continent, mainly from the Indian subcontinent to the Gulf countries and Saudi Arabia. A significant proportion of migration flows is made up of refugees who settle in countries bordering armed conflict zones.

Regarding *intercontinental* migrations, the main destinations are Europe (20.2 million) and North America (15.3 million). Migration flows from the rest of the world toward Asia remain at low levels. Over this same 25-year period, that is to say, between 1990 and 2015, the total number of migrants has been more or less the same in Europe as in Asia, but it is Europe which has largely welcomed the highest migration flows as a percentage of its population. Intra-European flows amount to nearly 40 million migrants. Most of these flows stem from movements from Eastern and Central Europe toward Western Europe, following the fall of the Iron Curtain, the dislocation of several warring countries and, as a consequence, the forced

2 Refugees are included in the calculation of the total number of migrants estimated by the UN. The once very clear distinction between migrants and refugees is tending to blur. According to the UNHCR (High Commissioner for Refugees), *migrants* choose to leave their country not due to a direct threat of persecution, but mainly in order to improve their lives by finding better jobs, by obtaining better education or due to family reunification. Unlike refugees, who cannot return home safely, migrants do not face such obstacles upon return. *Refugees* are persons fleeing armed conflict or persecution. Their status is defined by the 1951 Refugee Convention and its 1967 Protocol, as well as other legal texts. A significant portion of refugees are not registered in international flows because they have moved within their own countries.

displacement of populations. The other two continents of origin are Asia, representing 25% of migrants, and Africa, with 18% of migrants. North America (the United States and Canada) has mainly welcomed migrants from Latin and Central America (24.6 million), as well as from Asia (15.5 million). For centuries, North America has been primarily an immigration continent, to such extent that outgoing flows are minor. In Latin and Central America, flows are essentially unidirectional. About 69% of migrants went to North America, whereas immigration from other continents is virtually non-existent.

8.2.3. *The major migratory corridors*

Even if they offer initial indications for a general orientation, the migratory movements analyzed at the level of regions and continents necessarily obscure the extent and evolution of flows taking place between the countries that are the leading actors of migration. Similarly, the ranking of countries have received and sent the greatest number of international migrants over the past 25 years, while providing valuable indications about a country's receptive capabilities and its emigration propensities, does not make it possible for the main bilateral axes to emerge. As a matter of fact, the focus on larger countries characterized by the largest diasporas does not enable us to highlight the bilateral movements determined by the ups and downs of the economic situation, the new geopolitical constraints and the impact of unpredictable phenomena such as the Covid-19 pandemic.

Figure 8.2 shows the 15 main migratory corridors from a country of origin toward a host country in 2000 and 2017. Overall, the order of significance has remained stable over these 17 years and the trend indicates a significant increase in international migrants everywhere, with a few exceptions.

A first configuration reflects a situation with an almost exclusive link between country of origin and host country. This is the case of the Mexico–United States corridor, where nearly 13 million migrants represent 98% of the total emigration from this country. The same trend prevails, but with much smaller numbers, for the Algeria–France, Burkina Faso–Ivory Coast and Cuba–United States movements. A second configuration shows a greater diversification of flows from certain countries. Thus, India mainly sent migrants to the United Arab Emirates, Saudi Arabia and the United States. To a certain extent, a third migration pattern reflects bilateral population movements in both directions. This is the case for movements in the geographical unit corresponding to the former USSR. For the past 15 years, the number of "migrants" between Russia and Ukraine has included, in both directions and for each of the two countries, between 3 and 4 million people, and between Russia and Kazakhstan the figures total around 2.5 million people. This particular situation for these three countries is largely the result of the drawing of new borders, which have generated a population of "migrants" who have not actually crossed any border. The only notable change concerns the movement from Syria to Turkey, as a result of the war which has been tearing Syria apart for several years. Between 2000 and 2017, the number of Syrian migrants in Turkey increased from a few thousand to 3.3 million. The first European corridor concerns the migration between Poland and Germany, which has doubled over the past 17 years (2 million in 2016).

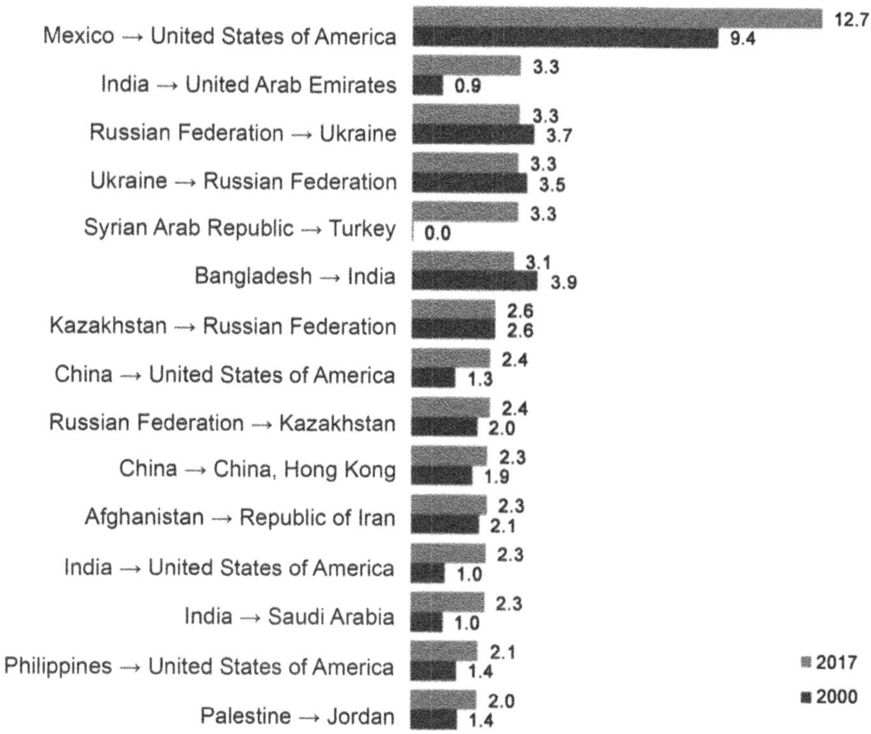

Figure 8.2. *The 15 most numerous migrant populations from a country of origin to a country of destination in 2000 and 2017 (in millions of migrants) (source: UN 2017). For a color version of this figure, see www.iste.co.uk/charbit/demographic.zip*

8.2.4. *Migration trends and the Covid-19 virus*

The Covid-19 virus, which has spread since the beginning of 2020, has profoundly transformed the volume of international migration stocks and flows. For the first time in decades, one can see a sharp shift in the international migrations growth curve. In some destination countries where the number of international migrants is very high and the result of properly integrated long-standing immigration, variations are unlikely to be very large. Contrary to this, recent labor immigration countries will certainly experience substantial return movements. On the one hand, migrants are widely represented in the most vulnerable and underpaid sectors, which have been fully affected by the shutdown of production and the effects of confinement. A large number of them work illegally or with very precarious contracts. There are significant return movements from Mexico to other Latin American countries, as well as massive migrant returns from Eastern Africa coming back from the Gulf countries and return migrations from Western Europe to Eastern Europe (World Bank KNOMAD 2020). On the other hand, it should be noted that a large proportion of migrants work in critical sectors such as hospital care and domestic services, for which demand will remain strong after the crisis period. While migrants represent, as reported, only 3.5% of the world's population, at the end of April 2020, they accounted for more than 10% of the population in 10 out of the 15 countries most severely affected by Covid-19 (World Bank KNOMAD 2020). Entry flows have stopped in all countries. According to data as of May 12, 2020, there were more than 60,700 global mobility restrictions in 207 countries and territories (International Migration Organization 2020). In addition to these very strict restrictions on entry, there are quarantines, sanitary confinements, and the suspension of humanitarian asylum and political programs, the suspension of international student exchange programs, etc. It is not yet possible to propose reliable hypotheses on this sudden reversal. Will the decline in international migration be temporary and will it be quickly followed by a rebound continuing with the growth of the past decades? Will the economic policies advocating for a slowdown on globalization also materialize in the field of international labor mobility? Can we reliably predict variations in the volume and intensity of bilateral migratory movements? The decline in migratory flows is already reflected in the decrease in remittances, which will have significant consequences for the economies of emigration countries.

8.3. Emigration of HQ workforce from developing countries

In the absence of data on an annual basis, the most recent and complete source is that provided by the latest update of the Database on International Migration DIOC OECD (2010/11). Most of the information presented in this chapter has been drawn from these data. In the light of this information, a few preliminary observations are needed as to the assessment of HQ immigration flows. First of all, these are HQ migration stocks for the year 2010/2011, compared to those from the year 2000.

Although this stock variation spanning 10 years provides general trends in migration flows, it does not make it possible to closely follow annual variations. Secondly, the data also only relate to migrations toward OECD member countries and therefore HQ immigration toward other developed countries and to developing countries is not taken into account. Thirdly, for a large number of countries, it is not possible to determine whether migrants have acquired all of their higher education in their country of origin or whether they have partially completed it in host countries or transit countries.

8.3.1. *Recent trends*

A brief comparison between migration flows of all skill levels and HQ migrants toward developed countries and the rest of the world makes it possible to identify the following major trends. As previously discussed, over the 27-year period between 1990 and 2017, the total number of global migrants increased from around 90 million to 258 million, a growth of around 69%, with a decrease in recent years. If one focuses on the period 2000–2010, the increase is 50 million migrants, equal to a growth of 29% in 10 years. Over the same 2000–2010 period, there were nearly 31.5 million migrants with higher education between all OECD countries, representing a considerable increase of over 70% in only 10 years, that is to say, more than double the increase in the number of migrants in all categories. Over the same period, the total number of migrants in all categories toward the group of developed countries increased by 17.5%. In 2010, HQ migrants accounted for more than one-third of the migration stock in all OECD countries, as well as in other developed countries. The number of HQ migrants greatly increased during this period, continuing the trend of previous years.

Table 8.3 collects the main data on the groups of countries and continents of origin of HQ migrants. The number of HQ migrants from OECD member countries increased by 50% during the decade 2000–2010. These internal migratory movements within the OECD area can refer to diverse situations. First, the strong attraction exerted by the United States and Canada for higher education graduates from European and East Asian developed countries. Secondly, one observes highly skilled workforce emigration movements continue from the former Soviet bloc countries. Finally, the magnitude of these flows also reflects to what extent the European Union has intensified the integration of the labor market as well as the free movement of people within its boundaries.

The second strong trend clearly reflects the scale and dynamics of the brain drain. In 2010, there were nearly 19.5 million migrants with a higher educational level coming from developing countries (middle-income countries as well as low-income ones), which represents 62% of the total HQ migrants present in OECD member countries. This represents a considerable increase of over 83% over 10 years. The selectivity of migration flows accelerated during this decade since the increase in HQ migration was higher than that represented by migration flows reuniting all educational levels. In addition, the share of developing countries among the countries of origin continues to grow significantly. These figures relate only to immigration toward OECD member countries. We should also add the other developed countries (especially the countries of the Arabian Gulf), which also receive a significant part of HQ migration flows from developing countries and for which data are often incomplete.

	1990	2000	2010	2015
		All migrants		
All countries	154.2	172.2	221.7	243.7
Toward the OECD	82.3	84.0	135.6	123.8
Toward other developed countries	-	31.2	-	48.7
		HQ migrants in the OECD		
Region of origin				
Africa	nd	1,705.5	3,060.6	nd
Asia	nd	6,110.0	10,914.9	nd
Europe	nd	6,767.2	10,887.4	nd
North America	nd	841.6	1,159.9	nd
Latin America	nd	2,680.3	4,929.3	nd
Oceania	nd	305.5	465.3	nd
		Country groups		
OECD countries	nd	6,491.5	9,923.2	nd
Non-OECD developed countries	nd	1,276.6	1,992.5	nd
Low/medium-income countries	nd	10,622.7	19,472.0	nd
Total	nd	18,390.0	31,387.7	nd

nd: no data available.

Table 8.3. *Migration stocks in the world and in developed countries 1990–2015. Migration stocks (thousands) having received higher education in the OECD, 2000 and 2010 (sources: Arslan* et al. *2015; OECD 2015; UN 2015b)*

A presentation by continent of origin reveals stark regional contrasts in how the dynamic stocks of HQ migrants have evolved, as well as the large differences in the ratio measuring the relationship between the category of unskilled migrants and that of migrants with higher educational levels[3].

Asia, with nearly 11 million HQ migrants in 2010, represents the most significant source. The increase in HQ migrations is over 78% over the 2000–2010 period. It is essentially supplied by three countries: India, China and the Philippines. Overall, for recent migrants (those having settled in host countries for five years or less), Asia is characterized by a very significant ratio, showing that the proportion of HQ migrants more than doubles unskilled labor: 47% HQ against 20% unskilled (and 33% for the intermediate level), compared to the total of migration stocks toward the OECD[4]. In India, the HQ/unskilled ratio is 63% versus 16%, and in the Philippines it is 62% versus 13%. With more than 4.9 million migrants, Latin America is the continent of origin with the highest number of HQ migrants toward the OECD (emigration from developing countries, detailed data for Europe and North America are not provided). For recent migrants, the HQ/unskilled migrants ratio is the reverse as it is for Asia, with a ratio of 20%–43%. This result reflects the preponderant weight of unskilled labor emigration from Mexico and Central America to the United States. Only Argentina and, to a lesser extent, Brazil have a higher proportion for the HQ migrants category. The situation is different for the much less numerous HQ migrants from Africa. They represent a lower proportion to that of unskilled migrants (30% against 40% and 30% intermediate level). However, the differences between countries in this continent are considerable and clearly reflect the great differences in the economic development and infrastructure levels of the higher education systems. Due to specific economic and political reasons, three countries – Nigeria (55%/13%), South Africa (54%/13%) and Egypt (52%/16%) – stand out from other countries, showing a higher proportion of HQ migrants than unskilled migrants.

A more precise examination at the regional level differentiating the first five years (2000–2005) from the following five (2005–2010) makes it possible to clearly highlight a marked inflection in HQ emigration flows over the entire period. Recent migrants are all migrants who have been present in the destination country for five years or less. While, at the global level, HQ migration growth over the whole period has remained largely positive, as is the case for all international migrations, it has also suffered a strong slowdown movement. In part, this shift was caused by the economic and financial crisis of 2007/2008, which, by negatively affecting the labor

3 The following data have been drawn from (OECD 2015; Arslan *et al.* 2015, Table 8 and Appendices).

4 According to the OECD nomenclature, unskilled migrants are the graduates from the lower middle level, the medium-skilled migrants from the upper middle level, whereas the HQ or highly qualified are those from the university level or High-Level Research Institutions.

markets of developed countries, reduced the hiring of new HQ migrants and accelerated the reverse movement of some of them returning home. This trend will probably be even more accentuated when all the post-Covid-19 data become available.

Thus, Asia experienced a 54% growth of HQ migrants between 2000 and 2005, and of only 15% between 2005 and 2010. In Africa, the decrease in growth was much stronger: it fell from 95% during the first period to 13% for the years 2005–2010. This trend reversal, probably related to particular economic fluctuations, was particularly evident in Latin and Central America, where the 74% growth between 2000 and 2005 was followed by a decrease of 18% between 2005 and 2010. As data are not available for the years after 2011, it is therefore not possible to determine whether this downturn continued or whether it was only a cyclical movement. A detailed presentation at the country level (rather than by region or continent) invites a better understanding of the weight represented by the main HQ emigration countries, at the same time it brings to light recent transformations of HQ flows.

8.3.2. *The main countries of origin*

Table 8.4 presents the top 30 countries of origin for HQ migrants living in one of the OECD countries in 2000 and 2010. It is important to bear in mind that these figures only relate to migration stocks. It is only by comparing these figures against the 2000 stock data that the most recent trends can be accurately assessed. This table presents a broader panorama, including the emigration from developed countries as well as from developing countries. Not only does it highlight the great diversity of emigration sources, but it also shows the convergences between large groups by country of origin. The emigration of HQ migrants from developing countries – a currently predominant trend in global migratory movements – took place within the general context of globalization, which encouraged the circulation of goods, capital and, to a lesser extent, labor. Nevertheless, assessing changes in the most recent flows could be overshadowed by the weight of migrants who have already been settled in the host countries for a long time. This list of the top 30 countries of origin presents the following characteristics:

– This list hardly varies between 2000 and 2010/2011. Two countries have disappeared from the list: Egypt and Costa Rica, whereas two new countries have appeared: Hong Kong and Brazil. The ranking of countries depending on the number of HQ migrants has not experienced significant modifications. This can be explained by a structural effect. Indeed, for many countries, emigration flows have been spread over a long period of time, resulting in well-established communities, with a high number of migrants. As a consequence, even the highly significant migration flows of recent years have not lead to sufficient migration stocks variations that are likely to substantially modify the classification of the countries of origin.

– The top three countries of origin are developing countries in Asia. India, China and the Philippines total more than 5.5 million HQ migrants residing within the OECD. These are followed by Mexico, Vietnam, Iran and Colombia. India is the country which has experienced the top HQ migration stock growth, with more than 123% in 10 years. The other developing countries of origin that have shown the strongest increase in HQ migrants over this period are Pakistan with 123% and Colombia with 116%.

– A second group, comprising of more than 3.3 million HQ migrants, is of a totally different nature from that of the emigration from developing countries. It includes the three largest European Union countries: the United Kingdom, Germany and France, countries where higher education institutions as well as research and development departments from large companies have long produced abundant scientific staff, with all the skills required to meet the demands of the HQ international labor market. With the exception of the United Kingdom (whose flows, due to economic and historical reasons, have largely gone to the United States and Canada), this number of HQ migrants is the result of the intensification of trade and the deepening of the internal market in the European Union. The supply's selectivity does not only result from the characteristics of the HQ. In turn, the demand for HQ personnel also modulates migration flows via restrictive migratory policies that operate on the basis of point and quota regimes.

– A third group consists of Eastern European countries which, until the fall of the Soviet Union, were subject to the Iron Curtain and whose workforce did not have access to the labor market of Western countries. The poor economic situation of these countries during the transition to a market economy, social unrest and the fear of political insecurity accelerated the outflow in recent years. The top three countries of origin are Poland, followed by Ukraine and Romania. Poland has over 1 million HQ migrants. It experienced a strong acceleration in emigration (115.6%) over the 2000–2010 period.

– In Latin and Central America, the three countries that have experienced the greatest increase in the number of HQ migrants during the same period are Colombia (+115.9%), Brazil (+102.8%) and Mexico (+86.4%). In order to avoid an underestimation of flows, it should be stressed that a significant portion of HQ migrants have emigrated to other developing countries on that continent. However, the available data only refer to HQ migrants settled in OECD countries. Insofar as migrants to other countries with a high GNP have not been taken into account, this reflects a second source of underestimation of HQ emigration from developing countries.

Country	2010	2000	Growth rate 2010
India	2,239,605	1,002,334	123.4
Philippines	1,545,206	889,072	73.8
China	1,529,414	822,793	85.9
United Kingdom	1,473,738	1,082,320	36.2
Germany	1,224,326	865,422	41.5
Poland	1,007,573	467,242	115.6
Russia	898,519	624,830	43.8
Mexico	885,232	474,970	86.4
Korea	811,062	517,087	56.9
Ukraine	654,491	372,688	75.6
France	619,110	377,431	64.0
United States	598,186	418,219	43.0
Canada	561,574	423,033	32.7
Romania	555,259	268,212	107.0
Vietnam	539,908	348,141	55.1
Iran	471,401	289,735	62.7
Pakistan	451,777	202,688	122.9
Italy	432,850	273,480	58.3
Morocco	425,917	233,734	82.2
Colombia	375,053	173,710	115.9
Japan	364,093	277,150	31.4
Cuba	341,999	222,430	53.8
China-Taiwan	336,400	263,209	27.8
Algeria	324,523	217,553	49.2
South Africa	297,200	162,288	83.1
Jamaica	292,963	190,722	53.6
Hong Kong	291,592	147,120	98.2
Brazil	291,510	144,119	102.3
Netherlands	282,124	187,381	50.6
Ireland	273,810	176,984	54.7

Table 8.4. *Top 30 countries of origin of highly skilled migrants toward the OECD (source: Arslan* et al. *2015)*

8.3.3. *The emigration rate of the HQ workforce: a relevant indicator for measuring brain drain*

The HQ emigration rate is defined as the total number of people with a higher level of education born in a country and living abroad (in an OECD country), divided by the total population with the same level of education and residing in that country. OECD data[5] do not include migrants toward other high-income countries on average, such as the countries of the Arabian Gulf, or the migrants who have moved to developing countries. The HQ emigration rate is undoubtedly the most relevant indicator for measuring brain drain, much more than the total number of HQ present in the host countries or the migration stock variations over a short period of time, which are only partial indications on the evolution of flows.

Table 8.5 presents the top 10 countries of each continent (Africa, Latin and Central America, Asia) depending on the level of HQ emigration rates in 2010/2011 and 2000. It also shows the total number of HQ migrants from 30 countries in 2010/2011. Only countries with more than 1 million inhabitants will be taken into consideration. These countries, along with a whole group of countries with small populations, are characterized by a significantly higher brain drain than other developing countries. This situation stems from their specific characteristics such as insularity, the insufficient level of development to sufficiently integrate the annual cohorts of graduates, the narrowness of the labor market for qualified personnel and the low remuneration levels. As a result, for most of these countries, around 50% of the HQ workforce whose training was funded by them works in an OECD country. For the 30 countries shown in Table 8.5, 10 of them have an HQ emigration rate greater than 25%. Furthermore, it is in countries where per capita incomes are the lowest that the largest gaps exist between the general emigration rate and that of HQ migrants. It should be noted that, according to the OECD calculation, the emigration rate for a given country of origin in a given year (i) is defined as the share of native population of country i living abroad at that moment: mi = Mi/(Mi + Ni), where Mi is the emigrant population of country i living abroad and Ni is the non-migrant native population of country i.

The main countries which, at the global level, are the origin of the largest HQ migration stocks do not appear in this ranking. The impact of these flows should also be assessed not only from the point of view of host countries but also from the country of origin's perspective. Only a few countries of origin account for the majority of the entire HQ migration stocks: India, 2.240 million; China, 1.530 million; Mexico, 885,000, but for many host countries, they represent a substantial contribution of HQ scientific manpower to numerous business sectors. However, the size of these countries, the size of their populations and the capacities of their higher education systems for annually producing trained graduates greatly reduce the impact of these departures on their academic and scientific workforce potential.

5 The following data have been calculated from (OECD 2015) and OECD, International Migration Data (2010 to 2014). In the latter document, Box 3 presents the methodology adopted and the reasons for choosing the "Barro-Lee 2013" database for the estimation of each country's population's higher education levels.

Country	HQ emigration rate 2000 (%)	HQ emigration rate 2010/2011 (%)	Number of HQ migrants 2011 (in thousands)
		Africa	
Mauritius	53.1	43.8	47.4
Zimbabwe	30.1	43.6	88.8
Congo	34.8	37.4	38.9
Sierra Leone	36.3	32.7	25.7
Zambia	16.3	29.9	30.3
Malawi	19.9	21.9	9.8
Mozambique	39.5	17.0	29.5
Ghana	11.6	15.9	116.0
Senegal	16.8	14.8	51.0
Cameroon	16.0	14.4	64.3
		Latin and Central America	
Haiti	47.1	75.1	167.4
Trinidad and Tobago	72.4	68.2	115.5
Jamaica	47.1	32.7	293.0
Honduras	13.7	32.2	59.6
Cuba	27.8	20.0	342.6
Salvador	14.2	20.0	128.6
Guatemala	18.9	17.4	80.1
Uruguay	8.3	14.1	41.7
Dominican Republic	10.1	11.8	167.5
Colombia	6.0	10.8	375.1
		Asia	
Papua New Guinea	16.4	20.6	12.6
Kuwait	10.0	17.8	30.3
Laos	25.3	14.9	52.0
Cambodia	Nd	14.8	52.7
Syria	Nd	17.5	75.4
Vietnam	18.3	10.6	539.9
Singapore	9.9	9.6	74.7
New Zealand	8.1	9.4	174.8
Nepal	2.2	8.9	60.4
Philippines	6.8	8.1	1545.2

Table 8.5. *Emigration rate and number of HQ migrants in the OECD (sources: Arslan* et al. *2015; OECD 2015, Table 16 and Appendix 6)*

The emigration rates of HQ migrants are between two and 15 times higher than the emigration rates for all migrants in all categories. These gaps became even more acute for almost all countries between 2000 and 2010/2011. They reflect the high selectivity of migration flows, which are characterized by a constantly increasing proportion of HQ migrants. The variation in the HQ emigration rates of most developing countries between 2000 and 2010/2011 results from two movements acting in opposite directions: on the one hand, the growth of HQ migration flows and, on the other hand, the increase in the number of HQ migrants produced by the education systems of these countries. As was the case with the OECD analysis, the increase in the level of higher education has been able to attenuate or even cancel out the growth in emigration rates, which would otherwise have taken place as a result of the increase in the number of HQ migrants. Thus, in Africa, the total number of HQ migrants from developing countries toward OECD countries grew by more than 80%, but HQ emigration rates remained relatively stable over the same period, because the population with higher education more than doubled (OECD 2015).

Globally, HQ emigration rates are higher in Africa (between 14.5% and 43%). This mainly concerns developing countries with the lowest total number of HQ migrants. The same happens with the small countries of Central America: Haiti, 75%; Trinidad and Tobago, 68%. In these developing countries, whose GNPs are among the lowest in the two continents, on average HQ emigration represents between 20% and 30% of the workforce having pursued higher education. In Asia, with one exception, the rates for the top 10 countries are between 9% and 18%, significantly lower than in Latin America. The Philippines, which has the highest total number of migrants, especially HQ migrants (1.545 million), nonetheless stands out with a relatively low HQ emigration rate. In Asia, HQ emigration rates probably decline due to a fast growth in the category of HQ personnel accessing the total workforce.

These general observations must be supplemented by more precise analyses at various levels, which are impossible to carry out within the boundaries of this chapter. First and foremost, it would be pertinent to analyze the HQ migration movements taking place outside the OECD. Next, it would be advisable to further examine the data particularly pertaining to certain professions, such as the medical or paramedical fields, whose emigration rates are much higher.

8.4. Theoretical perspectives

From time immemorial, people who were known as "clerks" circulated from one country to another in the search for more scientific and artistic knowledge, and also for more favorable living conditions in which to practice their art. Calling into question the economic consequences of the emigration of the HQ workforce did not appear significantly in the economic literature and in public opinion until the early 1960s (Berry and Soligo 1969). At the beginning, it was limited to Western countries, and it was only later that the problem was refocused with the emergence of flows from developing countries. The controversial question at the time was whether this HQ emigration was one of the causes for underdevelopment or if, conversely, it was one of its consequences, a symptom of the dysfunctions of these countries, and often reflected contradictory theoretical views and empirical evaluations.

8.4.1. Brain drain *or* brain gain?

The choice of the term *brain drain* reflects the conviction that this type of emigration leads to a loss in human resources, which are rare and essential for the development of developing countries. In particular, these losses could materialize in the area of public finances, technological capabilities and the reduction of human capital. On the other hand, the expression *brain gain* implies that one prioritizes the benefits potentially resulting from the greater international mobility of the HQ. Scientific production could increase worldwide and its consequences would be beneficial to all parties: first of all, for developed countries, which could save money funding the training of their skilled workforce, and, obviously, migrants who could receive higher salaries. However, they could also be beneficial to the countries of origin, which could benefit from positive financial (and, above all, technological) spin-offs resulting from the greater scientific production of migrants, which would be available to them thanks to the multiple channels used for knowledge transfer (Stark and Fan 2007a).

Critics of the brain drain argue that the decrease in the stock of human capital might reduce the levels in national production, the productivity of all the production factors and the economic growth of the countries of origin. The departure of a substantial part of the HQ would therefore deprive developing countries of an experienced workforce and also of younger graduates who had incorporated the latest technological advances during their studies. While they only have limited resources and low budgets, the departure of a high proportion of the HQ could also waste a significant part of the public investments that developing countries have devoted to raising the population's educational level and qualifications. In addition, developing countries would lose significant tax revenues, since they could no longer tax the HQ who have emigrated. On the contrary, these taxes they are no longer able to collect would benefit the host countries, which have saved the costs of training migrants. Finally, the brain drain would cause a dramatic decrease in the available quantity and quality of services that are needed to meet the population's essential needs in terms of health and education.

For the supporters of the brain gain, on the other hand, the return of some of the migrants trained abroad might help to raise the workforce's skills and productivity. In addition, HQ remittances would be particularly high and provide substantial resources to households, as well as foreign exchange earnings for the public authorities. HQ migrants would be important vectors of transfer of scientific knowledge and technology to the countries of origin at a negligible cost. HQ migrants would also stimulate international investment and, more specifically, investment in education and human capital in the countries of origin, which could further facilitate their integration into the globalization process. Finally, the countries of origin would benefit from the cooperation that their diasporas would bring in terms of political influence, economic and commercial connections and positive externalities.

Initially, these negative and positive arguments had the effect of stimulating questions on the specific impact of migrations on development, but beyond their controversial scope, they immediately showed their limitations, since they were based on fragmentary and insufficiently documented analyses.

8.4.2. *The new economics of labor migrations and the brain drain*

The "new economics of labor migrations" initiated by Stark and his co-authors at the end of the 1980s renewed socioeconomic reflection on the problem of internal and international migration, and enriched it with innovative perspectives (Stark and Bloom 1985). The original hypotheses of these authors have been the source of much empirical and theoretical research. However, other works, following this approach, turned out to be rather banal, contenting themselves with simply transposing the basic concepts of economic analysis to international migrations. The thesis defended in almost all of these works leads to the conclusion that globally speaking, HQ emigration has beneficial effects on the economies of developing countries. The negative aspects are largely downplayed or ignored.

As has been said, the main gains for the countries of origin would, first, be a very strong incentive effect to increase the demand for higher education in developing countries. Over the long term and for many countries, this would not result in a decrease, but on the contrary, rather in a substantial increase in the stock of human capital, a much higher increase had there been no international migration. Secondly, the return of a number of HQ migrants would enable their countries of origin to access scientific knowledge and technological expertise acquired in developed countries at zero or an insignificant cost. In fact, HQ migrants would be one of the best vehicles for technology transfer. In addition, the level of remittances from the HQ would be much higher than those from the other categories of migrants, and would provide a source of additional income. Finally, the well-established diasporas of HQ migrants would play a fundamental role in promoting international investment in their countries, thus establishing effective networks of scientific and political support.

However, the negative aspects (such as the loss of tax revenues or the risk of not being able to maintain a minimum scientific "critical mass" in the country) are generally underestimated or ignored. Nonetheless, many researchers believe that hasty and overly general conclusions based solely on cyclical factors should be avoided. Generalizing conclusions on the beneficial effects of HQ emigration to all developing countries would lead to ignoring the great diversity of countries classified in the "moderately developed" and the "less developed" categories, which are very disparate. In the analysis, it is also necessary to integrate the levels of development of these countries, the size of their labor market, the wage differentials with the host countries, the proportion of HQ migrants in relation to the entire migratory flow and the volume of their higher level workforce, in order to carry out a relevant assessment of the effects of the brain drain in each specific context.

Thus, introducing the temporal dimension within a long and complex migratory process was one of the fundamental contributions of Stark and Fan's analysis, who drew a distinction between short-term consequences – which are likely to be negative – and long-term consequences which, according to the authors, are inevitably positive. In the short term, they recognize the possibilities of temporary decreases in the stock of human capital, as well as the risks of underemployment of the HQ and the probabilities of overinvestment in higher education in the countries of origin (Stark and Fan 2007b). In the long run, however, these drawbacks would surprisingly become a "blessing in disguise" according to Stark and Fan, for three reasons which have been subject to much criticism. First, the level of over-education of parents would be a positive factor in the intellectual level and academic performance of children of HQ who did not choose to emigrate. Secondly, the underemployment of the HQ would encourage them to prolong their job search in the labor market until they find the job that best suits their qualifications. They are, therefore, more demanding that they maximize their productivity and they improve the efficiency of the labor market. Finally, the possibilities of emigration encourage the HQ to invest in training and in acquiring skills that best meet the technological demands of the labor market in developed countries. In this way, they contribute to the diffusion and increase of technological knowledge in developing countries. The two most frequently cited countries that symbolize this positive link between HQ emigration and growth are India and Ireland. However, it is very difficult to draw general conclusions from these two examples: is emigration actually the engine of their economic growth? And, on the other hand, do the current high rates of HQ migrants from these two countries not simply reflect diversified economies, open to the international economy and which, in any case, should not be generalized to the majority of developing countries?

8.5. Conclusion: HQ emigration, a growth engine for human capital?

Unanimity prevails among researchers and actors in development economics who generally admit that guaranteeing better education and health are essential conditions for the growth of developing countries. Therefore, the thesis that HQ emigration could be one of the main engines for their increase represented an important turning point in the literature. However, its paradoxical aspect has given rise to a varied theoretical and empirical research aimed at verifying it. It has also drawn a lot of criticism (Feld 2019).

Globalization has considerably extended the ease of access to the international market of HQ migrants, especially in the health professions, at the same time when the WHO expressed its concern about its global insufficiency, estimated at more than 4.3 million health workers in the world. This shortage is particularly acute in 57 developing countries. Out of these, 36 are located in sub-Saharan Africa. According to the WHO, this significant labor shortage might have considerably slowed down the achievement of several Millennium Goals, specifically those relating to health gains and mortality reduction. This warning was quickly incorporated into the development program agenda of several specialized agencies from the UN Economic and Social Council (primarily by those in charge of social development, the status of women and the population). By facilitating the international mobility of populations and the rapid diffusion of pandemic transmission risks, globalization has led to the encouragement of investment programs in all health-related sectors to benefit the most vulnerable countries. This has resulted in paradoxical situations where programs were organized to send teams of health personnel from developed countries to developing countries, yet all the while globalization favored massive departures of doctors and paramedical personnel from said beneficiary countries to the countries offering international aid. This sort of "crossover", in which the most failing developing countries contributed to the proper functioning of the hospital organization in developed countries, led to questioning the main determinants of the dynamics of the international medical labor market more deeply. This imbalance is most evident in African countries, which have lost 70% of their medical staff to the hands of developed countries. Certainly, these figures have to be interpreted within a global context, which also acknowledges all the other serious shortcomings of the entire health system infrastructure in these countries.

It would be a mistake to exclusively attribute all the deficiencies in the coverage of medical professional needs from developing countries to the emigration movements of doctors. This deplorable situation is mainly the result of the many inadequacies in infrastructure and the organization of public health services. It is aggravated by an unbalanced geographical distribution in the supply of medical services, which favors middle classe neighborhoods in urban centers to the detriment of poor populations in rural areas. In addition, the health situation in these countries can largely be explained by the serious deficiencies in preventive care programs, which should constitute a priority goal in health policies. Despite the shortages, many doctors are underemployed and lack the necessary environment in terms of equipment and resources to exercise their profession effectively. An ethical problem arises: on the one hand, guaranteeing the individual freedom of potential migrants and promoting their fundamental rights and, on the other hand, avoiding compromising the achievement of Goal 3 (“Good health and well-being”) from the sustainable development goals (SDG), adopted during the new United Nations Population and Development Program. However, these principles are clearly in conflict in developing countries, since certain highly targeted recruitment practices thwart the health programs initiated by international official development assistance. With this in mind, several “Ethical Recruitment Practices” agreements have already been put in place in order to prevent or restrict the large-scale recruitment of doctors and paramedical personnel from countries which are experiencing significant shortages in healthcare staff. These bilateral agreements have begun to regulate certain recruitment practices (for example: Great Britain has signed agreements with China and the Philippines, South Africa has agreements with Spain, certain Italian regions have agreements with regions in Romania).

Finally, the question arises as to the nature of higher education. It is generally accepted that in developing countries that are characterized by significant flows of HQ migrations – whether spontaneous or resulting from a policy for “exporting” skilled labor – the type and the content of the higher education offered tend to correspond much more to market needs in host countries than to those in the countries of origin. In public jobs, shortages are the result of a lack of investment in higher education or of restrictive practices in the access to certain professions. In private jobs, this is, in part, due to international competition for skills that are in high demand in the HQ market. The demand for higher education in the most advantaged sections of the population from these countries is probably fueled by the hope of increasing the chances of entering the market of developed countries than by the determinants of local labor supply. In developing countries that are large "exporters" of HQ migrants and in small countries with a narrow labor market, the academic system, in its main directions and according to the curriculum of the programs, tends to respond more to the demands of the economy from host countries than to needs in the countries of origin. The same trend is found in the curriculum of other scientific training courses that are better suited to the developed country market, to the detriment of specializations in agronomy and to the production of services required to meet basic needs. Thus, HQ migrants who are active in the scientific research field tend to focus on themes that correspond to the market needs of developed countries. Therefore, their contributions to R&D and innovation may not necessarily correspond to the economic and social priorities or to the environmental issues from their countries of origin.

8.6. References

Arslan, C., Dumont, J.-C., Kone, Z., Moullan, Y., Özden, C., Parsons, C., Xenogiani, T. (2015). A new profile of migrants in the aftermath of the recent economic crisis. OECD Social, Employment and Migration Working Papers, 160 [Online]. Available at: http://dx.doi.org/10.1787/5jxt2t3nnjr5-en.

Beine, M., Docquier, F., Rapoport, H. (2007). Measuring international skilled migration: A new database controlling for age of entry. *World Bank Economic Review*, 21(2), 249–254.

Berry, R. and Soligo, R. (1969). Some welfare aspects of international migration. *Journal of Political Economy*, 77(5), 778–794.

Carringon, W. and Detragiache, E. (1998). How big is the brain drain? IMF Research Department Working Paper, WP/98/102.

Docquier, F. and Marfouk, A. (2006). International migration by education attainment, 1990–2000. In *International Migration, Remittances and the Brain Drain. Trade and Development*, Özden, C. and Schiff, M. (eds). World Bank and Palgrave Macmillan, Washington.

Docquier, F. and Rapoport, H. (2012). Globalization, brain drain, and development. *Journal of Economic Literature*, 50(3), 681–730.

Dumont, J. and Lemaitre, G. (2005). Country immigrants and expatriates in OECD countries: A new perspective. Working Papers 25, OECD Social, Employment and Migration.

Feld, S. (2019). *Les migrations internationales et le développement. L'exode de compétences et les envois de fonds émigrés.* L'Harmattan, Paris.

International Migration Organization (2020). Global mobility restriction overview. 5DTM (Covid-19) [Online]. Available at: https://migration.iom.int/ [Accessed 20 May 2020].

OECD (2015). *International Migration Outlook 2015*. OECD Publishing, Paris [Online]. Available at: https://www.oecd-ilibrary.org/social-issues-migration-health/international-migration-outlook_1999124x.

Stark, O. and Bloom, D.E. (1985). The new economics of labor migration. *The American Economic Review*, 75(2), 173–178.

Stark, O. and Fan, C. (2007a). Losses and gains to developing countries from the migration of educated workers. *World Economics*, 8(2), 259–269.

Stark, O. and Fan, C. (2007b). International migration and "educated unemployment". *Journal of Development Economics*, 83(1), 76–87.

World Bank (2017). Migration and remittances. Migration and Development Brief, 27, Washington.

UN (2015a). Trends in international migration stocks, the 2015 revision. Department Economic and Social Affairs, POP/DB/MIG/Stock Rev. 2015.

UN (2015b). World Population Prospect, The 2015 Revision. Department Economic and Social Affairs, Population Division, POP/PD/WPP/Rev2015/POP/F-01.

UN (2017). International migration report 2017: Highlights. Department of Economic and Social Affairs, Population Division, ST/ESA/SER.A/404.

UN (2019). International migrants stocks. Department Economic and Social Affairs, Population Division, POP/DB/MIG/Stock/REV.2019.

World Bank KNOMAD (2018). Migration and remittances recent development and outlook. Migration and Development Brief, 29, Washington.

World Bank KNOMAD (2020). Covid-19 crisis through a migration lens. Migration and Development Brief, 32, Washington.

9

Aging

Frédéric SANDRON
CEPED, IRD, Paris, France

9.1. Introduction

In 2018, for the first time in human history, the proportion of people aged 65 and over in the world population exceeded that of children under the age of five (UN 2019a). This is one of the indicators of the demographic revolution our planet is experiencing: population aging, defined as the increase in the proportion of people aged 65+ in the total population. According to United Nations projections, one in 11 people were 65 or above in 2019 (9%), and this will be the case for one in six in 2050 (16%) and almost one in four in 2100 (23%). According to the central scenario projected by United Nations estimates (UN 2019a), the total population might increase from 7.7 billion inhabitants in 2019 to 9.7 billion in 2050, whereas the number of people aged 65+ might increase from 703 million in 2019 to 1,549 million in 2050, more than doubling the population.

One might think that the population aging phenomenon mainly concerns developed countries, but this is not the case. It is in developing countries that the number of people aged 65+ will increase the most, especially in East and Southeast Asia, where an additional 312 million people aged 65+ will increase the population between 2019 and 2050 (UN 2019b). In 2050, developing countries will become home to more than three quarters of people aged 65+, that is to say, 1.2 billion of them. In terms of population growth, this will be the strongest in sub-Saharan Africa, Northern Africa and Western Asia for the category of people aged 65+, since this age range will experience an increase of 220% between 2019 and 2050, compared to an increase of 48% for Europe and North America.

Demographic Dynamics and Development,
coordinated by Yves CHARBIT. © ISTE Ltd 2022.

Obviously, while population aging is taking place everywhere in the world, in the coming decades it will continue to do so in different ways depending on the countries' level of development, and more specifically on demographic, political, economic, sanitary, social and cultural conditions, specific to each of these countries. This is why in this chapter, by placing the emphasis on population aging in developing countries, their specificities will arise, trends which cannot simply be extrapolated from those in developed countries.

To do this, the first section will analyze the long-term dynamics of world population aging, as well as its causes and consequences. The second section will go into detail by presenting the differentiated paces of population aging, identifying major regions and countries throughout the 21st century, as well as the resulting sanitary, social and economic issues. A third section will provide details on thematic case studies in countries or regions with contrasting aging levels. Finally, the conclusion will show that, while population aging is universal, the differences in the demographic pace of its advent, development levels, as well as the degree of commitment from public authorities imply that the demographic, social and economic dynamics of this demographic revolution are and will be different in various countries and regions.

9.2. The aging of the world population: a demographic revolution

Following the decline in fertility and mortality (section 9.2.2), the aging of the world population is a fundamental transformation in global demographic dynamics (section 9.2.1). Its consequences reverberate in many areas of society (section 9.2.3). The statistical data used here have been drawn from the United Nations, both to assess the current state-of-the-art and establish demographic projections.

9.2.1. *The demographic dynamics of aging*

Loriaux (2002) wrote:

> One thing is certain: aging is a process, and like many others, is undergoing the process of globalization. It should be considered as a heavy, unavoidable and irreversible current, to which reason has to adapt as best as possible, rather than trying to stop it in vain (Loriaux 2002, p. 25).

Ten years later, after interviewing a panel of 970 demographers around the world, Van Dalen and Henkens (2012) concluded that for this scientific community, demographic aging is a major topic for the future. Finally, for Zimmer and McDaniel (2016), "it is not hyperbole to say that the aging of the global population will be among the most important phenomena driving policy around the world over the next number of decades" (p. 1).

These references indicate that demographic aging must be considered as a global scope phenomenon, in that it concerns all countries and also has repercussions on the entire planet. In this regard, it seems reasonable to consider its importance at the same level as that of climate change, whose evolution has also been observed over several decades. However, despite its unprecedented, universal and irreversible character, global aging is far from having a media impact as strong as that of global warming.

Beyond the statistical data proposed in the introduction, world population aging began around the 1960s and has accelerated since the 2010s (Figure 9.1). In 70 years, between 1950 and 2020, the share of the population aged 65+ increased from 5% to 9%, and is expected to reach 16% in 2050, in just 30 years. The current period is, therefore, the one that will experience the strongest growth rates of the population aged 65+. Later on, during the second half of the 21st century, population aging will continue, although at a slower growth rate than in the first half of the century (UN 2019a). Please note that the indicated population projection figures are those provided by the United Nations median scenario and that, from a technical viewpoint, these world population demographic projections – and especially those concerning population aging – are relatively robust, insofar as the elderly of tomorrow have already been born. In reality, these projections are based on reasonable hypotheses: it is impossible to integrate the demographic consequences of probable catastrophic health, environmental or confrontational events.

To better understand the extent of world population aging, it is pertinent to compare the evolution of the number of people aged 65 years+ with those of young people under 20 years old. As previously indicated, for people aged 65+, their number could rise from 703 million in 2019 to 1,549 million in 2050, an increase of 120%, whereas the number of young people under 20 could increase from 2,484 million to 2,728 million, an increase of less than 6% over the period 2019–2050 (UN 2019a). Showing the cross-changes in the proportion of people aged 65+ and children under the age of five, Figure 9.2 is particularly revealing in terms of the ratio reversal between these age groups during the period 1950–2050.

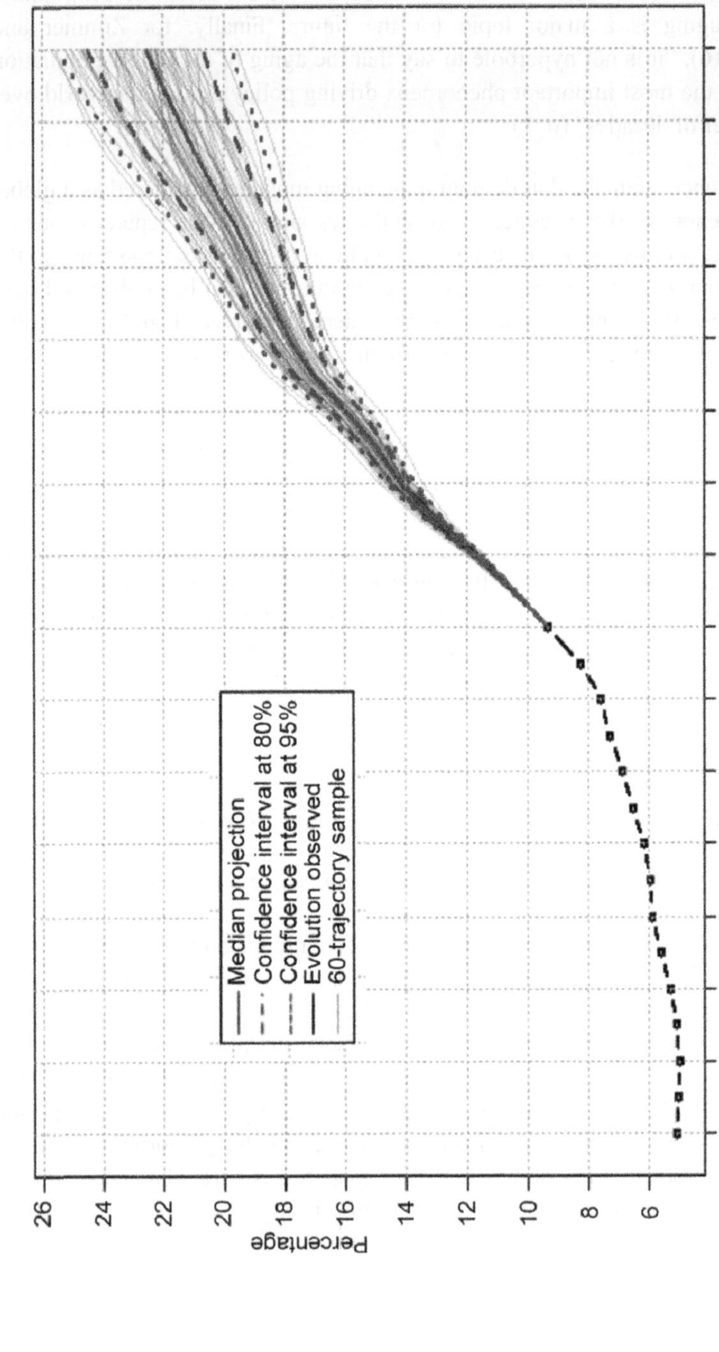

Figure 9.1. *Evolution of the proportion of people aged 65+ (world population 1950–2100) (source: UN DESA, World Population Prospects 2019), see: https://population.un.org/wpp/). For a color version of this figure, see www.iste.co.uk/charbit/demographic.zip*

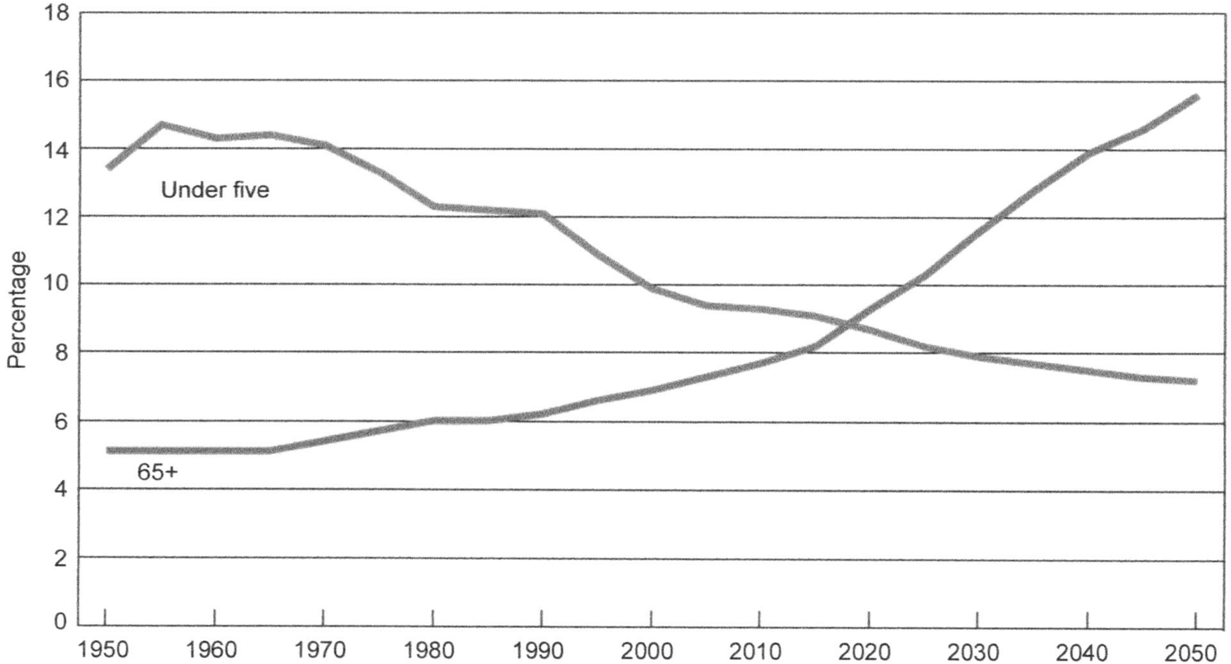

Figure 9.2. *Evolution of the proportion of people aged 65+ and under 5 (world population 1950–2050) (sources: UN 2013; He* et al. *2016). For a color version of this figure, see www.iste.co.uk/charbit/demographic.zip*

A consequence of aging is the increase in the population's median age (Table 9.1). In 1975, it was 22 and it increased to 31 in 2020. United Nations projections indicate that it could reach 42 in 2100.

	Median age
1975	21.9
2000	26.3
2025	32.0
2050	36.2
2075	39.2
2100	41.9

Table 9.1. *World population median age evolution (1975–2100) (source: UN DESA, World Population Prospects 2019, see: https://population.un.org/wpp/)*

Note that the proportion of women increases with age. In 2020, although the total number of women and men on the planet was globally equivalent, women actually represented 55% of people aged 65 years+, 65% of those were aged 85 years+ and 78% were centenarians (UN 2019a). Another striking feature of demographic aging is that, even within the 65+ age range, growth rates in the upcoming decades are all the more important as ages become higher (Table 9.2). The 21st century will see an impressive increase in the number of centenarians and what are called the *old-old*. As will be shown in the following paragraphs, the gender composition of the population aged 65+ and the strong growth in the oldest age ranges are a direct consequence of the increase in life expectancy.

	2020 Population	2050 Population	Growth 2020–2050 (%)
0–64 years	7,067,193	8,186,182	16
65 years+	727,606	1,548,854	113
85 years+	63,573	204,641	222
100 years+	573	3,195	458

Table 9.2. *World population growth by age range expressed in thousands (2020–2050) (source: UN DESA, World Population Prospects 2019, see: https://population.un.org/wpp/)*

9.2.2. *The causes of aging*

Demographic aging is a direct consequence of the demographic transition (He *et al.* 2016). The decline in fertility and then in mortality were the two driving forces at work (Lee and Zhou 2017; Agree 2018). Between 1950 and the end of the 2010s, fertility decreased from 5 to 2.5 children per woman (Bloom *et al.* 2018), contributing to what has been called "aging from the bottom" (Dumont 2016). The other essential factor of demographic aging is the decline in mortality. Since the 19th century for some developed countries, and the 20th century for developing countries, progress has been observed in terms of reducing death rates at a global level, in all life ages, and especially in young children. For each year between 1840 and 2007, there was an additional 3-month gain in life expectancy, earned for the world population as a whole (NIH 2011). For the first time in human history, the majority of humans in contemporary times live beyond the age of 60 (WHO 2016), whereas most people born in 1900 did not live up to the age of 50 (NIH 2011).

At the origin of the decline in mortality, one can identify a series of factors that have greatly improved living conditions, such as water sanitation, personal hygiene, public health policies, advances in medicine, economic development and more nutritious diets (NIH 2011; He *et al.* 2016; Bloom *et al.* 2018). Thanks to vaccinations, public health policies have made it possible to reduce the incidence of infectious diseases that were devastating for young children, such as measles or pertussis, or even fully eradicate them, as was the case with smallpox in 1980 (NIH 2011). Over the past century, the world structure in causes of death has radically changed. The epidemiological transition stipulates that infectious and parasitic diseases are gradually giving way to non-communicable diseases (cardiovascular diseases, cancers, chronic respiratory diseases and diabetes) as the main causes of death. The World Health Organization attributed 71% of deaths worldwide to non-communicable diseases at the end of the 2010s (see: www.who.int). With the sharp decrease in infant mortality rates, there has been a shift in mortality with a concentration in older ages. Therefore, for countries with a complete demographic transition, with fertility rates of less than two children per woman, and therefore not subjected to notable variations (Lee and Zhou 2017), population aging is increasingly related to the reduction in mortality at older ages (WHO 2016).

There is a third structural cause that specifically explains the rapid demographic aging during the 2010–2050 period: the aging of the large cohorts born after the Second World War, including those in developing countries (Bloom *et al.* 2018). The existence of these large cohorts with improved survival rates contributes to the world population's "top-down aging". For developing countries alone, Preston and

Stokes (2012) have indicated that the cohorts born in the 1940s and 1950s have particularly benefited from progress in terms of survival.

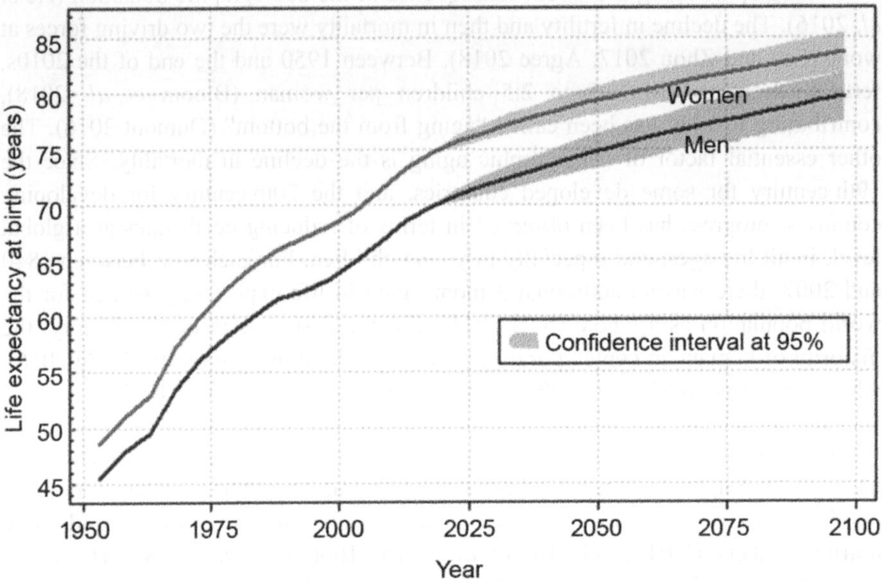

Figure 9.3. *Evolution of life expectancy at birth (world population 1950–2100) (source: UN DESA, World Population Prospects 2019 https://population.un.org/wpp/). For a color version of this figure, see: www.iste.co.uk/charbit/demographic.zip*

Alltogether, despite the appearance of new risk factors having an impact on the advent of non-communicable diseases (smoking, obesity, pollution) (He *et al.* 2016), life expectancy of the world's population continues to grow and experts speculate that this will be the case throughout the 21st century (Figure 9.3). Some even estimate that life expectancy in developed countries could be around 100 years by the end of the 21st century (Bloom *et al.* 2018).

Without making any more predictions about the future, it should be noted that these hypotheses are based on a currently observed phenomenon, the "compression of mortality", an expression according to which "a given proportion of deaths occur between shorter age intervals" (Martel and Bourbeau 2003, p. 44), and incidentally, at increasingly older ages (Bloom *et al.* 2018). The survival curve then becomes progressively rectangular, thereby connoting the eradication of "premature deaths" (Garcia *et al.* 2019).

These technical aspects should be supplemented with a semantic distinction. Until now, the terms "demographic aging" or "population aging" have been used to describe the growing weight of people aged 65 years and over in a population. Subsequently, we will also need to focus on "individual" aging, defined as a biological process affecting aging individuals (Pison 2009; Hentic-Giliberto and Stephan 2018). As will be shown, many demographic aging implications are directly correlated with individual aging characteristics.

9.2.3. *Main consequences and implications*

Demographic aging is an irreversible movement that cannot be thwarted by any public policy and its scale is such that minor adjustments in public policies would not be enough to curb the profound changes it brings about in societies (Héran 2016; Bloom *et al.* 2018). This is all the more significant as these transformations affect many essential sectors for society, such as labor and financial markets, the demand for goods and services, housing, transportation and social protection, as well as family structures and intergenerational relationships (UN 2015).

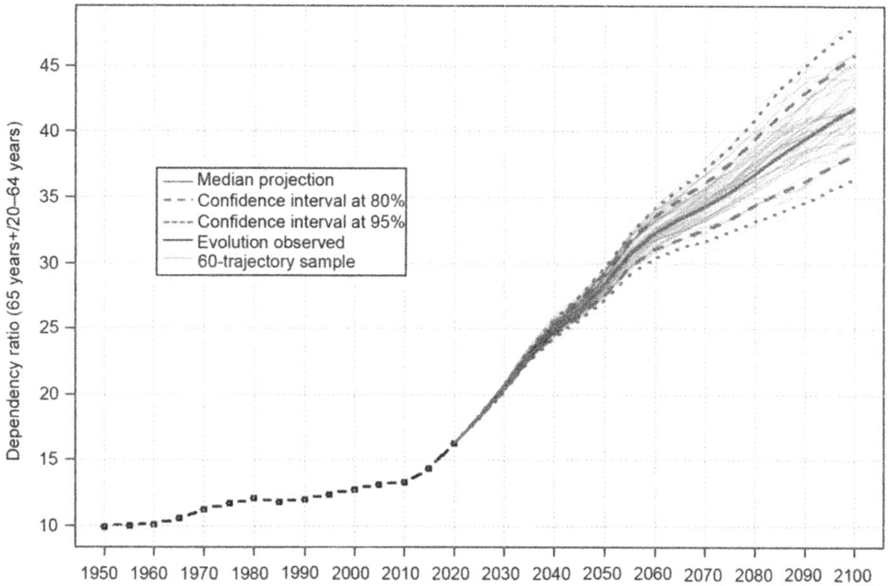

Figure 9.4. *Evolution of the dependency ratio (65 years+/20–64 years) (world population 1950–2100) (source: UN DESA, World Population Prospects 2019, see: https://population.un.org/wpp/). For a color version of this figure, see www.iste.co.uk/charbit/demographic.zip*

On the economic level, a recurring preoccupation about demographic aging concerns the risk of secular stagnation, that is to say, the weakness or even the absence of economic growth in the long term. Empirical studies indicate a negative correlation between population aging and GDP growth (Kydland and Pretnar 2019; Lee and Shin 2019).

First of all, this might result from a growing proportion of retirees in relation to the number of working people. The dependency ratio, measured by the ratio of the number of people aged 65+ over the number of people aged 20–64, has sharply increased since the 2010s for the entire world population (Figure 9.4). This ratio changed from 13% in 2010 to 16% in 2020, and is estimated to reach 28% in 2050 and 42% in 2100. This structural modification leads to a deep questioning of initial retirement systems, even if different solutions have been suggested: raising the age for retirement, taxing work income or promoting funding by capitalization (generally quite unpopular measures). It is also possible to bet on an increase in capital intensity (capital/work ratio), but this depends in part on the behavior of savings and retirees investment (Lee and Mason 2016). The hypothesis is often made that retirees prefer savings to investment because, as they age, individuals are more averse to risk (Sunde and Dohmen 2016), but the empirical results are not so clear-cut (Lee and Mason 2016).

A second mechanism responsible for secular stagnation is related to the supply and quality of the workforce. The workforce supply could become insufficient, unless the retirement age is raised, but this proposal would require people over 60 or 65 to be in good health so as to be able to continue working. As for the quality of the workforce, a decline in individual productivity is commonly observed as age goes by (Acemoglu and Restrepo 2017). This last argument is clearly more related to the individual aspect of aging. Finally, many other variables, such as real interest rates, house prices or household debt, can be analyzed in light of demographic aging (Lisack *et al.* 2019), thereby indicating the profound changes that the latter is imposing on the economic systems of countries around the world.

Not only does population aging have repercussions on the social sphere, but also on intergenerational relations. The demographic and sociological changes underway are both quantitative and qualitative in nature. They are quantitative, because there are profound transformations in family structures, in particular through the number of members involved in intra-family relationships. They are qualitative in that they call into question the modes of solidarity and cohabitation within families. First of all, with the decline in fertility, the number of siblings and families is reduced. The number of children/siblings is less important than in the past and the density of intergenerational relationships is decreasing, together with the number of people potentially able to take care of the elderly. On the other hand, the increase in life expectancy results in the appearance of four-generation families (NIH 2007). All in all, intergenerational relationships within families are increasingly vertical, involving more generations, but smaller numbers (Bengtson 2001; NIH 2011). From a more sociological point of view, inter-generational relations are transformed in the face of modernization, urbanization, globalization and the development of information and communication technologies (NIH 2011; Khan 2019). Independent accommodation between generations, and in particular, no longer living together with the elderly, is a major trend observed all over the world.

Population aging, therefore, raises new questions about the relationships that the elderly have with other members of their family and society. Historically, these relationships were organized in such a way that the elder members of the household were to be taken care of by the youngest ones, since the family was the only institution capable of ensuring this function. Nowadays, in developed countries, but also more and more in developing countries, this function is performed by the public authorities who take charge of the dependency risk of seniors. Indeed, individual aging is accompanied by a decline in physiological and cognitive functions, whose onset and modalities are extremely variable depending on populations, but also within the same population (Berr *et al.* 2012). As previously seen, the compression of mortality tends to push the most serious damage toward the end of life. Another characteristic of individual aging is the increasing occurrence of multiple and cumulative pathologies with advancing age (Khan 2019). The growing challenge for public authorities is to guarantee older people the best possible conditions for "healthy aging", that is to say, good health and a satisfactory quality of life (UN 2015). This requires adapting social security systems and health structures to the particular features of old age diseases, for example, neurodegenerative diseases whose occurrence is strongly correlated with age (NIH 2011). More generally, Khan identified four major areas of risk for older retired people (Khan 2019): the morbidity burden, financial security, family resources for care (specific aids and props related to age) and the availability of professional *care* workers. It is clear that the general issue of helping older people in need will only be tackled through a combination of solutions and practices combining the individual and collective, private and public levels (Agree 2018). They find their source in social programs, social assistance, retirement pensions, personal savings, capital and family support (Weil 2006; NIH 2007).

By focusing too much on the confirmed and potential problems of population as well as individual aging, there is a risk of reinforcing a catastrophic view of old age, which has been denounced by Bloom (2019), for example:

> Population aging is setting off alarm bells all over the world. Some of the alarms take the form of apocalyptic visions of mass numbers of

> lonely, insecure, vulnerable, abused, and exploited older people, deprived of their dignity, fearfully vegetating in their rockers and wheelchairs, and in holding patterns waiting to die (Bloom 2019, p. 9).

This catastrophic view in turn contributes to maintaining ageism. According to the World Health Organization:

> Ageism is the stereotyping of and discrimination against individuals or groups based on their age. Ageism can take many forms, including prejudicial attitudes, discriminatory practices, or institutional policies and practices that perpetuate stereotypical beliefs. Negative ageist attitudes are widely held across societies and are not confined to one social or ethnic group. Research suggests that ageism may now be even more pervasive than sexism and racism. This has serious consequences both for older people and society at large (WHO 2016, p. 11).

To offer a more optimistic perspective than the one usually presented in the literature, some more positive facets of population aging are herein discussed.

First, the preconceived and negative idea that the elderly are dependent and constitute a burden on society needs to be nuanced. Regarding this, the majority of retirees are doing well, are active and do not need help with their daily lives. Second, whether in developed or developing countries, the elderly can continue to participate in the formal and informal labor market, they pay taxes, consume, execute financial transfers to younger generations, do volunteer work and provide many services to their families and the community (Beard *et al.* 2018; Khan 2019). The direction of intergenerational support is becoming more and more often reversed. In Africa, for example, the elderly house their children or grandchildren in urban areas, when they face financial difficulties in finding accommodation (Antoine and Golaz 2010). As for the additional health-related costs provoked by an older population structure, several studies have indicated that it is not aging itself that determines the strongest increases in expenditure, but rather the technicization of care, wages, the price of drugs, etc. (Kingsley 2015; Grangier 2018).

The idea that the category of “seniors” offers new economic opportunities is becoming increasingly popular. In the 2000s, it even gave rise to the creation of the term *silver economy*, which refers to a set of potential sectors that could reap the benefits of working with an elderly clientele (Blanchet 2018). This could involve either adapting existing offers to an elderly clientele (tourism, health, leisure), or developing new products and services specifically intended for this clientele

(Malochet 2013). According to Kubiak, the privileged sectors are as follows: the new technologies of information and communication in care systems, home furnishings, prevention in the field of health, the leisure, tourism and cultural sectors, physical activity adapted to the elderly, and specific financial and insurance products (Kubiak 2016). The service sector for the elderly is rapidly expanding (Guérin 2018). Obviously, the effective existence of a silver economy at the national level requires a sufficient number of senior citizens with a certain purchase power. It is an option rather intended for countries with a certain level of development.

Prevention policies and the action of public authorities to promote healthy aging are another type of proactive approach that can be envisaged in order to not suffer from demographic aging, but on the contrary, to support it, or even make it a lever for economic and social development:

> Two international policy instruments have guided action on ageing since 2002: the *Political Declaration and the Madrid International Plan of Action on Ageing* and the World Health Organization's *Active ageing: a policy frame-work.* These documents sit within the context of an international legal framework afforded by human rights law (WHO 2016, p. 4).

Political will is important in this matter, because, as previously stated, demographic aging data and projections are easy to establish. It has been shown that inaction in the face of society's adaptation to aging entails a social and financial cost (NIH 2007; Ferranna 2019). Many initiatives are taken to promote innovative policies specifically geared to cater the needs of the elderly in terms of health, housing, social protection, employment (UN 2015), urban planning, daily mobility, the fight against social isolation (Nader *et al.* 2018), affording the dependency burden, volunteering and participation in city life (Pilon and de Lapasse 2018). These initiatives can be part of *age-friendly* labels for shops and products particularly adapted for the elderly (Malochet 2013), or of a more global approach, such as that of the World Health Organization that promotes "Age-friendly cities" when these take concrete actions to promote active aging and healthy aging (WHO 2007). For example, we could think of the multiplication of prevention policies aiming to detect the frailty of the elderly at an early stage in order to try to delay the most deleterious effects (Woo 2018).

9.3. A strong heterogeneity in aging and its consequences

Population aging increasingly concerns developing countries, in particular those whose demographic transition was fast, like China or Tunisia. Statistics on the proportion of people aged 65+ are available for all countries, as well as the projections over the next decades. They indicate that the extent of aging projected over the 21st century will be different depending on the continent, but it will be universal nonetheless (section 9.3.1). Beyond its quantitative aspects, the differentiated impacts of demographic aging on society depending on a countries' development level will be addressed in section 9.3.2.

9.3.1. *Aging by region*

Following a fast demographic transition, Japan is currently the "oldest" country in the world, with a proportion of people aged 65+ equal to 28% in 2019. Next come the European countries, and in particular, Italy (23%), Germany, Portugal, Greece and Finland (22%). At the other end of the spectrum, the countries with the lowest proportions of older people are the United Arab Emirates (1%), Burundi, Kenya, Zambia, Angola, Chad, Burkina Faso, Mali, Qatar, Oman (2%), as well as Iraq, Yemen and Afghanistan (3%). In between, Tunisia, Turkey, North Korea, Jamaica, Brazil and Colombia are placed in the world average with a proportion of people aged 65+ equal to 9% (UN 2019c). While the aging process is currently further advanced in high-income countries (UN 2015), an analysis of demographic projections shows that middle-income countries will experience the fastest aging by 2050 (Bloom 2019). The growth rate of the population of people aged 65+ will double between 2020 and 2050, and it will be higher than that of high-income countries and that of low-income countries (Table 9.3).

By 2050, for upper middle-income countries, the proportion of people aged 65+ will be close to that of high-income countries (respectively, 22.5% and 26.9% of the population). Middle-income countries are also the most populated and will host most of the growth of the world's elderly population in the coming decades.

The observation of demographic aging by region indicates that in 2020, demographic aging was most advanced in Europe, followed by North America and Oceania. The situation in Asia and Latin America is intermediate, whereas the African continent as a whole is only at the beginning of this process. By 2050, demographic aging will continue in Europe, North America and Oceania, but it is in Latin America and Asia that the growth rates of the proportion of people aged 65+ will be the highest. Africa will also experience the process of population aging, with significant differences depending on the continent's sub-regions (Sajoux *et al.* 2019). By 2050, even if the dispersion of the median age depending on continents slightly narrows compared to that of 2020, it still shows strong disparities with the two extremes: 25 years on the African continent and 47 years in Europe (Table 9.4).

	65+ Population (millions)			Proportion of 65+ in the region's total population (%)		
	2000	2020	2050	2000	2020	2050
Regions						
Africa	27.2	47.1	143.1	3.4	3.5	5.7
Asia	216.7	411.6	954.7	5.8	8.9	18.0
Europe	107.0	142.9	199.9	14.7	19.1	28.1
Latin America and the Caribbean	29.7	58.7	144.6	5.7	9.0	19.0
North America	38.6	61.9	96.3	12.4	16.8	22.6
Oceania	3.1	5.4	10.3	9.8	12.8	17.9
Income levels						
High income	150.7	231.8	355.6	13.5	18.4	26.9
Upper middle income	154.9	287.6	630.3	6.8	10.8	22.5
Lower middle income	102.0	182.2	482.7	4.5	5.9	11.7
Low income	14.5	25.7	79.6	3.2	3.3	5.4

Table 9.3. *Population aged 65+ by region and level of development (2000–2050) (source: UN DESA, World Population Prospects 2019, see: https://population.un.org/wpp/)*

Regions	Median age		
	2000	2020	2050
Africa	18.3	19.7	24.8
Asia	26.0	32.0	39.9
Europe	37.7	42.5	47.1
Latin America and the Caribbean	24.2	31.0	40.8
North America	35.4	38.6	43.0
Oceania	30.8	33.4	37.2

Table 9.4. *Median age of the population (large regional sets 2000–2050) (source: UN DESA, World Population Prospects 2019, see: https://population.un.org/wpp/)*

As previously indicated, the dynamics of population aging over the long-term depends on several factors pertaining to the demographic transition. In some countries, such as France or Sweden, it started as early as the 19th century. In most developed countries, the transition started at the beginning of the 20th century and the entire process spanned several decades. In Asia and Latin American countries, the demographic transition, which took place later, in the second half of the 20th century, was quite fast, hence a faster demographic aging. As for the African continent, the majority of countries started their demographic transition more recently and it is taking place more slowly (Dumont 2016; He *et al.* 2016). These differences in the advent, tempo and modalities of the demographic transition explain the national heterogeneities of demographic aging. While it took more than a century for France to shift from 7% to 14% of people aged 65+ in the total population, the same phenomenon only took 25 years in China (Pison 2009). Globally and historically, this doubling time is, or will be, much lower in developing countries than it has been in developed countries (Figure 9.5). This means that developing countries will have a shorter time than developed countries to economically and socially adapt to population aging, and this with lower national income levels (UN 2015).

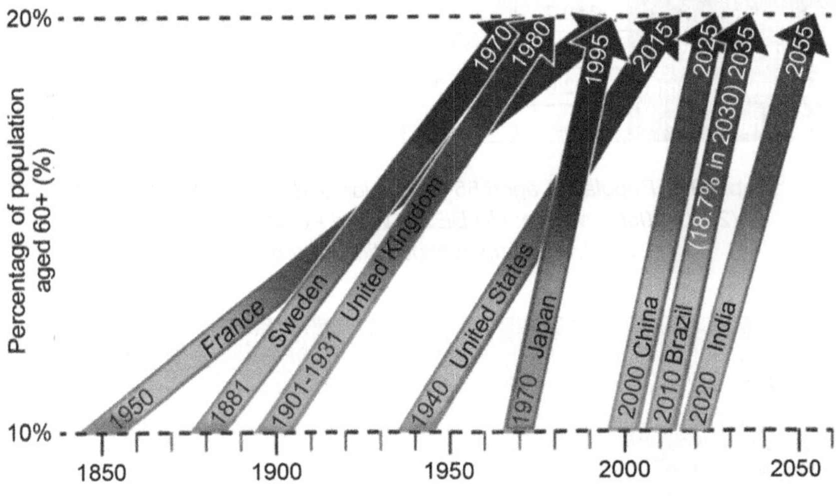

Figure 9.5. *Period of time required for the 60+ population to increase from 10% to 20% of the total population for a selection of countries (source: WHO 2016)*

This finding is all the more important since it is especially in the least developed countries that the proportion of the *old-old* (people aged age 85+) will increase the fastest, reaching growth rates close to 300% in Africa, Asia and Latin America (Table 9.5). In contemporary times, the current and expected gains in life expectancy between 2000 and 2050 are more related to the improvement in survival at age 60 in developed countries, and to the reduction in mortality at younger ages in developing countries (UN 2015). All things considered, while there are still persistent inequalities among continents, these are expected to decrease between 2000 and 2050. In 2000, there was a 24-year gap in life expectancy at birth between the African continent and North America, but this will probably have been reduced to 13 and a half years by 2050 (Table 9.6). The results for life expectancy at age 65 are less clear-cut.

Regions	Growth over the period (%)	
	2000–2020	2020–2050
Africa	133	295
Asia	167	283
Europe	75	114
Latin America and the Caribbean	163	274
North America	67	192
Oceania	115	200

Table 9.5. *Increase in the population aged 85+ (large regional sets 2000–2050) (source: UN DESA, World Population Prospects 2019, see: https://population.un.org/wpp/)*

Care for elderly patients and/or dependents is of crucial importance in developing countries where palliative care is much less established than in developed countries. Bloom *et al.* (2018) noticed that this is a massive problem in China and India, the two most populated countries in the world. Again, there are big differences between countries in how people age, as well as in the morbidity burden, insofar as years of life expectancy are gained over time (Chang *et al.* 2019; Peterson and Ralston 2019).

Regions	Life expectancy at birth			Life expectancy at 65		
	2000	2020	2050	2000	2020	2050
Africa	53.5	64.1	70.5	12.2	13.8	15.4
Asia	68.3	74.2	78.5	14.7	16.7	18.9
Europe	73.8	79.1	83.3	16.5	19.2	22.0
Latin America and the Caribbean	72.2	76.1	81.3	16.8	18.6	21.2
North America	77.4	79.5	84.1	18.1	20.1	23.2
Oceania	74.9	79.2	82.5	18.1	20.5	22.2

Table 9.6. *Life expectancy at birth and at age 65 (large regional sets 2000–2050) (source: UN DESA, World Population Prospects 2019, see: https://population.un.org/wpp/)*

9.3.2. *Diversified social and economic issues depending on the country*

From a strictly demographic, "technical" point of view, population aging is a universal phenomenon. On the other hand, the precise course of demographic aging, as well as its implications, varies greatly depending on the context in each country or region (Peterson and Ralston 2019).

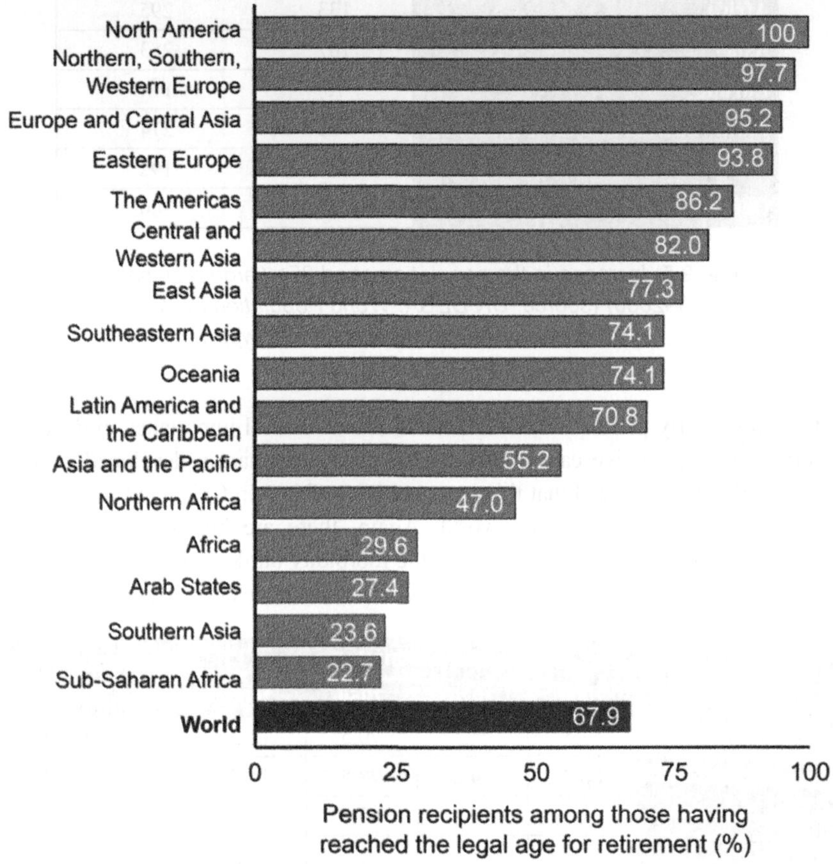

Figure 9.6. *Proportion of pension recipients among those having reached the legal age for retirement (large regional sets around 2017) (sources: ILO, database on social protection in the world; OECD SOCR; national sources)*

An important difference between developed and developing countries is that, for the former, population aging has taken place in a manner consistent with economic development, as well as with health and medical progress. Taken together, these countries can ensure effective coverage of retirement pensions, care systems and social security for the elderly. On the contrary, in developing countries, the speed of demographic aging and the level of available financial resources hamper the possibilities of comprehensive care for the elderly. Thus, in the mid-2010s, while people over the legal age for retirement were more than 90% in North America, Europe and Central Asia, they represented less than 25% in Southern Asia and sub-Saharan Africa (Figure 9.6).

However, we should not generalize the adage according to which "some countries will get old before they get rich" nor oversimplify this dichotomy (NIH 2007; Sudharsanan and Bloom 2018), as indicated by the vast geographical group represented by Central Asia, Western Asia, East Asia, Southeast Asia, Latin America and the Caribbean, where more than 70% of retirees receive a pension. The small amounts of pensions in developing countries are sometimes singled out, but their existence often constitutes a first palliative measure against extreme poverty. In Latin America and the Caribbean, for example, the poverty rate for the elderly who receive a public pension (5.3%) is five times smaller than that of people who do not (25.8%) (He *et al.* 2016).

Several challenges present themselves to the public authorities of southern countries in the face of population aging. As already pointed out, the first is the speed of aging. The equilibrium point or the fragile solutions found to finance a small volume of elderly people over the years is challenged by the growing proportion and numbers of people aged 65+ (Pison 2009). This is the case, for example, for the demographic giants China and India (Sudharsanan and Bloom 2018). In terms of income and health, the costs of financial support systems for the elderly are increasing rapidly under the influence of the factors related to the demographic transition, often leaving governments with the sole possibility of playing on adjustment variables, such as eligibility age, contribution rates or the amount of aid (NIH 2007).

A second challenge encountered by southern countries is simultaneously having to take into account the needs of older people and the expectations of the younger generations, still very numerous, particularly in sub-Saharan Africa, in terms of education, health and employment (Sajoux *et al.* 2019; Tabutin and Schoumaker 2020). There is a whole range of strategic choices made by the public authorities depending on the priority given to the youngest or the oldest age ranges (Lee and Mason 2016). It is legitimate and easy for a government to be generous with the elderly when these are not very numerous, but such an initial system may not prove to be sustainable in the long term, insofar as population ages. The labor market can also become the object of competition among generations, with union demands in certain southern countries asking for an increase in the retirement age so as to avoid the impoverishment of the elderly, who have little or no social assistance or retirement pensions (Antoine and Golaz 2010). Continuing to work after 65 is far from being marginal in developing countries, but, here again, the observed national activity rates reflect a political, economic and social history that cannot be reduced to the sole country's income level. Thus, within the African continent itself, and this is a perfect illustration of the heterogeneity of countries in terms of the elderly's living conditions, the participation of people aged 65+ in the labor market is extremely variable, as participation rates fluctuate by more than 70% for Malawi, Mozambique, the Central African Republic or Zimbabwe to less than 15% for Algeria, South Africa, Egypt or Tunisia (Figure 9.7).

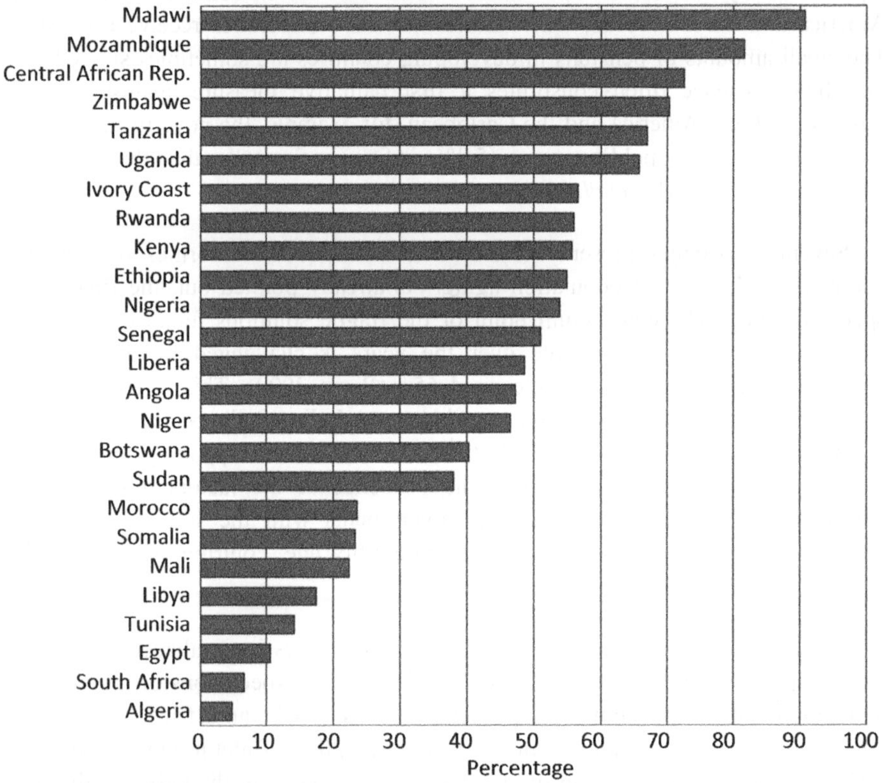

Figure 9.7. *Activity rate of the population aged 65+ (various African countries 2011) (sources: He* et al. *2016; 2013 World Bank data)*

Finally, understanding the economic, sanitary and social contexts where national demographic aging processes take place is essential to anticipate them, and thus be able to take proper action. In the most disadvantaged southern countries, in the absence of social assistance and sufficient retirement pensions, it is often the people's health conditions that will determine when they withdraw from the (formal or informal) labor market. The issue of caring for elderly dependents then arises with all the more acuteness, as social and cultural transformations are moving toward a lesser valuation of the elderly status, an increased emancipation of the younger generations, a refounding of intergenerational relationships and obligations and a predominantly urban lifestyle in smaller housing facilities (Golaz *et al.* 2012). The rural exodus of young working people in the southern countries creates a "local aging" phenomenon, resulting in villages where only the elderly live (UNFPA 2002). In addition, regarding the services supply for the elderly, the low income of private prospective customers does not act as an incentive for workers in the medico-social sector to choose this type of public, especially since there is a competing demand in developed countries, which are subject to a significant structural population aging (NIH 2007).

Finally, a reference was previously made to the weight of demographic aging in light of climate change. There is another relationship between these two planetary phenomena: the elderly are more vulnerable to climate change than others, since narrow mobility and fragility increase with age, as well as polypathologies or impairments (Harper 2019). The elderly are especially sensitive to dehydration and heat, and are less resilient than younger people. However, it has been shown that it is the poorest countries and the poorest individuals who are the most vulnerable to the impacts of climate change (Guivarch and Taconet 2020), hence the current and future particular exposure of the elderly in those countries.

9.4. Responding to population aging: three case studies

Thc particular situation of each country means that its precise aging methods and socioeconomic contexts in which they occur are widely diversified. This is why such diversity will be illustrated by three case studies in developing countries and regions, showing how public authorities are confronted with the problem of population aging.

9.4.1. *The health system in the face of aging in Cuba*

A Caribbean island state with a population of 11.3 million, Cuba is classified as an upper middle-income country. In 2000, the proportion of people aged 65+ was 10%, it was 16% in 2020, and is expected to reach 22% in 2030 and 30% in 2050 according to the central scenario of the United Nations[1] projections. By 2050, Cuba will not only be the oldest country in Latin America and the Caribbean region, but also one of the oldest in the world.

These particularly high figures for a southern country bear witness to a demographic aging that is already well advanced. This is primarily the result of an ancient decline in fertility, dating from the first half of 20th century, which accelerated in the 1970s, and then stabilized in the early 1990s with around 1.7 children per woman (Ham-Chande and Nava-Bolaños 2019). Cuba then experienced a dramatic drop in mortality because of a health policy developed by the new government following the 1959 Revolution. Truly revolutionary in itself, this public health policy has been globally recognized as a success (Lage 2019). Thus, in 2017, infant mortality was extremely low (four per 1,000 live births), the number of doctors per capita was one of the highest in the world (82 per 10,000 inhabitants), whereas life expectancy at birth was 79 years old, the same level as that of its American neighbor.

With free and universal access to health and social services, retirement pensions for those who have had contributory careers and social assistance for others, and thanks to quality medicine, the elderly benefited from the spirit and achievements of the 1959 Revolution, of which the health system and social justice were then the spearheads (Salazar and Jenkins 2018). Since the 1980s, many programs specifically aimed at gerontology have been developed, not only in the field of care for the elderly in hospitals and health-related environments, but also in the research field (Destremeau 2019). In 2016, with a "Healthy Life Expectancy" of 70 years, Cuba ranked in 30th place on the world scale of the 183 countries listed following this criterion (WHO 2020). This ranking, decorrelated from the country's low economic level, has been an original political mix for more than half a century, based on massive investment in the field of biomedicine, more oriented toward individual medicine, and on a public health ethic inherited from the Revolution (Graber 2019).

However, since the 1990s, this health and social system, as well as the situation of the elderly have changed. Indeed, at that time, Cuba suffered economic difficulties due to the disappearance of the European socialist allied bloc and following the United States' embargo. The ensuing economic degradation and the

1 UN DESA, World Population Prospects 2019, see: https://population.un.org/wpp/.

continued aging of the population made it increasingly difficult to apply the health system universally and generously. According to Destremeau (2019), the main obstacles to be faced are as follows: the decline in public investment capacities and the functioning of health institutions and services; the expatriation of Cuban doctors and the reduction in the number of paramedical personnel, as well as their reassignment to the private system; the evolution of the health and social services system toward new non-communicable pathologies, in particular those related to aging.

In this context, while the Cuban health system and actions in the gerontological field were initially oriented toward universal coverage and social justice, the diversification of the situations of retirees and the progression of inequalities have resulted in new practices that make it possible to compensate for the shortcomings of the health system and the devaluation of retirement pensions. Thus, in 2008, the Cuban Parliament authorized retirees to continue working, which was the case for 20% of them in 2010–2011 (Graber 2019). For old people who do not work, whether in the formal sector or in the informal petty trading sector, family support and local solidarity networks have become an essential asset, all the more so if a family member sends money transfers from international migration. Faced with the growing difficulties of access to the public health service and *care*, self-medication practices are spreading, as well as recourse to black market drugs and non-conventional medicines (Graber 2019).

Today in Cuba, the health culture among the public authorities and the population make room for preventive practices, which are at the heart of new public policies regarding healthy aging. For the next decades, with the proportion of people aged 65+ almost doubling between 2020 and 2050, a challenge for the public authorities in health and social matters will be the distribution of contributions and transfers to fight both against social exclusion and intergenerational inequalities.

9.4.2. *The "Age-Friendly Cities" program, with a focus on southern countries*

In addition to population aging, another major trend in the 21st century is world urbanization. Today, 55% of the population is urban, and this will be the case for 66% of the planet's inhabitants in 2050, according to United Nations projections (UN 2019d). Due to the growth of the world's population and an increasingly urban-oriented lifestyle, an additional growth of 2.5 billion people is expected by 2050, 90% of this growth taking place in Africa and Asia and more than one-third in India, China and Nigeria. By 2030, Delhi will have overtaken Tokyo in the number of inhabitants, which at that moment will be the only city from a developed country among the 10 largest megalopolises in the world (UN 2019d).

In this double context of demographic aging and planet urbanization, having an interest in the living conditions of the elderly in towns becomes essential. In 2007, the United Nations launched an initiative entitled *Age-friendly Cities* whose goal is:

> to engage cities to become more age-friendly, so as to tap into the potential that older people represent for humanity An age-friendly city encourages active aging by optimizing opportunities for health, participation and security, in order to enhance quality of life as people age. In practical terms, an age-friendly city adapts its structures and services to be accessible to and inclusive of older people with varying needs and capacities (WHO 2007, p. 1).

For example, in the health sector, age-friendly cities orient their actions toward specific issues for older people: health promotion, disease prevention, disability and frailty, management of co-morbidities, provision of long-term care and avoidance of unjustified institutionalization (WHO 2015). In all, there are eight major topic areas age-friendly cities must be alert for, or even proactive: transportation, housing, social participation, respect and social inclusion, civic participation and employment, communication and information, community support and health services, outdoor spaces and buildings.

The original Age-Friendly Cities initiative in 2007 incorporated 35 cities, almost half of which are in developing countries. Among them are Amman (Jordan), Islamabad (Pakistan), Kingston (Jamaica), Mexico City (Mexico), Nairobi (Kenya), New Delhi (India), San Jose (Costa Rica), Shanghai (China) or Udaipur (India). The "Vancouver protocol" approach was designed upstream to propose an assessment method evaluating the quality of the living environment for the elderly, which can be standardized and valid either for developing, transitioning or developed countries (Petitot *et al.* 2010). Later, a guide from the World Health Organization was developed in order to further formalize the process for building pertinent indicators (indicators of equity, resources, products, results, impact) (WHO 2015). These indicators enable candidate cities or cities which are already a member of the network to better understand the level of friendliness their environment offers for the elderly. In 2015, the initiative was extended to communities to create an "age-friendly world". In 2018, the network included 780 age-friendly cities and communities (WHO 2018).

An Age-Friendly City initiative was undertaken by Indonesia, the fourth most populated country in the world, in 14 cities. Based on the grid drawn up in 2007 by the WHO, 95 indicators describing the above-mentioned eight thematic fields were identified (Suriastini *et al.* 2019). The cities chosen to implement the program in 2013 had a population of 125,000 to 10 million inhabitants, with proportions of people aged 65+ ranging from 3% to 10%. The program collected these indicators and raised awareness in decision-makers around the issue of population aging in the cities. An assessment was carried out in 2017 by Suriastini (Suriastini *et al.* 2019). Here are a few brief results. Between 2013 and 2017, nine out of 14 cities launched public policies specifically aimed at the elderly, in varied areas including regulations, financial aid or the extension of services. The capital city, Jakarta, has carried out several orchestrated actions in the service of the elderly (green spaces favoring intergenerational meetings, dedicated bus lines, creation of medical teams, provision of accommodation on the ground floor, free recreational and cultural services, etc.), thereby reflecting the plurithematic nature of healthy aging. Another city, Surabaya, facilitated the access of the elderly to health services and religious sites, built a retirement home, distributed healthy and suitable food, remodeled sidewalks and built green spaces. From 2013 to 2017, it seems that the most active cities serving the elderly were those in which one or more high-level decision-makers (mayor, deputy) were personally involved in the program. Another criterion is the city's size, the most populated having also been the most dynamic in designing initiatives for the seniors. On the other hand, the proportion of seniors in each city does not seem to have been a decisive criterion in this matter.

Like other United Nations initiatives, the reports and recommendations of the Age-Friendly Cities program do not act as an injunction to states, which remain sovereign in their decisions. Alltogether, raising awareness in decision-makers and public authorities on the issue of "age-friendly" environments is one of the proactive elements that can help promote healthy aging in the long term, understanding it in its broadest aspects. This is all the more relevant in southern countries where, as has already been indicated, population aging will take place faster than in northern countries.

9.4.3. *Living conditions of the elderly in rural sub-Saharan Africa*

With 43% of its population living in urban areas in 2018, the African continent is the only one still predominantly rural (UN 2019d). Faced with bad employment prospects and poor income in African rural areas, people in their active age perform internal and international migrations towards urban areas, which has the effect of "aging" rural areas. For their part, older people often reside in rural areas; this is the case, for example, for 77% of older people in Cameroon (Djouda Feudjio and Leumaleu-Noumbissie 2019). While older people in urban areas were able to work in the formal sector and thus benefit from a retirement pension, this is rarely the case in rural areas. This is all the more problematic since it is in sub-Saharan Africa that the age at which pathologies and health problems arise is the earliest. Thus, out of the 27 countries in the world with a "healthy life expectancy" of less than 50 years, 26 of them are in Africa.

In addition to these economic and physiological variables, there are many obstacles or constraints that the elderly have to face in African rural areas: the obligation to continue working for lack of a retirement pension; absence of specific social policies for the elderly (Sajoux and Macia 2017); poor or no coverage from social security systems (Nsiamalembe and Nowik 2019); low mobility of the elderly in having access to care; fatalism in the face of the process of senescence; little interest in hospitalization; non-existence of geriatric care and specialized medicine (Djouda Feudjio and Leumaleu-Noumbissie 2019). In rural Cameroon, it is common for health centers to be 15–20 km from villages, with rudimentary transport available to the elderly. They must pay for their consultation, treatment and medication. There is rarely a doctor in these centers. In the end, for the elderly, renouncing and resorting to ethno-medicine and/or self-medication remain the most usual options (Djouda Feudjio and Leumaleu-Noumbissie 2019). While there may sometimes be legislative texts governing elderly care, it is very rare in practice for these to actually reach rural areas (Sawadogo *et al.* 2019). With the help of associations, NGOs or the private sector, occasional operations for supporting the elderly are sometimes carried out, but most often, these concern the urban environment (Djouda Feudjio and Leumaleu-Noumbissie 2019).

In summary, the living conditions of the elderly in rural sub-Saharan Africa are often precarious, with poor or virtually non-existent support from the public institutions. All of this affects the ability of the elderly to heal and effectively take care of themselves (Djouda Feudjio and Leumaleu-Noumbissie 2019; Nsiamalembe and Nowik 2019). Under these conditions, the role of the family and village solidarity is essential, whether from an economic or a social point of view. Interpersonal networks are the only guarantors of care and effective help given to the elderly. But does the rural exodus of the young generations still make it possible to maintain this intergenerational solidarity?

Overall, in rural sub-Saharan Africa, the answer is "yes", or more exactly "yes, but…", since intergenerational solidarities are reconfigured depending on specific situations and opportunities within villages, regions and countries. We should not hide behind clichés or overly idyllic representations of the "remarkable family solidarity that reigns in Africa". Solidarity can only evolve under the transformations already mentioned, which are migration to the cities, encouraging the nuclear family model, reducing family size, monetizing exchanges. Solutions to help dependent or not very autonomous elderly family members are numerous: the elderly person lives with one of their children already living in a rural area; goes to live with one of their children in town; a child having migrated returns to the village to settle with their parent(s); care for the elderly is provided by a solidarity network which is off-center from the immediate family. In the event that a migrant child, most often a son, comes back to settle in the village to take care of a parent, the other children contribute financially to the maintenance of the two people. This generates more or less simple and more or less tense situations depending on the amount of remittances and the attributions of each member when negotiating the transmission of the patrimony and the maintenance of the family social status (Douglass 2019; Sawadogo *et al.* 2019). When the direct descendants cannot or do not want to take care of one or more elderly parents on site, other levels of solidarity are then mobilized. They can take the form of family in the extended sense (nieces, nephews), the community, as well as territorial or even religious associations (Nsiamalembe and Nowik 2019). In his study of the villages in Benin and Togo, Häberlein (2018) showed that the "intergenerational contract" – taking care of or looking after parents after having been brought up by them – is still present, either directly or indirectly in the form of cash remittances, accompanied by support from neighbors or other people in the village. With this reconfiguration of the intergenerational contract, there are no really destitute elderly people, all of them have access to basic goods and a minimum of care.

The healthy and independent elderly in African rural areas can, nonetheless, keep their prerogatives. It is common for them to look after and educate their grandchildren (Djouda Feudjio and Leumaleu-Noumbissie 2019; Nsiamalembe and Nowik 2019) and work as mediators or advisers in local affairs and conflicts (Macia *et al.* 2019). As the elderly are perceived as possessing qualities of wisdom, knowledge and the ability to transmit this knowledge, they still play a social regulation role, serving as a guide in everyday life and perpetuating the values of society (Macia *et al.* 2019; Sawadogo *et al.* 2019).

9.5. Conclusion

It will not have been said enough, population aging is above all a success. Reflecting an unprecedented and still ongoing increase in life expectancy, it testifies to the progress in the sanitary and medical fields, which is visible on the whole planet. But this universal phenomenon is not happening in all countries at the same rate or to the same extent. In addition, it does not intervene in the same cultural, socioeconomic, cultural and political contexts. The first consequence is that its effects on societies are and will be heterogeneous; the second one is that the awareness of governments in anticipating these demographic changes is also varied.

It seems unfortunate, even damaging, to not take hold of this very simple observation from a political point of view. While scientists have had to patiently convince decision-makers and the public opinion about the anthropogenic impacts on the environment and climate change, the fairly basic arithmetic of population aging does not leave any room for doubt as to its actual and immediate reality, including the great majority of developing countries that have already started to age. The reasons for this timid acknowledgment often rely on the long time horizon along which demographic aging takes place, whereas inter-temporal and intergenerational choices only focus on the short term.

The cost of inaction, although difficult to quantify in hard currency, not only leads to a loss of opportunity regarding healthy aging on an individual level, but also to macroeconomic dysfunctions in terms of retirement pensions, social aid or medical care for the most fragile elderly. There is also a real risk – particularly in the context of rapid development – of perpetuating and amplifying the stereotype that young individuals bring innovation, while older individuals bring conservatism and stagnation. And behind this risk looms that of the stigmatization of the elderly and of ageism, with the mass of the "old" or of retirees becoming an easy new argument for non-economic development, as was the case with high demographic growth in developing countries in the 1960s and 1970s (Sandron 2012).

Integrating population aging further into the reflection on development would therefore have proactive virtues, which would make this unprecedented demographic change not only a problem, but also an asset, or at least a lever. In the context of compression of morbidity, the evolution of intergenerational relationships and the opportunity to develop a new interior service-oriented labor market does not sound too unrealistic.

9.6. References

Acemoglu, D. and Restrepo, P. (2017). Secular stagnation? The effect of aging on economic growth in the age of automation. *American Economic Review*, 107(5), 174–179.

Agree, E. (2018). Demography of aging and the family. In *Future Directions for the Demography of Aging*, Hayward, M.D., Majmundar, M.K. (eds). The National Academy Press, Washington.

Antoine, P. and Golaz, V. (2010). Vieillir au Sud : une grande variété de situations. *Autre-part*, 53, 3–16.

Beard, J.R., Pot, A.M., Peeters, G. (2018). Implications of population ageing for societies and governments. In *Oxford Textbook of Geriatrics Medicine*, 3rd edition, Michel, J.-P., Beattie, B.L., Martin, F.C., Walston, J.D. (eds). Oxford University Press, Oxford.

Bengtson, V.L. (2001). Beyond the nuclear family: The increasing importance of multi-generational bonds. *Journal of Marriage and Family*, 63, 1–16.

Berr, C., Balard, F., Blain, H., Robine, J.-M. (2012). Vieillissement, l'émergence d'une nouvelle population, *Médecine/Sciences*, 28, 281–287.

Blanchet, M. (2018). Gérontocroissance et territoires : quel potentiel pour la silver économie ? *Population et Avenir*, 739(4), 4–7.

Bloom, D.E. (2019). The what, so what, and now what of population ageing. In *Live Long and Prosper? The Economics of Ageing Populations*, Bloom, D.E. (ed.). CEPR Press, London.

Bloom, D.E., Mitgang, E., Osher, B. (2018). Demography of global ageing. In *Oxford Textbook of Geriatrics Medicine*, 3rd edition, Michel, J.-P., Beattie, B.L., Martin, F.C., Walston, J.D. (eds). Oxford University Press, Oxford.

Chang, A.Y., Skirbekk, V.F., Tyrovolas, S., Kassebaum, N.J., Dieleman, J.L. (2019). Measuring population ageing: An analysis of the Global Burden of Disease Study 2017. *Lancet Public Health*, 4 March, e159–e167.

Destremeau, B. (2019). Les défis du secteur de la santé et de la prise en charge du vieillissement à Cuba : enjeux éthiques et sociaux. *Droit, Santé et Société*, 1(1), 40–45.

Djouda Feudjio, Y.B. and Leumaleu-Noumbissie, U. (2019). Accessibilité sanitaire chez les personnes âgées en milieu rural au Cameroun. *Gérontologie et société*, 41(158), 41–55.

Douglass, R.S. (2019). Economic crisis of opportunity? The ageing of Africa 2015–2050. *Ashesi Economics Lecture Series Journal*, 2(1), 3–8.

Dumont, G.-F. (2016). Vieillissement de la population et géopolitique. *Politique étrangère*, 2, 157–170.

Ferranna, M. (2019). Happiness at old ages: How to promote health and reduce the societal costs of ageing. In *Live Long and Prosper? The Economics of Ageing Populations*, Bloom D.E. (ed.). CEPR Press, London.

Garcia, M.A., Garcia, C., Markides, K. (2019). Demography of Aging. Report 635, Sociology Department, Faculty Publications.

Golaz, V., Nowik, L., Sajoux, M. (2012). L'Afrique, un continent jeune face au défi du vieillissement. *Populations & Sociétés*, 491, 1–4.

Graber, N. (2019). L'éthique des biotechnologies à Cuba : un regard socio-anthropologique. *Droit, Santé et Société*, 1(1), 68–76.

Grangier, J. (2018). Le vieillissement de la population entraîne une hausse des dépenses de santé liées aux affections de longue durée. *Études et Résultats de la DREES*, 1077(September), 1–6.

Guérin, S. (2018). La silver économie. Levier au service d'une société de la longévité douce ou eldorado numérique pour économie déclinante ? *Pour*, 233(1), 195–201.

Guivarch, C. and Taconet, N. (2020). Inégalités mondiales et changement climatique. *Revue de l'OFCE*, 165(1), 37–70.

Häberlein, T. (2018). Complexities of elder livelihoods. Changing age-inscriptions and stable norms in three villages in rural West Africa. *Anthropology & Aging*, 39(1), 33–47.

Ham-Chande, R. and Nava-Bolaños, I. (2019). Convergence toward demographic aging in Latin America and the Caribbean. *Annual Review of Sociology*, 45, 607–23.

Harper, S. (2019). The convergence of population ageing with climate change. *Journal of Population Ageing*, 12, 401–403.

He, W., Goodkind, D., Kowal, P. (2016). An aging world: 2015. International Population Reports, United States Census Bureau, P95/16-1.

Hentic-Giliberto, M. and Stephan, S. (2018). Les impacts du vieillissement de la population française sur les systèmes sanitaires et médico-sociaux : une analyse des revues académiques et professionnelles depuis la loi ASV. *Management & Avenir Santé*, 2(4), 99–123.

Héran, F. (2016). The population ageing process in global perspective. In *Global Ageing in the Twenty-First Century*, McDaniel, S.A., Zimmer, Z. (eds). Routledge, London.

Khan, H.T.A. (2019). Population ageing in a globalized world: Risks and dilemmas? *Journal of Evaluation in Clinical Practice*, 25, 754–760.

Kingsley, D.E. (2015). Aging and health care costs: Narrative versus reality. *Poverty & Public Policy*, 7(1), 3–21.

Kubiak, M. (2016). Silver economy. Opportunities and challenges in the face of population ageing. *European Journal of Transformation Studies*, 4(2), 18–38.

Kydland, F. and Pretnar, N. (2019). Who will care for all the old people? In *Live Long and Prosper? The Economics of Ageing Populations*, Bloom D.E. (ed.). CEPR Press, London.

Lage, A. (2019). Science and challenges for Cuban public health in the 21st century. *MEDICC Review*, 21(4), 7–14.

Lee, R. and Mason, A. (2016). Conséquences macro-économiques du vieillissement de la population. *Revue d'économie financière*, 122(2), 83–101.

Lee, H.-H. and Shin, K. (2019). Nonlinear effects of population aging on economic growth. *Japan & the World Economy*, 51, 1–17.

Lee, R. and Zhou, Y. (2017). Does fertility or mortality drive contemporary population aging? The revisionist view revisited. *Population and Development Review*, 43(2), 285–301.

Lisack, N., Sajeni, R., Thwaites, G. (2019). Les impacts macro-économiques du vieillissement de la population. *Bulletin de la Banque de France*, 223(2), 1–8.

Loriaux, M. (2002). Vieillir au Nord et au Sud : convergences ou divergences ? In *Jeunesses, vieillesses, démographie et sociétés*, Gendreau, F., Tabutin, D., Poupard, M. (eds). Academia-Bruylant/L'Harmattan, Louvain-la-Neuve.

Macia, E., Ka, A., Duboz, P. (2019). Les représentations des plus âgés (Nayédio) chez les Peuls ruraux du Sénégal. *Gérontologie et société*, 41(158), 57–70.

Malochet, G. (2013). Le vieillissement démographique : quelles promesses économiques ? *Gérontologie et Société*, 36(2), 119–127.

Martel, S. and Bourbeau, R. (2003). Compression de la mortalité et rectangularisation de la courbe de survie au Québec au cours du XXe siècle. *Cahiers québécois de démographie*, 32(1), 43–75.

Nader, B., Prandato, L., Mobillion, V., Bochaton, A., Charreire, H., Baron, M. (2018). Vieillissement de la population et ville durable : quels enjeux ? *Pollution atmosphérique*, 237/238, 1–12.

NIH (2007). Why population aging matters: A global perspective. Report, National Institute on Aging, National Institute of Health, NIH Publication, 07(6134).

NIH (2011). Global Health and Aging. Report, National Institute on Aging, National Institute of Health, World Health Organization, NIH Publication, 11(7737).

Nsiamalembe, A.-C. and Nowik, L. (2019). Vieillesses urbaines et rurales au Gabon. *Gérontologie et société*, 41(158), 23–40.

OIT (2017). Rapport mondial sur la protection sociale 2017–2019 : protection sociale universelle pour atteindre les objectifs de développement durable. Report, Bureau international du travail, Geneva.

Peterson, L. and Ralston, M. (2019). Aging well in an aging world: The impact of material conditions, culture, and societal disruptions. *Social Science & Medicine*, 220, 245–253.

Petitot, C., Beard, J., Kalache, A., Plouffe, L., Cox, J., Powell, S., Tahrat, A.-M. (2010). Vers des environnements amis des aînés. *Gérontologie et Société*, 33(132), 229–242.

Pilon, C. and de Lapasse, B. (2018). Les territoires au cœur du défi de l'adaptation au vieillissement. *Pour*, 233(1), 37–44.

Pison, G. (2009). Le vieillissement sera plus rapide au Sud qu'au Nord. *Populations & Sociétés*, 457, 1–4.

Preston, S.H. and Stokes, A. (2012). Sources of population aging in more and less developed countries. *Population and Development Review*, 38(2), 221–236.

Sajoux, M. and Macia, E. (2017). Hétérogénéité territoriale des vieillissements en Afrique : approche globale et études de cas au Sénégal. *Retraite et société*, 76, 89–114.

Sajoux, M., Macia, E., Kâ, O., Reguer, D. (2019). Étudier les vieillissements en AfriqueS : entre nécessité et complexité. *Gérontologie et société*, 41(1), 13–22.

Salazar, P. and Jenkins, L. (2018). Poverty, social protection and participation of ageing adults in working spaces. A description of eight countries. *International Journal on Ageing in Developing Countries*, 2(2), 114–127.

Sandron, F. (2012). Population et environnement : 50 ans de débat. In *Population, mondialisation et développement. La fin des certitudes ?*, Cambrezy, L., Petit, V. (eds). La Documentation Française, Paris.

Sawadogo, N., Randall, S., Bazié, F. (2019). Mobilités familiales face à l'isolement des personnes âgées au Burkina Faso. *Gérontologie et société*, 41(158), 99–112.

Sudharsanan, N. and Bloom, D.E. (2018). The demography of aging in low- and middle-income countries: Chronological versus functional perspectives. In *Future Directions for the Demography of Aging*, Hayward, M.D., Majmundar, M.K. (eds). The National Academy Press, Washington.

Sunde, U. and Dohmen, T. (2016). Aging and preferences. *Journal of the Economics of Aging*, 7(1), 64–68.

Suriastini, W., Buffardi, A.L., Fauzan, J.B.A. (2019). What prompts policy change? Comparative analyses of efforts to create age-friendly cities in 14 cities in Indonesia. *Journal of Aging & Social Policy*, 31(3), 250–270.

Tabutin, D. and Schoumaker, B. (2020). La démographie de l'Afrique subsaharienne au XXIe siècle. Bilan des changements de 2000 à 2020, perspectives et défis d'ici 2050. Working document 10, Centre de recherche en démographie, Louvain-la-Neuve.

UN (2013). World Population Prospects 2012: Highlights and advance tables. Report 228, Department of Economic and Social Affairs, Population Division, ESA/P/WP, New York.

UN (2015). World population ageing. Report, Department of Economic and Social Affairs, Population Division, ST/ESA/SER.A/390, New York.

UN (2019a). World Population Prospects 2019: Highlights. Report, Department of Economic and Social Affairs, Population Division, ST/ESA/SER.A/423, New York.

UN (2019b). World population ageing. Report, Department of Economic and Social Affairs, Population Division, ST/ESA/SER.A/430, New York.

UN (2019c). World Population Prospects: Data booklet. Report, Department of Economic and Social Affairs, Population Division, ST/ESA/SER.A/424, New York.

UN (2019d). World Urbanization Prospects 2018: Highlights. Report, Department of Economic and Social Affairs, Population Division, ST/ESA/SER.A/421, New York.

UNFPA (2002). Population ageing and development. Social, health and gender issues. Report, Population and Development Strategies Series, 3, United Nations Population Fund.

Van Dalen, H.P. and Henkens, K. (2012). What is on a demographer's mind? A world-wide survey. *Demographic Research*, 26, 363–408.

Weil, D.N. (2006). Population aging. NBER Working Paper, 12147.

WHO (2007). Global age-friendly cities: A guide. Report, World Health Organization, Geneva.

WHO (2015). Measuring the age-friendliness of cities: A guide to using core indicators. Report, World Health Organization, Geneva.

WHO (2016). World report on ageing and health. Report, World Health Organization, Geneva.

WHO (2018). The global network for age-friendly cities and communities: Looking back over the last decade, looking forward to the next. Report, World Health Organization, Geneva.

WHO (2020). World Health Statistics 2020. Monitoring health for the SDGs, sustainable development goals. Report, World Health Organization, Geneva.

Woo, J. (2018). Challenges of population ageing: Putting frailty as a cornerstone of health and social care systems. *European Geriatric Medicine*, 9, 273–276.

Zimmer, Z. and McDaniel, S.A. (2016). Global ageing in the twenty-first century: An introduction. In *Global Ageing in the Twenty-First Century*, McDaniel, S.A. and Zimmer, Z. (eds). Routledge, London.

Conclusion

Complex Relationships Between Demographic Dynamics and Development

Yves CHARBIT
CEPED, University of Paris, France

Considering that in the context of a brief conclusion it is impossible to account for the richness of the preceding chapters, here will be presented a summary of the main lessons drawn from them, before concluding on the need to avoid two pitfalls: on the one hand, not jumping to hasty generalizations, but on the contrary, contextualizing demographic facts as much as possible, and not overestimating the role of demographic dynamics as a brake on development.

C.1. Main lessons drawn from the chapters

C.1.1. *The demographic transition*

The demographic transition (Chapter 1, Maria Eugenia Cosio Zavala) describes the passage from a regime of high mortality and high fertility to one with low mortality and reduced fertility. Demographic transitions began in European countries, widely spread around the world, slightly earlier or later in the majority of Asian and Latin American countries, and then in Africa, where they are still underway.

Demographic transitions were first associated with the "modernization" of economies and societies, but this explanation has proven to be insufficient. Many authors have highlighted other dimensions, such as spoken language, religion, education, gender relationships, family role models, the value of children, social interactions, intergenerational relationships, social inequalities, etc. The wealth of concepts brought forward to explain the multiple relationships between demographic transitions and economic and social changes offers an extremely stimulating field of study for the history of world population spanning more than three centuries. The chapter also offers analytical frameworks and proposes explanatory variables to understand the complexity of relationships between population and development in the past as well as today. On the basis of some of the major works of specialists, one observation stands out: the great variety of demographic transitions, the diversity of forms of demographic changes over time and in different territories. The in-depth case study is devoted to Latin America and other countries illustrating the heterogeneity of developments.

C.1.2. *Demographic dividend and dependency ratios*

The concept of a demographic dividend (Chapter 2, Vincent Turbat), which was developed in the groundbreaking article by Bloom *et al.* (2003), is based on rapid economic growth (around 7% per year) which resulted from an equally rapid demographic transition experienced by four East Asian countries (the four Asian Tigers) between the early 1960s and the 1990s. The question is whether sub-Saharan Africa can implement the policies that have enabled Asian countries to benefit from the demographic dividend. Three dependency ratios make it possible to analyze the dividend: the demographic dependency ratio (DDR), the employment dependency ratio (EDR) and the socioeconomic dependency ratio (SDR), for which the author provides estimates. Several dependency ratios from sub-Saharan Africa are then compared to those from East Asia: the prospects for sub-Saharan African countries to benefit from a first demographic dividend; the main actions that should be taken to benefit from a demographic dividend. The prospects for the countries from sub-Saharan Africa to benefit from a first demographic dividend by 2035 are not certain.

C.1.3. *From the demographic dividend to generational economics*

Chapter 3 (Latif Dramani) is part of the intergenerational economics methodology proposed by Lee and Mason. It measures the contribution of cohorts to consumption or conversely, to production, and identifies the ages when they switch from consumption to production. The chapter proposes an estimate of the support ratios and phases of the first demographic dividend in sub-regions of the African continent using microeconomic survey data. The results show that the window of opportunity of the first dividend is already open in all regions of Africa, regardless of the fertility scenario based on the United Nations demographic projections. Northern and Southern Africa will complete the first dividend phase before the end of the century. The comparison between consumption and labor income profiles from African countries with those of East Asian countries reveals the low productivity of young people in Africa. These results imply that African States must play a more active role in this critical period for the continent's development.

C.1.4. *Fertility and nuptiality*

While in the past mortality was a major brake on population growth, nowadays fertility (Chapter 4, Yves Charbit) is undoubtedly the key variable of current demographic dynamics, much more so than international migration. A brief presentation of the mean number of children born to women in the different continents and according to the countries' income level clearly shows that declining fertility has become a global reality, with the exception of three of the five sub-regions of the African continent and a few countries in Asia. Several sociodemographic theories have been proposed to explain the progressive control of fertility in the world: insularity, the relationship with the decline in infant mortality, receding religion, the effect of land overcrowding, the modernization of behavior and the rationality of the numerous family. One thing is clear: there is no single, universally valid explanation. However, along with contraception, nuptiality is the major variable that governs fertility. Once again, from a sociodemographic perspective, the second part of the chapter shows a widely spread behavior in developing countries – often considered a public health problem in itself – namely early marriage and one of its consequences, the advent of pregnancies and births among teenagers. Their vulnerability is analyzed and illustrated by the case of Benin.

C.1.5. *Contraception and reproductive rights*

Next to nuptiality, contraception appears to be the other major variable that regulates fertility (Chapter 5, Aisha Dasgupta). As for the relationship with development, which is at the heart of this book, the major question is to explain the use or refusal of contraception. This chapter does not provide an inventory of the sociological, anthropological or economic factors of contraceptive use, which are discussed in the previous chapter. It analyzes what specialists call fertility preferences. These have given rise to numerous data collections around the world and to a rich stream of research. Three major quantitative contributions from this chapter deserve to be recalled. Preferences are by no means individual, but are influenced by the conformity to social norms of the environment where each couple lives. From the 1960s onwards, the fear inspired in rich countries by the hasty demographic growth of developing countries led to an interventionism which sometimes resulted in ethically unjustifiable sterilizations. Fortunately, the recognition of reproductive rights has now been acquired and the freedom of couples is respected, with one exception: in several countries, women encounter violent hostility if they want to have an abortion. Finally, using the example of Pakistan and Bangladesh, the chapter shows that alongside international cooperation – both bilateral and multilateral – the importance of State voluntarism in the implementation of population policies should not be forgotten.

C.1.6. *Mortality and health, the factors involved in population dynamics*

The decline in mortality is generally considered to be the driving force behind the demographic transition and its development is highly dependent on the health status of populations (Chapter 6, Maryse Gaimard). In different world regions, life expectancy has increased everywhere, although deep inequalities still exist between continents, within a continent, and even within the same country. These disparities are due to socioeconomic contexts, but are also due to the health status of populations. While developed countries have eradicated infectious diseases, these still weigh heavily in developing countries, particularly in sub-Saharan Africa and Asia. In addition, in these regions, the adoption of so-called "modern" lifestyles and behaviors results in the diffusion of chronic diseases (cancer, cardiovascular diseases). Thus, the majority of developing countries face a double morbidity burden. In the poorest countries, the most vulnerable people are children and women. The second part focuses on infant and child mortality, as well as on maternal mortality, which remain abnormally high in developing countries. The reduction in the number of these preventable deaths requires improvement in the health context and a general access to healthcare.

C.1.7. *Dynamics of migration history in Western Europe*

A detailed understanding of past migrations should simultaneously take into account structural factors (attachment to home countries rooted in property, employment opportunities, capitalist accumulation), individual characteristics (age, sex, skills, etc.) and finally, the role of families. In this rich panorama (Chapter 7, Leslie Page Moch), which covers several regions in five Western European countries (France, Belgium, Italy, Prussia and England), large migration systems are identified and analyzed: local, circular, chain, forced and military migrations. Over the centuries, these have evolved: during pre-industrial times (1650–1750) and the first industrialization period (1750–1820), migrations in the era of massive urbanization and the triumph of industry on agriculture (1820–1914), and finally migrations during the 20th century. Many observations are perfectly relevant for current migrations.

C.1.8. *Current international migrations*

There is consensus on the importance of the world context to understand international migration, characterized by the persistence of inequality between Northern and Southern countries and by the extent of movements from the global South to the global North, while South–South migration remains less studied (Chapter 8, Serge Feld). The changes that occurred during the first three decades of the 21st century were analyzed using data on migration stocks as defined by the United Nations. Current global migration trends, the volume and relative weight of South–South and South–North flows in relation to the populations of origin and destination, as well as their composition by sex, are analyzed in relation to the inequalities between sending and receiving countries. The second part of the chapter is devoted to the migration of the highly skilled: workforce by continent, by country income level and by major country of origin. The emigration rate of skilled labor is an indicator for measuring *brain drain*. The debate remains open as to the development of the countries supplying this highly qualified workforce: do they actually experience a *brain drain* or rather a *brain gain*?

C.1.9. *Aging*

The aging of the world population describes the demographic dynamics underlying an unprecedented increase in the share of people aged 65 and above in the population (Chapter 9, Frédéric Sandron). This demographic revolution, whose importance for the 21st century is sometimes compared to that of climate and environmental change, has consequences on many societal levels. The chapter highlights its sanitary, sociological and economic implications, with a particular focus on Southern countries. A global analysis of population aging, an analysis by major regions and three territorialized case studies, illustrates the diversity, extent, rates and consequences of aging on societies. While the phenomenon is universal, these variables may explain the different awareness levels of governments regarding the anticipation of these demographic changes for society as a whole.

C.2. Avoiding two pitfalls

The first pitfall is that of simplistic visions and hasty generalizations, and one cannot insist enough on a key contribution of this work which hovers over all the chapters: the demonstration of the complexity of the relationships between population and development. As soon as the researcher leaves the strictly quantitative observation, which is at the heart of demographic dynamics, they must broaden reflection and extend it to the various factors underlying changes in fertility, mortality, nuptiality, geographic distribution and age structures. Not only are these factors of a diverse economic, sociological, anthropological and geographical nature, but it is necessary not to be satisfied with analyzing them only at the level of the individual. On the contrary, the interactions between the micro-level of man, woman and couples in question and two other levels should be taken into account: the meso-level of the family the individual belongs to (since intergenerational solidarity contributes to determining behavior), and the communities and social classes which play a role in shaping beliefs, standards and values. Then, the macro-level which comprises the cultural, political and ideological factors prevailing in the country considered, and which are reflected in national population policies, keeping in mind that demographic developments have taken on an international political dimension. This is why, beyond the apparent universality of the processes, one cannot underestimate the complexity of the relationships between population and development and the diversity of societal issues involved, notably poverty and inequalities, where the interplay of economic and political dimensions is striking.

The second pitfall is to overestimate the role of demographic dynamics in development issues. Another work (Charbit 2022) conclusively showed that the demographic variable could not be considered as the sole cause of two major current issues: poverty and inequalities, and environment and natural resources. The political choices in developing countries, and in particular the priority or not given to education, health and the fight against corruption, are much more decisive than demographic growth. Likewise, population is mistakenly presented as a major ecological risk factor, while the modes of production, of consumption, the way in which societies are organized, and finally territorial inequalities are much more serious. What has just been mentioned implicitly concerns the management of the population issue by the governments of developing countries. But this would mean overlooking the international dimension of the problem, and more precisely, the responsibility of developed countries, which keep the corruption of governments alive in order to maintain their domination over these countries – let us recall here the plundering of natural resources. If some countries are still unable to escape underdevelopment, are demographic dynamics the real problem?

C.3. References

Balandier, G. (ed.) (1956). *Le Tiers-monde, sous-développement et développement.* PUF/INED, Paris.

Casterline, J.B. and Bongaarts, J. (eds) (2017). *Fertility Transition in Sub-Saharan Africa.* The Population Council, New York.

Charbit, Y. (1983). The fate of Malthus's work: History and ideology. In *Malthus Past and Present*, Dupaquier, J. (ed.). Academic Press, London.

Charbit, Y. (2009). *Economic, Social and Demographic Thought in the XIXth Century. The Population Debate from Malthus to Marx.* Springer, Dordrecht.

Charbit, Y. (ed.) (2022). *Population Issues and Development.* ISTE Ltd, London and John Wiley & Sons, New York.

Ehrlich, P. (1968). *The Population Bomb.* Ballantine Books, New York.

Goode, W.J. (1963). *World Revolution and Family Patterns.* Collier-Macmillan, New York.

Malthus, T.R. (1798). *An Essay on the Principle of Population, as it Affects the Future Improvement of Society, with Remarks on the Speculations of Mr. Godwin, M. Condorcet and Other Writers.* Penguin Book, Harmondsworth.

Mandelbaum, D.G. (1974). *Human Fertility in India.* University of California Press, Berkeley.

Notestein, F.W. (1953). Economic problems of population change. In *Proceedings of the Eighth International Conference of Agricultural Economists.* Oxford University Press, London.

Piketty, T. (2013). *Le Capital au XXIe siècle.* Le Seuil, Paris.

UN DESA (2019). World population prospects. The 2019 revision. Key findings and advance tables. Report, United Nations, New York.

List of Authors

Yves CHARBIT
CEPED
University of Paris
France

Maria Eugenia COSIO ZAVALA
El Colegio de México
Mexico
and
Paris Nanterre University
France

Aisha DASGUPTA
United Nations
Geneva
Switzerland

Latif DRAMANI
CREG-CREFAT
University of Thiès
Senegal

Serge FELD
University of Liège
Belgium

Maryse GAIMARD
LIR3S Laboratory
University of Burgundy
Dijon
France

Leslie Page MOCH
Department of History
Michigan State University
East Lansing
USA

Frédéric SANDRON
CEPED
IRD
Paris
France

Vincent TURBAT
Georgetown University
Washington, DC
USA

Index

D

E

F

G

H, I

L

M

N

O, P

R

S

T, U

V, W